The
Direct
Path

Creating a Journey to the
Divine Through the
World's Mystical Traditions

Andrew Harvey

Broadway Books
New York

BROADWAY

A hardcover edition of this book was published in 2000 by Broadway Books.

THE DIRECT PATH. Copyright © 2000 by Andrew Harvey. All rights reserved. Printed in the United States of America. No part of this book may be reproduced or transmitted in any form or by any means, electronic or mechanical, including photocopying, recording, or by any information storage and retrieval system, without written permission from the publisher. For information, address Broadway Books, a division of Random House, Inc., 1540 Broadway, New York, New York 10036.

Broadway Books titles may be purchased for business or promotional use or for special sales. For information, please write to: Special Markets Department, Random House, Inc., 1540 Broadway, New York, New York 10036.

BROADWAY BOOKS and its logo, a letter B bisected on the diagonal, are trademarks of Broadway Books, a division of Random House, Inc.

Visit our website at www.broadwaybooks.com

First trade paperback edition published 2001.

Grateful acknowledgment is given to the following for permission to quote:

HarperCollins for *The Essential Tao* translated by Thomas Cleary (HarperCollins, 1991).

HarperCollins for *The Tibetan Book of Living and Dying* by Sogyal Rinpoche (HarperCollins, 1993).

Nilgiri Press for *The Upanishads* by Eknath Easwaran (Nilgiri Press, 1987).

Nilgiri Press for *The Dhammapada* by Eknath Easwaran (Nilgiri Press, 1986).

The Library of Congress has cataloged the hardcover edition as:

Harvey, Andrew, 1952–
    The direct path / by Andrew Harvey.
      p. cm.
    1. Spiritual life. 2. Mysticism. I. Title
  BL625.H34 2000
  291.4'4—dc21
  99-048805

Designed by Ralph Fowler

ISBN 0-7679-0300-5

01 02 03 04 05 10 9 8 7 6 5 4 3 2 1

Additional Praise for *The Direct Path*

"A rich offering from Andrew Harvey's deep cup. A book to work and live with, a cornerstone for the direct transmission from the heart to the open mind." —Stephen Levine, author, *Embracing the Beloved*

"*The Direct Path* is a divinely inspired guide to the heart of the spiritual practice by one of the twentieth century's most passionate and tender mystics. If I were stranded on a desert island with one book, this would be my choice. Andrew has given a treasured gift to all seekers—across all paths." —Gabrielle Roth, author, *Sweat Your Prayers*

"*The Direct Path* arrives at the perfect time in human history. This *practical spirituality* can turn our species around and tame our violence. In this way our reptilian brains can learn to develop the peace and energy we so desperately need to celebrate and heal our planet and its children." —Matthew Fox, author, *Original Blessing*

"Andrew Harvey is an enlightened spirit—a messenger from the Divine. *The Direct Path* reveals how on every level we can release the passion, the divine fire within, and, thereby, find and integrate into our everyday lives the love, the order, the balance, and the happiness that should be our birthright. This book will change your life." —Gloria Vanderbilt

"A beautiful book that is also useful in the most profound way. Andrew Harvey is one of the world's irreplaceable resources." —Lance Morrow, writer, *Time* magazine

"This wonderfully bold book is Harvey's latest offering, his song of faith and praise . . . He offers a rich compendium of exercises taken from the world's traditions, from prayer to tantric lovemaking to a Taoist laughing dance. Harvey describes each practice with a down-to-earth clarity and simplicity, writing not as a guru but as a spiritual friend eager to share the tools that others have shared with him." —*Publishers Weekly* (starred review)

"The breadth of [Harvey's] knowledge about the world's religions impressively and substantively underpins his work. Firmly grounded and clearly articulated, Harvey's arguments offers inspiration to those searching for such a life." —*Booklist*

"Harvey's advice is uncommonly practical and balanced . . . Indeed, what stands out most about this book is not Harvey's fervor and passionate lyricism, but his generosity. Harvey extends his experience and his learning life a light, showing us that there is nothing to fear and that the sacred is indeed close at hand." —*beliefnet.com*

"Harvey is probably the greatest living scholar and practitioner of mysticism. There are others more deeply steeped in individual traditions, but few, if any, have so extensively explored such a variety of mystic paths, not just as an academic observer but also as a participant . . . *The Direct Path* reaches beyond the trappings and rituals of the world's great mystic traditions, to present what he believes is the essential message of them all." —*Worchester Magazine*

Also by Andrew Harvey

A Journey in Ladakh
Hidden Journey: A Spiritual Awakening
The Way of Passion: A Celebration of Rumi
The Return of the Mother
Son of Man: The Mystical Path to Christ

With Patrick Gaffney and Sogyal Rinpoche

The Tibetan Book of Living and Dying

For my mother, *for all her truth and passionate goodness*

For Eryk, *my husband and Beloved*

For Mara, *sister of my spirit*

For Leila, *incomparable heart-friend*

Acknowledgments

To Lauren Marino, brilliant and indefatigable editor and superb spiritual midwife.

To Tom Grady, dear friend and the best of agents.

To Leila and Henry Luce, for all their tender generosity.

To Kelly O'Quinn and family, for their wise neighborliness.

To Dorothy Walters, for the beauty of her presence.

To Tracy Cochran, for her extraordinary help.

To Rose Solari, for the courage of her witness.

To Barbara Groth, for hours of delight.

To Paul Todisco, for his patience and excellent work.

To Mary and Axel Grabowsky, for the depth of their love.

To Harold and Carol Weicker, for their warmth and support.

To Mollie Corcoran, for her brave friendship.

To Purrball, my darling and heart-friend.

Contents

Everything is laid out for you.
Your path is straight ahead of you.
Sometimes it's invisible, but it's there.
You may not know where it's going
But you have to follow that path.
It's the path to the Creator.
It's the only path there is.

CHIEF LEON SHENANDOAH

A way can be a guide,
but not a fixed path:
Names can be given,
but not permanent labels.

TAO TE

However innumerable sentient beings are,
I vow to save them.
However inexhaustible the defilements are,
I vow to extinguish them.
However immeasurable the dharmas are,
I vow to master them.
However incomparable enlightenment is,
I vow to attain it.

BODHISATTVA VOWS

Introduction

YOU ARE READING THIS PAGE, so you have come to what could be the most transformatory discovery of your life—that of the Direct Path.

The Direct Path is the Path to God without dogma or priests or gurus, the Path of *direct* self-empowerment and self-awakening in and under God in the heart of life. You do not have to go anywhere or take a new name or sign up for expensive intensives to begin it; whether you yet know it or not, you have been on this path since the day you were born.

When you discover for yourself how real the Direct Path is and how it can transform you faster, and more completely and integratedly than any other, your whole life will change and you will discover with wonder and delight why you are here and what you are here for. You will start to become free from all the political, social, and religious systems that constrain you, with the freedom that is yours by right of being a child of God, the freedom of your divine nature and your divine truth, and this freedom and this truth will make you increasingly an empowered agent of change in every arena in the world.

I know the truth of these words for myself. Looking back on my life, I can see clearly the different steps, missteps, and revelations that led to the vision that informs this book. I can see how life, its inner meaning, and the writing of this book, and the imparting of sacred knowledge it contains have all, through grace, begun to come together; I feel as if I understand at last why I searched and suffered and worked and prayed, and for what.

The great Greek philosopher Plato wrote in *The Republic:* "When the souls had chosen their lives they went before the Goddess of Necessity, Lachesis. And she sent with each as the guardian of his life and the fulfiller of his choice the daimon he had chosen."

For many years I could only guess confusedly as to what my "guardian" and "fulfiller" was up to. Now, more and more often, I can see his face clearly and see, with wonder and delight, that it is becoming more and more my own.

THE REVEALING OF THE SECRET New Delhi, India, 1958.

I was six years old, a skinny, precocious, gangly-legged little boy with large deep-set brown eyes and jumbo ears that glowed brickred if I sat with my back to the sun. My parents had departed for a dinner party on the other side of the city; I still remember how regal my father looked and how my mother, thin and radiant in a flame-red taffeta dress, seemed to float down the stairs as she left.

It was a cloudless Indian summer night, brilliant with stars; the moon was huge, almost full; the light warm wind that billowed the drawing room's ghost-white curtains smelled of monsoon rain, car fumes, and jasmine. Antony, the cook, prepared a little table for me on the balcony of our house with my favorite dinner on it—scrambled egg with tomato followed by vanilla ice cream smothered with hot chocolate sauce.

As I was eating, Antony came and sat down on the ground beside me. He was a tall, always unshaven man with high cheekbones and the wild, bloodshot eyes of a drunk. That night I could tell he had been drinking; his breath reeked of gin and his eyes had a glazed, faraway look and his hands shook slightly. I never minded when he drank; although I sometimes had heard him screaming and shouting at his wife, Mary, my nanny, or ayah, he was always loving to me and when drunk would tell me fantastical stories in broken English about princes and princesses, flying horses, and yogis who would walk on the sun.

That night, however, he did not speak at all. He brought out onto the veranda a small, battered-looking drum, a tabla, and began to play. I shall never forget the way he played—passionately, moaning slightly, swaying from side to side, the sweat drenching the armpits of his dirty khaki shirt and pouring down his face, his heart, mind, body, and soul fused in a dark flame of concentration. On and on Antony played, faster and faster, until the balcony seemed to shake and tremble and the stars to start to run down the night sky.

And then he stopped, and putting his tabla to one side, clasped his hands together and bowed down and touched the floor of his balcony with his forehead.

"What are you doing?" I asked. "Are you all right?"

His lips were moving and strange, garbled words were coming out of them.

"What are you doing?" I said again, a little scared by then.

"O my dear," he said, taking my hands and kissing them. "O my dear, what I am doing is thanking."

"Thanking who?"

"Thanking the God. The God is listening when I am playing. I am playing for the God. I am playing for the God and I am saying 'I know I am no good but I play for you, I love you, you must forgive me because I play so good.' Understand?"

"And you think God hears you?" I asked.

Antony looked at me genuinely shocked. "God is everything. God is everywhere." He started waving his hands. "God is the moon. God is the garden. God is you. God is me. God all around. God always seeing. God always listening. All you need to do is to whisper and God will hear." He started to laugh hysterically. "Men not good always, but God always good. God love everyone. God understand Antony. God know that Antony cannot help drinking. God know Antony love God. I play for God and God clapping, clapping."

Antony froze still as a cat, and, his eyes blazing, leaned forward into the still-ringing silence. He was listening, I knew, to a sound of God clapping that I couldn't hear. Then, satisfied, he rubbed the palms of his hands together, belched, yawned, stretched, and stood up.

"You Antony's friend too. You my friend. Tonight you and Antony and God all happy. This is good life."

He staggered off into the moonlit house, balancing the tabla on his head and banging against the walls. I stayed out on the balcony, startled and shaken. I knew that Antony that evening had revealed to me a secret I had never begun to suspect before; God was in everyone and everything, and in me, and I could be with God directly and talk to God directly whenever I wanted and in whatever state or condition I was in. Why had no one told me this secret before? I gazed up at the moon swimming in the dark, and it seemed to smile down at me; I gazed down at the jasmine bushes streaked with moonlight in the garden, and they seemed to smile up at me. I looked at my six-year-old hands gripping the balcony railings and saw that they, too, were shining with God.

FROM THE BEGINNING of my life, India initiated me into an awareness that God is One, present everywhere, alive in all events and all things. I grew up in a Protestant family with a Muslim driver, Catholic ayah, and Hindu servants; no one mocked anyone else's religion; everyone felt free to worship in whatever way they wanted. My Muslim driver would speak to me of Allah; my ayah would talk to me of the mercy of Mary and show me how she worshipped her; our Hindu servant would take me to the local temple and put garlands of marigold around my neck and red tilak spots on my forehead and spoil me with fat orange and purple sweets blessed by the priest. Although my parents and grandparents were Christians, I never heard them patronize Indian religion; my mother told me at an early age that God spoke to different peoples and different cultures in different ways but that it was always the same God speaking, and the only finally important thing about life was whether you loved deeply.

The result of such a tolerant atmosphere was that my sacred

imagination flowered naturally. I realized very young, without being able to formulate it in words, that my driver and ayah and the Hindu servants were all talking in different—and wonderful—ways about the same God and that if I listened to them, I would learn great secrets and be led into rich mysteries. So I would deliberately draw our thin, austere driver out to tell me how Muslims prayed and what they meant by bowing five times a day to Allah; I would get my ayah, Mary, to tell me what she knew and felt about Jesus and the Mother of God; I would ask my Hindu servants and the priests of the temples they took me to to tell me the fantastical and baroque legends of Krishna and Kali and Durga and Saraswati.

My reverence grew for all religious traditions, and my sense that each of them was holy was deepened by the way in which all the people around me lived their spiritual lives quite naturally. I saw that my parents' Christian values translated themselves into kindness and consideration for all the people they met and that they did not make them in any way life hating or judgmental; parties and fancy dress balls and expeditions to the beach and present giving were clearly just as "religious" to them as praying in church or singing hymns. Once I saw my father praying as he was making up his bow tie in the mirror. I saw how much strength and endurance faith gave our driver and how even in the middle of a shopping trip in the bazaar he would get on his knees and bow toward Mecca without any self-consciousness or theatricality whatsoever. I saw the tender emotion that softened my ayah's face when she talked about Jesus, and her Mother in heaven, while making curry on our roof. I saw with what relish and fantasy our Hindu servants prayed in the temple and how much they enjoyed the more flamboyant Hindu festivals, like holi, when everyone flings brightly colored water at everyone and everything else, and dances and sings all day from house to house.

From all this I derived quite naturally the awareness that worship was normal and could and should be done in all circumstances and everywhere.

It was natural for me, too, in such an atmosphere to imagine that the whole purpose of life was to live with God and praise God.

The first poems I ever wrote were love poems to Jesus, astonishingly bad but personal and fervent. From about five years of age onward, I loved to sing, especially in church: I think now that my first experiences of mystical absorption were when I sang, at the top of my voice, and with my whole heart and soul, "Onward, Christian Soldiers" or my favorite, "Abide with Me." I never doubted that I was singing directly to and for Jesus, or that he liked what he heard.

I loved the religious themes of Hindu and Persian art also, and the tombs and monuments of ancient India. I still remember the awe I felt when I first saw the Taj Mahal, glittering like mother-of-pearl in the early dawn light. When our Muslim driver said to me "Shah Jahan loved his empress, Mumtaz Mahal, with a divine love and so he built for her—he had to—this work of divine beauty," I knew and felt quite simply what he meant; it was obvious that only a God-given love could inspire a building of such mind-deranging loveliness.

IT WASN'T ONLY by stories or art or spiritual instruction that I was led to see the presence of God. India also revealed to me that God was present in the sometimes savage glory of nature. Just behind our Delhi house there was a wilderness full of snakes and tangled brambles that was haunted by what seemed like thousands of peacocks. Almost every evening, as dusk started to fall, I would badger my ayah to take me for a walk there because I knew that this was the time when the peacocks would start to dance, fanning out the turquoise-blue-gold splendor of their tails. I still dream of those peacocks, appearing suddenly in the doorway of a ruined tomb or from behind a darkening bush; the rapture their outrageous beauty filled me with as a child has come for me to be a sign of how the Divine threads all of the Creation with its secret splendor. As a child I was in love, in fact, with all aspects of nature, with the delicacy of fuchsias, with my Dalmatian, Joey, whose ears flapped like prayer flags in the wind, even—my mother tells me—with the hippopotamuses in the Delhi zoo, that I found, for some reason I have forgotten, far more beautiful than the snow leopards and gazelles.

This natural sense of the presence of the Divine in nature made it impossible for me, I see now, ever to accept a purely transcendental version of God; I knew from my earliest childhood that God was in India's extreme and extraordinary beauty. Long before I could start to articulate what I knew and felt, I understood that loving, and living in, God was a supremely sensual as well as a spiritual experience, that, in fact, real spirituality led to an experience of the world in which all the senses danced, as at a perpetual marriage feast of heart and mind, soul and body.

India initiated me also into what Keats called "the holiness of the heart's affections." For me as a child, God was as much in the sweetness of familial and friendly relationship as in the glory of the Himalayas or of the Taj Mahal or in the Sanskrit chanting of the temple priests.

I remember how easy it was to talk to anyone in my childhood world, how accessible everyone, from servants and wandering holy men to politicians and plump, silver-haired maharanis, always was despite my endless questions. For all its terrible inequalities and religious restrictions, the India of my childhood was for me a place where I felt utterly at home with others and enjoyed the simple truth of an easy communication with everyone, regardless of social station or religion.

I KNOW NOW and see that India's divine gifts to me and its initiations were not simply "golden" ones. No one can live in India with an open heart and open senses—especially as a child—and not also be introduced—and in a fierce, unmasked way—to the pain of things, the horror and misery of life and of the world.

Although I was a protected and privileged child, I could not help but see the poor huddled and starving under the rotten bridges in winter, the corpses floating bloated down the Jamuna, the dogs with their faces eaten away by cancer and their ribs poking out of their skin. Even the stories my ayah told me were full of danger—full of poisonous flying fish and snarling, carnivorous yetis.

India's lethal, violent, macabre aspects, then, did not escape me, nor did the sense of tragedy and sad illusion that permeates so much of India's music, poetry, and philosophy of life. I was aware early on that I was being brought up in the twilight of one empire surrounded by the ruins of many others; crumbling medieval Turkish and Mogul tombs ringed the house in Delhi where we lived.

I saw every year how quickly the monsoon rains could stain and eat away the freshly plastered outer walls of our flat; books that I opened in my grandmother's bookshelves fell apart in my hands, hollowed out by years of heat and the secret incessant attrition of insects. Many years later, when I read the Hindu and Buddhist mystics with their vision of the world as maya, as a passing dream or phantasmagoric film, I realized just how deeply my childhood had initiated me into such an understanding without my knowing it. In India, nothing would last long, nothing was stable, everything was continually shifting shape, vanishing. My childhood in India made it certain that I could never believe in the pride of the merely human; I would always know that its boasts were empty, and that all purely human dreams have to end. From early on, something in me knew—without being able to formulate it—that only the divine in us is permanent and only the truth of the eternal spirit can triumph over the mockeries of time.

WHAT INDIA AND my Indian childhood gave me, then, was an overwhelming sense of paradox and of the secret unity of opposites—priceless gifts to someone searching for the truth of life and God. The enormous scale and power of India's beauty and agony opened me at the beginning of my life to the presence of both at the heart of life and to their mysterious interrelationship. My child-heart and child-imagination knew what my early mind could not have been able to formulate—that India, and therefore life itself and God himself, contained both wonder and terror, as well as extreme splendor and bliss and death and madness and anguish.

And in the haunting smile of the dancing Shiva my aunt Bella kept in her apartment surrounded always by flowers and lit with hanging lamps, I encountered for the first time a hint of the knowledge of unity that reconciles all opposites and transcends them. As Bella often used to say to me, "At the heart of the dance of life, there is calm, the calm of God. India shows you everything—all the beauty and all the horror, together. It also reveals to you the divine smile behind them both."

AT NINE YEARS OLD, the second stage of my journey to the Direct Path began, when I left India and went to England to be put through the military rigors of English private education. I felt as if I had been driven out of Eden to be locked in an airless and dark refrigerator; nothing in the warm extravagance of my Indian childhood prepared me for the bizarre rituals and snobberies of England. I felt alien and separate from the beginning. To survive in the jungles of prep and private school, I overworked my mind, slaved to win as many academic prizes as possible, and cultivated a scathing wit as protection. My games worked; I won a top scholarship to the Sherborne School at thirteen, another scholarship to Oxford at eighteen, where I took a congratulatory first in English literature three years later. Then, at twenty-one, I was elected a fellow of All Souls College, Oxford, England's highest academic honor.

The world I then entered was in many ways an extraordinary one. I was given long medieval rooms wedged between the chapel and the dining room with T. E. Lawrence's prayer mat on my bare bedroom wall; I made friends with such inspiring people as Isaiah Berlin, Michael Howard, and Iris Murdoch; I was able to travel to Italy and Greece and Turkey and read deeply in the whole European literary and philosophical tradition.

Oxford was ancient and glamorous and the All Souls High Table flowered with fine wines and sometimes electric conversation, but my sense of alienation from England grew more and more obsessive, and I became suicidally lonely and depressed. I had all the outer trimmings of success and seemed to have a glittering career to look forward to; the education I had received both at school and at Oxford could not have been more comprehensive or rich; why, then, did I want to die? I had no idea; all I knew was that I had to get back to India. I had no clear notion of what India would be for me; all I obscurely understood was that my life was coming to a dead end and that I would be able to survive only if I returned to India and drank deeply again from the springs of my childhood.

At twenty-five I won a traveling scholarship from a college in Cambridge that gave me just enough money to go back to India for nine months. Aunt Bella met me in a blond wig and red jump suit in the middle of the night at the airport in Delhi: I cried with joy when I saw her. For two weeks I sat with her on her balcony in Old Delhi, watching India parade past, too overwhelmed to move out of the flat. Then, one evening, in front of the dancing Shiva I had so loved as a child, Bella poured me a stiff gin, took my hands in hers, and said, "I know why you are terrified. You know that everything is going to change on this trip; one Andrew is going to die and another is going to be born. But you can't just stay paralyzed like a mouse in front of a cobra. You must dive into India and let her give you what your destiny is preparing for you, whatever dangers or heartbreaks it brings."

And so, tenderly, Bella threw me out the next day, and I began a long, meandering trip through India. I went to Sarnath and Bodh Gaya and Benares and traipsed around all the great Shiva temples of the south; I read the major Hindu and Buddhist scriptures in some detail for the first time; I met and quizzed and traveled with Buddhist monks, Hindu pilgrims, western seekers of every conceivable spiritual persuasion and level of eccentricity. I listened and studied hard but understood little; my mind had become hardened by years of too-scrupulous training in Oxfordian skepticism and irony. I made "scholarly" notes in a series of black notebooks in tiny handwriting, as if I were still back in the Bodleian Library at Oxford writing a "thesis" on "religion": I laugh out loud when I read these notes now; they reek of fear and uneasy smugness.

But then, thank God, my mind and heart were forever shattered open by a series of direct mystical experiences that forever altered my perception of the universe and compelled me to become a seeker. The third stage of my evolution began.

OVER THE COURSE of two months, while I was based in a small hut by the sea in the ashram of Sri Aurobindo at Pondicherry, I was graced three "visions" that opened a new world to me. The first two were "dreams"; the third happened when I was in a waking state.

In the first "dream" I found myself part of a million-voiced choir of voices singing ecstatically in a cloud of light "O my Beloved, I hate to leave you but I have to go." Immediately I was given to understand that I was hearing the voice of my soul as it parted from the Source to enter embodiment. The music that filled me and the light-cloud around me was the most marvelous I have ever heard; all music of this world pales before what I remember of its rapture. After singing with the other voices for a long time, I then, suddenly, fell down what seemed to me like a large black chute and entered my body and woke up. As I lay in ecstasy and grief on my bed, I realized that the whole meaning of my life would be in "reentering" consciously that divine music here on earth and in a body; my task would be, then, to bring each part of my being—my mind, heart, body, and soul—consciously back into the singing unity from which I—and all other beings—had come.

It was a profoundly confusing experience because I knew I could not refute its clarity and intensity. I knew that I had been "erupted" into a dimension I had never previously encountered and hardly believed existed. For two weeks I wandered around Pondicherry in a comic daze, my head and body ringing with the divine music I had heard.

Then I had another "vision." This time I was on a beach, feeling very calm. Toward me, across the sand, was floating a most beautiful being, of indeterminate sex, smiling and surrounded by gold light.

My whole being seemed to break into a flame of love for this creature, and I allowed him or her to come and hold me and lie down in my lap. I found the courage to ask the being who he or she might be. A voice replied laughingly, "I am you," and I awoke, bathed in joy. I was made to understand that I had been given a direct glimpse of my "complete" self, my inmost human divine identity in all its androgynous perfection.

Three weeks later I was walking by the sea in a nearby seaside town. It was night, and I was walking along the beach on my way back to the hotel. All at once my mind seemed to split apart like a coconut flung against a wall, and I saw with open eyes all the fishermen's boats and the beach itself glitter with brilliant white light. I heard the waves singing *om* as they crashed on and on. The experience lasted for at least fifteen minutes. Reality, I realized, was revealing to me its divine face without a mask, its face of light.

These three experiences began the third stage of my journey to the vision that inspires this book, a stage of intense mystical searching in many of the world's major mystical traditions. I knew I had to find out the truth of mystical reality for myself and to study and live it from as many different angles, and as richly and comprehensively, as possible, beyond any dogma of any kind, and unconfined to the interpretations and insights of any one tradition. I knew, too, that living such an adventure would demand and cost everything; there was nothing in my immediate world that could encourage it or help me: I would not be protected by any church or any one spiritual system: I would have to trust to the mercy of God and to my own vision, level of realization, and destiny.

Three things characterized my search during this period—a sense of the essential unity of all mystical traditions that derived from my experience of my Indian childhood and also from my own increasing inner understanding; a concentration on the "feminine" aspect of God, on God as mother in all the different religions, and on the "feminine" mystical virtues of devotion, passion, and surrender; and an uncritical embrace of the Indian tradition of the guru. I am profoundly grateful for the first two of these "drives"; the third, as I will show, initially seemed to help and then almost destroyed me.

During these years my deepest guide was the nineteenth-century Bengali mystic Ramakrishna, whose pioneering experience of the inner unity of all mystical traditions inspired everything I undertook; Ramakrishna wrote in a passage I returned to constantly:

> I say that all are calling on the same God . . . it is not good to feel that my religion is true and the other religions are false. All seek the same object. A mother prepares dishes to suit the stomachs of her children. Suppose a mother has five children and a fish is brought for the family. She doesn't cook the same curry for all of them . . . God has made religions to suit different aspirants, times and countries. All doctrines are only so many paths.

With this marvelous and wise vision of God as all-tolerant and all-loving Mother as my guide and inspiration, I dived into a radical exploration of the mystical traditions and practices of Hinduism, Buddhism, Sufism (the mystical aspect of Islam), and Christianity. For almost twenty years I saw my life's purpose as being to experience the truth and inner relationship of these traditions and to use my skills as a writer to communicate to others the essence of what I was learning.

In 1978 I met and became a disciple of a young Indian woman then living in Pondicherry, Mother Meera. In 1983 I traveled to Ladakh, a remote Himalayan Buddhist kingdom in the north of India, where I met a great Tibetan mystic Thuksey Rinpoche and studied the philosophy and practices of Tibetan Buddhism: I wrote about my encounter with Thuksey in my first spiritual autobiography, *Journey in Ladakh*. In 1984 I started a ten-year exploration of the mystical works of the Persian poet Rumi, and the Sufi mystical heritage helped by a group of French Sufis and fine Islamic scholar Eva de Mitray Meyerovitch.

In 1987 I had a breakdown after a miserable love affair and went to live with Mother Meera in Germany for almost a year. During this year all the many minor mystical insights I had been gathering over the previous years of search and practice coalesced into a solid and permanent inner possession of the beginnings of divine awareness. In my book *Hidden Journey* I describe in detail the many linked revelations that led to this "awakening."

In 1990 I was invited by an English filmmaker to travel with him to Nepal to work on a film about the Tibetan Book of the Dead; during that trip I met several Tibetan adepts, studied the Mahayana teachings about death in detail, and was asked by Sogyal Rinpoche to collaborate with him and his assistant, Patrick Gaffney, in the writing of *The Tibetan Book of Living and Dying*, which later became a worldwide best seller and introduced the major Tibetan mind-practices to seekers of all kinds.

In 1992 I was asked by an Australian filmmaker to help him make a film on the then eighty-six-year-old Bede Griffiths, a Catholic monk who lived in South India. Meeting a great Christian mystic—and a man whose humility, brilliance, and tenderness profoundly moved me—completed the circle of mystical seeking for me by introducing me to the deepest truths of the Christianity of my childhood. It did not seem a coincidence that Bede Griffith's ashram should be on the road from Tanjore to Coimbatore—the place where I was born in Madras state.

In 1993 I was invited by the California Institute of Integral Studies in San Francisco to give a class on Rumi. For the first time in public, I was able to speak without shame or fear as a developing mystic about one of the greatest of all mystic poets; it was an extraordinarily happy and fulfilling experience and excited a great deal of interest in my work. During that year, too, Channel Four in England produced a television film about my life and work, *The Making of a Mystic*, which aired in November 1993 and was received with, to me, a surprising degree of respect.

Eight months earlier, in March 1993, another grace had enriched me; I had met in Paris a man fifteen years younger than myself, Eryk Hanut, with whom I had fallen deeply and reciprocally in love. I had always believed that one of the deepest fulfillments of the mystical life would lie in a divine human love, but many miserable and frustrating experiences had deprived me of any hope of realizing this, and I had resigned myself to an uneasy celibacy. Meeting Eryk changed that; here was a beautiful, fiercely honest, fearless, and religious young man, entirely open to everything I had explored and learned, who loved me back and offered me his heart and his life. Loving him and being loved back, I began to experience directly the beginnings of the alchemical fusion of heart, mind, body, and spirit I had long believed possible but never experienced.

At the end of 1993, at the age of forty-one, I felt happier and more fulfilled than I ever imagined I could be. I had written several books that were helping other seekers; I had begun a wholly new kind of teaching career; I had, in Mother Meera, what I imagined to be a superb and compassionate "divine master": I had, in Eryk, the loving, artistic, and spiritual companion I was looking for. It seemed to me that at long last, every aspect of my life was being brought by the grace of the Divine Mother into creative harmony.

I was deluded. The worst, most frightening, and painful period of my entire life and search was just about to break upon me and transform both beyond recognition.

ON DECEMBER 27, 1993, Mother Meera told me to leave Eryk, get married, and write a book claiming that her divine force had transformed me into a heterosexual. After a period of terrible struggle, I was compelled to realize that she could not possibly be the divine master I had believed her to be and that her actions showed her to be prejudiced and destructive.

The horror of the next years only confirmed this; when I started, back in San Francisco, to make public my split with Meera, she denied that she had ever told me to leave Eryk in the first place, plunging Eryk's and my life into danger. Death threats from various disciples and "nuts" followed; my career was menaced by the denunciations of various of my fellow disciples, whom I had counted as spiritual friends; the pupils at the California Institute of Integral Studies who had "adored" my Rumi classes now tried to get me expelled as a heretic and liar from the institute and filled my letterboxes with hate mail. Eryk developed cancer under the strain, and my back went out, putting me in permanent physical pain. Everything I had loved and worked for for over fifteen years, it seemed, lay in ruins.

In the middle of 1994 I heard, too, that eleven of Sogyal Rinpoche's woman pupils were suing him for sexual abuse. I had devoted a year and a half of my life to him and to helping him and Patrick Gaffney convey the greatness of the Tibetan tradition to the world. Given my own circumstances, the news of what Sogyal was alleged to have done, as well as the various ways in which the leading American Buddhist teachers tried to explain it away or cover it up, disgusted and scared me and shattered my faith both in the traditional "master" system and in the New Age.

THE FOURTH AND HARDEST and most transformatory stage of my journey of the vision of the Direct Path had begun. Agony and extreme and prolonged crisis would compel me to clarify for myself—and in the deepest, most fundamental sense—what I believed to be true; I had, for the sake of my own inner survival, to refine, deepen, purify, and essentialize everything I had learned about mystical reality. I had also to face—and in the most unsparing way—all my illusions about myself and about my own inner search. I had, after all, through writing about Mother Meera helped to make her a worldwide cult; now I had, for the sake of my own spiritual future and on behalf of all those I had unwittingly misled, to undergo a fierce self-analysis and self-exposure, nothing less, in fact, than an incineration of all the illusions and projections that had driven me to exalt Meera in the first place. Nothing less would be honest or useful; nothing less would enable me to be able to bear myself or redeem the pain I had plunged myself and Eryk into.

Now, five grim and amazing years later, I can see just how vast and comprehensive a blessing this period of "annihilation" has been. It has stripped me, my psyche, my life, my beliefs, and my work down to their essentials, and in return for the multiple humiliations and deaths I have suffered given me the certainties that illuminate this book.

Without the radical disillusion with the guru system in all of its aspects that I have endured, I would never have discovered the force, passion, and transforming power of the path of *direct* communion with God without the need for any mediation of any kind; I would have continued to project, probably in more and more subtle ways, my own divine truth and essence onto Meera or Rumi or the Dalai Lama, and so have avoided the ultimate adventure—which is to claim complete responsibility, in and under God, for one's own spiritual development. If I had not made the decision to choose my love of Eryk over all the spurious loyalties to a system of power that I had once advocated, I would never have been initiated, as I have been, systematically and sometimes miraculously, into the truths of tantric sexuality and so never have glimpsed the depth and potential of that sacred marriage of heart and mind, body and soul that is the reward and goal of the Direct Path. If I had gone on believing that my spiritual development was an effect of Meera's grace, I would never have claimed the depths of my own realization or known that I would make far faster, deeper, and more honest spiritual progress outside the guru system that kept me, in subtle ways, diminished and a slave.

Suffering, in a prolonged and devastating way, the corruption of one accepted system of power—that of the master system and its advocates—has made me far more sensitive than I was before to the ruthless effects of power in general. This, too, has been a blessing; I now see clearly the connections between authentic mystical awakening and political, social, and economic transformation. Fighting against the guru system and surviving its lies and cruelties has greatly expanded my vision of the possibilities of mystical activism. I have seen and known in my own life the tremendous radical creative energy that is unleashed when you allow yourself to claim your divine identity in a direct relationship with God, free of all damaging and limiting controls; I have seen and known in my own heart and mind and soul the prophetic realizations and revelations that come directly to the being—*any* being—who dares to be authentic in this way; experiencing these has helped me begin to understand just how immense a force for transformation of all existing world conditions could be unleashed if human beings freed themselves from *all* systems of mind manipulation. Because I have begun to live its truth in my own life, I have come to know just how empowering on every level—emotional, sexual, social, political—the Direct Path can be and what an opportunity for radical change it could make possible if human beings were willing to slip the chains of their conditioning and claim the rigors and glories of authentic relationship with the Divine.

TWO AND A HALF YEARS AGO the full radical potential and true direction of the Direct Path became clear to me through what I consider to be the most important inner experience of my life. It occurred, as so much of importance has in my journey, in India, and in Coimbatore, the place of my birth.

In November 1996 I flew from San Francisco to Coimbatore in South India to be with my father, who was dying. I had not seen him for several years; we had always loved and respected each other, but my strange life bewildered him and we had grown apart. My mother faxed me in California and made it clear that if I did not go to India to be with him, I might never see him again.

I arrived to find my father close to death. There was no time to do anything but exchange love. For a long time every day I sat by his bedside and told him how grateful I was that he had been my father and how much his goodness and dignity had meant to me.

Most of our conversation, however, was about Christ. The depth and simplicity of my father's Christian faith shook me deeply. One day I asked him, as he lay white and exhausted from a night of suffering, "Which Jesus are you praying to now?" He looked at me and said, "I am praying to Jesus in Gethsemane because it is then that he needed help."

As the days went by, I and my father opened up more and more to each other; the deep love we had always felt but never expressed was at last expressed and filled us both with tremendous joy. Many times I sensed the living presence of the Christ in the room with us and in the force of the love that flowed between us.

I arrived in Coimbatore on a Tuesday; the following Sunday I went with friends to a local Catholic church. It was the Feast of Christ the King, and a short, soft-voiced Indian priest gave a moving sermon about how the true "kingship" of the Christ lay not in any form of worldly or religious power but in the passion of his love and in the self-sacrificing abandon of his desire to serve and save all beings.

After the priest had finished, I happened to look up at the crucifix at the back of the church. There is only one way I can describe what happened then; the Christ on the cross became alive. For fifteen astounding minutes, with open eyes, my entire being racked by the glory of what I was witnessing, I saw the Christ on the cross extending his arms in a gesture of all-embracing, absolute, and final love to the whole of reality.

Wave after wave of divine love invaded me; nothing in any of the many experiences of the Divine I had had up to that moment prepared me for the volcanic ecstasy and passion and sheer frightening force of what streamed to me from the living Christ. It took all the strength I possessed not to crumble under the fiery intensity of what was being given me; I gripped the pew in front of me as involuntary sobs of gratitude shook me from head to foot.

After the service I said nothing about what I had experienced to anyone, but went quietly with my friends to their car. Then I glimpsed sitting in the dust at the gate of the church the most wretched and derelict human being I have ever seen—a young Indian man, probably in his early twenties, in shredded khaki pants and a disgustingly filthy white shirt, with no arms or legs. I had seen the living Christ in splendor on the cross; now I saw him, just as vividly and unforgettably, in the shattered, abandoned being before me. I knew that this young man who could not defend himself or even move without being helped and who was totally at the mercy of others was none other than the Christ himself. I went up to him and gazed into his eyes a long time; he gazed back at me with the most gentle helpless and resigned look I have ever seen, full of an inexpressible pain and a kind of final dignity. As I put everything I had on me into his shirt pocket, I heard a voice say within me softly, "Now you have seen me in everyone, you must serve me in everyone. Now you have seen that I live especially in the poor and derelict of every kind, you must devote all of your gifts and the rest of your life on earth to working to change the conditions that create misery."

Silently I vowed to the voice within me that I would do as it asked. Two days later, when my father was blessing me for the last time with his hand on my head, he said to me, "I do not wish you money or fame or even happiness, although I hope and pray God will be good to you and give you all these things. I wish you the constant living presence of the Christ at the heart of your life now and always."

This immense meeting with the Christ, which has continued to grow within me, has not made me a "Christian"; there are no possible labels or dogmatic containers for the vast force of divine love that I experienced that Sunday and continue to experience, steadily and more and more intensely burning in the core of my body and trying to infuse everything I write or do. The Christ I know is beyond all religion, all dogma, all churches, especially perhaps the ones created in his name; he is nothing less than the love force at the heart of every human being, the love force that is at the heart of the Direct Path, the volcanic, all-transforming nuclear power of active divine human love that is waiting in everyone on earth to be released and expressed and lived and incarnated in every law and institution, in every creative and scientific and political activity.

All the great mystical revelations speak of and describe in their own terms something of this force. In Hinduism, it is celebrated as the Ananda—the blazing bliss of the Godhead; in Sufism it is known as the heart power of the Beloved, the direct inner experience of the love that creates and infuses all things; in Mahayana Buddhism it is known as Bodhicitta, the enlightened compassion that fuels the vow of the bodhisattva to return again and again to this reality to help free all sentient beings from its illusions.

What my experience of this final and all-consuming love made clear to me was that mystical experience has to be made real in active service of all beings everywhere and in a burning commitment to transform the conditions of earth life in every way and on every level. Through my encounter with the Christ in Coimbatore, the Direct Path revealed itself to me as not merely a path of direct private communion with God but as one also of *public* commitment to political, social, sexual, and economic transformation. What do all the highest meditations and revelations mean if they do not alter those conditions that keep billions below the poverty line and allow the horrible rape of nature to continue? How can we even begin to speak of a mystical renaissance in our time—as so many do so glibly—if millions of people are not being galvanized to claim their divine identity not merely in "private" inner experience but also in a living commitment to fight for the *transformation* of existing conditions? What happened to me on that Sunday in Coimbatore two and a half years ago is that I saw, with no possibility of ever being able to turn away from what I saw, that nothing in my or anyone else's inner journey would be anything more than narcissistic fantasy if the love we were receiving from the Divine were not also being given out to all beings, and not in a purely emotional or even spiritual way either, but in a dynamically *practical* way also, a way that demands of all of us a stark look at real conditions and their remedies.

What I saw—and saw chillingly clearly—in other words was the limitation of all purely otherworldly inward or private forms of mysticism. My father's final blessing, his death, and the force of what I experienced in the church at Coimbatore compelled me to plunge into an exploration of the historical Jesus and the authentic Christian mystical tradition. In my previous work I had made available, as richly as I could, the transforming insights and visions and practices I had myself learned from Hinduism, Buddhism, and Sufism; in my most recent work, especially in *Son of Man: The Mystical Path to Christ,* I have tried to do for the Christian mystical tradition what my work with Sogyal Rinpoche and Patrick Gaffney did for the Tibetan Buddhist in *The Tibetan Book of Living and Dying*—to make available to all seekers everywhere the transformatory passion and practices that stream from realization of the Christ. What drove me in this labor was the increasingly strong belief that it was essential for all beings who truly have the good of the world at heart to listen to the challenge of the Christ to make love real in the most radical and revolutionary way in every arena and at every level of society.

The richness, complexity, and comprehensiveness of my own journey had taken me deep into middle eastern and eastern mystical disciplines to return me to the living heart of my own Christian tradition; what I discovered there was in many ways the truth that focused and made coherent and practical everything I had learned from Rumi and Ramakrishna and Aurobindo and the Tibetans.

Through my confrontation with this truth—that mystical knowledge and love must be made active, radical, and transformatory at every level in the real—the vast potential of the Direct Path has at last come into focus, and in a way that consummates and fulfills, I believe, the highest and richest truths not only of the world's mystical and religious but also of its political, scientific, and artistic traditions.

The Vision of
the Direct Path

WHAT IS ATTEMPTING to be born, I believe, through the agony and terror of this extremely dangerous but also extremely creative and fertile period, is a new humanity, one that is in direct and un-mediated contact with the Divine, free of the divisiveness, body hatred, and bias toward transcendence that disfigures all the inherited patriarchal religions, and so is able at last to inhabit time, the body, and the earth with ecstatic consciousness and a passionate and radical sense of responsibility toward all living things.

It seems to me (and to increasingly greater numbers of people) that *all* the major religions have failed in one essential task—the reducing of human anxiety and aggression through the instruction of human beings in their essential divine nature. Each of them, in different but fundamentally similar ways, controls believers and claims to broker the relationship between the believer and God in ways that both subtly and blatantly keep the believer from claiming the full range of his or her innate divine powers.

The guru system too—as the epidemic of scandals over the last thirty years in *all* the major mystical transmission systems makes clear to anyone honest enough to confront the facts—also disempowers the seeker in a subtle way: Worshipping another person as divine can *seem* a means to realize your own individual divinity, but in the overwhelming majority of cases it just re-creates ancient patterns of dependence and old habits of giving away one's own power to another. It is also clear that almost all those currently claiming to be enlightened—and therefore beyond karma and criticism of any kind—are nothing of the sort; they are using an ancient and sacred language of mystical truth to justify ways of getting rich, accruing personal power, and acting as "stars" in what has tragically become a kind of international Hollywood star system.

What this failure of the traditional ways of reaching God means is that the sacred energy now being released in a worldwide opening to the Divine *cannot* reach its full expression because it is being siphoned off into inadequate systems or exploited by unscrupulous gurus for their own very temporal purposes. A potential birth—on a gigantic scale—is being, or is in danger of being, aborted. This is potentially disastrous, for as I and many others now believe, if there isn't a vast raising of human consciousness very soon and on a scale that influences all major political and environmental decisions, nature and thus the human race are in danger of being destroyed. The future of the entire human race may depend on whether large numbers of the human race can now take the *Direct* Path into claiming humbly their divine humanity and acting from it in order to preserve the environment and see that justice is done to the poor and starving and depressed. What is needed on a large scale, I believe, is an army of servant-warriors for peace and justice, an army of practical visionaries and active mystics who work in every field and in every arena to transform the world.

This is a radical vision, of course, but it is not a new one. Christ's real teaching was *not,* as the church has claimed, about worshipping *him* as son of God; it was an attempt to transmit to everyone else the intimate, *direct,* totally transforming relationship he had himself realized with God, an attempt to empower all beings with their own human divine identity and to begin a mystical and political revolution. The ancient shamanic cultures (as we can see from the remnants of them that survive in the Aboriginal and American native peoples) believed that *all* beings were entitled, by virtue of being born into this world, to a *direct* relationship with the Source, and they developed elaborate and poignant rituals for

every stage of life. Early Hinayana Buddhism had no time f
elaborate master worship that so infused the Mahayana s
the Buddha made it clear that he was *not* a god and that all who
wanted enlightenment as passionately and pointedly as he had
wanted it could have it if they were prepared to give, suffer, and
work enough. His dying words, after all, were "Go and work out
your own salvation, with diligence."

Most of the schools of Judaism have stressed the necessity of
going to the Divine directly. Even in Hinduism, which has extolled
and worshipped the guru concept, there have been many sects and
movements profoundly critical of all intermediaries between the
human heart and its origin. The *Direct* Path, then, has always been
known and followed by a certain part of humanity. If many religions and mystical systems have played its significance down, it is
because the Direct Path is inherently radical. After all, if everyone
is able to be in unmediated contact with the Divine, to be taught
in the terms of their own lives directly by the Divine, then what
need is there for a priest class, monasteries and temples, or gurus?
And if everyone is in the highest sense equal before God, then very
soon the idea that the historical Christ proposed—that people
should also be equal in society—becomes unavoidable and the
whole hierarchical system of patriarchal cultures and religions is
menaced. We are now being strangled to death, I believe, by these
authoritarian systems that no longer have any rationale or spiritual innocence; it is time for the revolutionary energy of the Direct
Path to be released and Christ's and Buddha's vision of a free, empowered humanity to be born at last. On that birth depends the
future.

The Birth

THE RULES OF THIS BIRTH the Direct Path makes possible
are simple; *everything* that divides one human being from another
or from nature must now be revealed as the convenient social, cultural, or religious fiction it is; *everything* that in any way disempowers or depresses the divine power and consciousness innate in
every human being must be unmasked as a lie of power; *everything*
that provides authentic help and truth and wisdom from whatever
area of human experience or pursuit must be embraced and fused
with every other source of awareness and empowerment to provide
the human race in this, its hour of danger and need, with the resources of an integral wisdom, a wisdom that unites the highest
mystical understanding of the transcendent with the highest
scientific, political, technological, economic, social, and psychological knowledge of how to shape the immanent to mirror and
enshrine the ideals of equality, justice, and compassion on every
level.

What does this mean in practice? It means that the essential
truth of the innate divinity of all human beings, beyond all dogma
and religious difference, must become the ground of all human
knowledge and practice. It means that all the valuable insights and
transformative practices of all the mystical traditions must be preserved outside the systems that still try to mediate or control
them. It means that a marriage must take place, at the highest,

most lucid level, between mystical and scientific knowledge, the tremendous achievements of western science and technology and the ancient wisdom of the middle eastern and eastern mystical systems. It means that the modern western achievements of psychoanalysis, democratic government, sexual freedom—the great liberating work of Marx and Freud and Jung—must be fused with the richest, deepest, and most transformatory work of the Tibetan, Hindu, cabalistic, and Christian mystics and all the shamanic truths preserved, against so many odds, by the native peoples. It means that the fatal separation between mysticism and politics, between a sacred cultivation of inner character and a commitment to act in the world to radically transform all existing social, economic, and political conditions, must end in a marriage of prophetic vision and purpose with steady and passionate political action to stop the killing of nature and the proliferation of the horrors of mechanized war and abysmal poverty.

This great marriage and electric, dynamic fusion of everything that has traditionally been kept apart—East and West, religion and science, masculine will and order and feminine sensitivity and commitment to life in all its forms, sexuality and spirituality, mystical initiation and political action—is the goal and alchemical work and challenge and potential of the Direct Path. If it can be realized—and it must be, I believe, for the human race to have a chance of surviving the many dangers and problems that afflict it—a wholly new humanity will be born, a truly universal humanity respectful of the best insights and practices of all the religions and mystical transmission systems but enslaved to none of them, tolerant of all forms of healthy and love-empowered diversity, awake to the finest discoveries of every field of knowledge, in harmony both with nature and the glory that is always manifesting nature.

For the first time in human history, such a birth on a massive scale is now possible. All the wisdom of all the mystical systems is now available to anyone with the willingness, stamina, and discipline to absorb it; the Internet and other forms of world communication make open to everyone potentially the most recent and transformatory discoveries in every domain; forms of world government exist in however fragmentary fraught and imperfect shapes; the very extent of the catastrophe that threatens us all has the power to make us awake to the necessity for total transformation if we have the courage and the willingness to let it.

A great Christian visionary, Hildegard of Bingen, summed up the highest and most challenging wisdom of all the mystical traditions when she wrote; "Humanity, full of creative possibilities, is God's work. Humanity is called on to assist God. Humanity is called to co-create with God." This call to "co-create" with God a new future is the central, and glorious, challenge of our time and of the Direct Path. It involves, and demands, great sincerity, passion, humility, and discipline; its potential is as boundless as divine love itself.

As the great modern Sufi mystic Iqbal wrote:

Who can tell what miracles
Love has in store for us
If only we have the courage
To become one with It?
Everything we think we know now
Is only the beginning
Of another knowing that itself has no end.
And everything we now can accomplish
Will seem derisory to us
When the powers of our divine nature
Flower in glory and act through us.

One

The Map

The soul grows by its
constant participation in
that which transcends it.

GREGORY OF NYSSA

You have to climb the stairs and
rest your feet firmly on each step
in order to reach the summit.

SRI AUROBINDO

Between me and You,
there is only me.
Take away the me,
so only You remain.

AL-HALLAJ

Why We Are Here

Take courage.
The human race is divine.

PYTHAGORAS

THE FIRST THING we must understand if we are to take the Direct Path in full awareness is why we are here in the first place and who and what we really are.

The great mystical traditions are astonishingly united in their answers to these questions; they each claim, in different ways, that we are essentially sparks of Divine Consciousness, emanated by the Divine out of itself, and placed here in this dimension to travel back to conscious union with the Godhead.

Thus, for the Buddhist mystics, the purpose of being incarnated here is to unfold our innate Buddha nature and enter into conscious possession of its timeless peace, bliss, power, and all-seeing knowledge. For the Hindu mystics of the Gita and the Upanishads, the whole meaning of human life lies in realizing the essential unity of our individual soul, the atman, with Brahman, the eternal reality, that timeless and spaceless and placeless bliss-truth-consciousness that is at once manifesting everything in all the worlds and beyond all manifestation. Sufi mystics claim that the human being has a unique relationship to God because God fashioned us with his own hands, while creating all other things by the Divine Word and its fiat; they believe that God, while making us, breathed into us his own being, sowed in our innermost core a memory of our origin in him, and ordained that the whole purpose of our lives on earth should be to return in full awareness to the Origin, whose children we are. For Christian mystics such as Meister Eckhart and Teresa of Avila, the soul is placed in a body and in matter to undertake the immense journey to a living aware "marriage" with the inner Christ and his divine love and knowledge. For Taoists like Lao-tzu and Chuang-tzu, the whole of the universe is a manifestation of the the mystery of the Unnamable—which for convenience's sake they name the Tao—and the one who realizes his or her own nature realizes his or her own essential unity on every level with this Tao in its original peace, harmony, and boundless fecundity.

When you look past the different terminologies employed by the different mystical systems, you see clearly that they are each talking about the same overwhelming truth—that we are all essentially children of the Divine and can realize that identity with our Source here on earth and in a body. Although each of the mystical systems expresses it in subtly different ways, this realization that we can all have of our essential identity with the Divine is always described as a nondual one—that is, as a relationship in which we wake up to the overwhelming and glorious fact that our fundamental consciousness is "one" with the Divine Consciousness that is manifesting all things, all worlds, and all events. In other words, we are each of us parts of Godhead who, when we are aware of it, enter into a naked, nonconceptual identity-of-consciousness with the Source from which all things and all events are constantly streaming.

Each of the major systems has a different way of characterizing this astounding truth. Jesus in the Gospels says; "The Kingdom is within you." The seers of the Hindu Upanishads describe the awakening in three interrelated short formulas: *tat tvam Asi, aham Brahmasmi,* and *sarvam Brahmasm,* which mean "You are That," "You are Brahman," and "Everything that is is Brahman."

A Tibetan Buddhist, Nyoshul Khenpo Rinpoche, describes this nondual realization of essential unity with all things in the following way:

Profound and tranquil, free from complexity,
Uncompounded luminous clarity,
Beyond the mind of conceptual ideas

This is the depth of the mind of the Victorious Ones.
In this there is not a thing to be removed
Nor anything that needs to be added.
It is merely the immaculate
Looking naturally at itself

A great Sufi mystic, Rumi, speaks of the mystery of this union when he writes:

Love is here; it is the blood in my veins, my skin
I am destroyed; He has filled me with passion.
His fire has flooded the nerves of my body
Who am I? Just my name; the rest is him.

A Jewish mystic, Ben Gamliel, says of this ultimate truth state that it is the "seamless being-in-place that comes from attending to Reality."

All these formulations are stammering attempts to put into words what can never be adequately expressed but can be experienced—and has been over the course of human history by millions of true seekers in all traditions.

The Paradox of the Journey

All major mystical traditions have recognized that there is a paradox at the heart of the journey of return to Origin.

Put simply, this is that we are *already* what we seek, and that what we are looking for on the Path with such an intensity of striving and passion and discipline is already within and around us at all moments. The journey and all its different ordeals are all emanations of the One Spirit that is manifesting everything in all dimensions; every rung of the ladder we climb toward final awareness is made of the divine stuff of awareness itself; Divine Consciousness is at once creating and manifesting all things and acting in and as all things in various states of self-disguise throughout all the different levels and dimensions of the universe.

The great Hindu mystic Kabir put this paradox with character-istic simplicity when he said:

Look at you, you madman,
Screaming you are thirsty
And are dying in a desert
When all around you there is nothing but water!

And the Sufi poet Rumi reminds us:

You wander from room to room
Hunting for the diamond necklace
That is already around your neck!

The "Sublime Joke" of the Journey

Knowing that we are looking for something we already have and are does not, of course, mean that the journey is unnecessary, only that there is a vast and sublime joke waiting to be discovered at its end.

There is a story that I was told by an old Greek Orthodox monk that describes this joke deliciously. I was twenty-five when I met him in a monastery in central Greece; he took me to his room and gave me thick black coffee and we talked of God. He said, "Have you heard the story of Stassinopolos Street?" When I said I hadn't, he threw up his hands in mock horror. "Then you still don't know the meaning of life." And he began:

"There was a poor young man who lived in a village in the Pelepponese who had a dream. In it he saw a courtyard with turquoise tiles with an old man sitting on a vast pile of treasure. The old man said to him, 'All this treasure belongs to you. Come and get it! You'll find me at 3 Stassinopolos Street in Salonika.' When the poor young man woke up, he leapt for joy. 'God is good! God has told me how I can become very rich! And in such a de-tailed way too!'

"So he set out immediately for Salonika. Well—to cut a long story short—everything conceivable happened to him to stop him getting there for years. He was robbed, beaten, left for dead, kidnapped, sold into slavery for two decades on the Barbary Coast. As a middle-aged man, weary, disillusioned, he found himself in Salonika at last and decided, 'What the hell, I'll see if Stassinopolos Street really exists.'

"Well, it did exist and there was a number 3. And, sure enough, when he entered through the door, he saw an old man sitting on a bench in the sunlight in a courtyard with turquoise tiles just like the old man in the dream. His heart leapt with joy.

"The old man looked up at him and clapped his hands. 'Oh, you have come at last! You are the man I saw in a dream I had many years ago! Many years ago I dreamed of a poor young man who lived in a village somewhere in the Peleponnese. He was sitting on his broken-down cot, and underneath his cot there was a gleaming pile of treasure. I meant to set out and see if I could find the man, but life intervened and I never did.'

"All at once, the man who had been looking all his life for Stassinopolos Street understood; the treasure he had been hunting for so long was all the time within his own deepest self."

The old monk wiped away tears of joy and held my hands in his.

"My son," he whispered. "Please never forget this story."

I remember asking him rudely, "Well, if the poor young man always had the treasure within him, why did he have to go on such a long, harsh, complex journey to find that out?"

The old monk laughed. "That is just how it is. You have to go through a million different experiences to discover what you already are. It is God's joke."

One serious explanation of this joke at the heart of the journey is, of course, that our essential self is hidden from us by what the Sufi mystics call "a hundred thousand veils of illusion." Placed in this dimension of time and space and matter, we forget who we are; we identify our essential nature with what surrounds us and with what our culture and society and parents and ordinary senses tell us about ourselves; a massive journey is then needed for us to "dis-identify" with everything we have falsely learned about ourselves so that we can experience, with the "hundred thousand veils" burned away, the glory of our true identity.

This is one explanation, and it is true as far as it goes. The trouble with it, however, is that it subtly devalues the experience of being created at all and dismisses too easily the whole of human experience and creation itself as what the Hindu mystics have called maya, illusion. Why would the Divine have created us in the first place if the only meaning of our being created is to *escape* the "illusion" of Creation, transcend all its particulars and events to enter into what is beyond it?

Perhaps the deepest and richest answer to this question—and it is an "answer" that the Direct Path embraces in its difficulty and challenge—is that we are placed here as a *seed* of the Divine within time, space, and matter to *unfold* fully all our divine powers and capacities within them: We do this not to escape the "illusion" of creation but to *divinize* not only ourselves but also reality *from within it*.

This explanation—that is at the heart of certain schools of Jewish, Sufi, and Christian mysticism, and which has inspired the work of great modern evolutionary mystics such as Teilhard de Chardin and the great Hindu sage Aurobindo—has the advantage of treating the whole journey of the Path not just as a marvelously witty joke—which it, of course, partly is—but also as an opportunity for the Divine *through us* to permeate, infuse, and transfigure its own creation.

What *this* version of the meaning of the journey makes of each of us is what Hildegard of Bingen calls "co-creators with God of a New World." We undertake the tremendous journey of return to Origin not to vanish into Origin or simply rest in its peace and glory but to be infused with its sacred passion and power and become so saturated with its energy and love that we can "reenter" reality and become agents with and in God of a massive transformation of *all* the conditions of the Creation. In other words, we are created by the Divine to participate with it in its "plan" of bringing the whole of the Creation consciously into the glory of its eternal being.

The Truth of Reincarnation

Such a massive and all-demanding enterprise is bound to fail if we do not try to be as clear as we possibly can be about what it entails.

All those who take the Direct Path need to be clear about the truth of reincarnation. Reincarnation in one form or another has been accepted by nearly all the world's major mystical transmission systems—by Buddhism and Hinduism primarily but also by certain schools of Sufism, Cabalism, by the majority of the Christians of the first three centuries of the development of Christianity, and by many of the native shamanic traditions.

Reincarnation has been accepted as a reality not because it is "exotic" or "mysterious" but because it makes sense and because at certain levels of awareness it becomes self-evident; just before he attained enlightenment, it is said, for instance, the Buddha saw clearly all the lives that had led up to this finally liberating experience in all their detail and necessity.

Reincarnation makes sense because when you see just what is entailed in the journey of return and just how many levels of fantasy, false identification, and illusion have to be penetrated and transcended, it becomes clear that most beings are most unlikely to be able to accomplish *all* of the journey in one lifetime. It *is* possible to do so, but only by the rare being who is willing to give and risk and suffer everything that is necessary with almost unimaginable singleness of purpose.

How Reincarnation "Works"

I was six years old when the truth of reincarnation was exposed to me casually by Shantih, an Indian saint whom I met at the house of my mother's great friend Bella, in Delhi. She was a big, serene woman who worked with the poor and always wore a white sari. Eating chocolates on Bella's big bed, Shantih and I sat and I plucked up my courage to ask her about what my mother had already told me, that Shantih had, as a little girl, walked up to a stranger in the street and claimed him as her husband in a previous life and told him where she had hidden some money in their house.

I asked Shantih to tell me her story. Quite matter-of-factly, Shantih told me how, when she was six, she had clearly recognized a man in a town near her village as her husband in a previous life and how everything that she "remembered" about that life had been checked by priests and even some "very skeptical English journalists with spectacles" and found to be true.

She then told me of how she had remembered, soon after meeting her former husband, what had happened between the life she was living then and the life she had lived before. Everything she told me so simply that afternoon I later uncovered in my research with Tibetan mystics for *The Tibetan Book of Living and Dying,* and in my reading in other mystical traditions and in accounts of the near death experience.

Shantih settled back on the bed, popped a chocolate into her mouth, and started:

"When you die, you will meet a great white light which is God. If you live a good life, you will have the courage to dive into this light and choose it and become one with it and you will be free forever in God. Last life I was good and so when this light came up I just jumped into it.

"What happened then was that I met Krishna. Everyone meets the holy being they believe in. If you are a Christian you meet Jesus; if you are a Buddhist you meet Buddha.

"I met Krishna and he said, 'You could stay with me here forever but I want you to go down and be a healer and tell everyone about what you have seen so that they can have faith. I want you to teach people about the truth of reincarnation and so I will arrange for you to meet the people you knew in your last life and have everything you say checked and believed.'"

Shantih paused, closed her eyes as if still seeing her God, and then went on.

"And then Krishna explained to me how the system of rebirth works. You come into this world with *two* souls, one inside the other. The outer one is the one that you will evolve and develop in *this* life; the inner one will go on and on traveling until you reach final union with God. The outer one, Krishna told me, will die at the end of this life; everything you learn about God will however penetrate the inner one and so help it grow in wisdom and understanding on its journey."

The Two Souls or "Drops"

What Shantih told me that wonderful afternoon is echoed, I discovered, in the descriptions of the death process in the Egyptian Book of the Dead and even more precisely in the Tibetan Book of the Dead. Tibetan mystics also describe, just as Shantih did, *two* souls: They do not call them souls, however, for Buddhists do not believe in an "entity" that continues from life to life. They call them *tigle,* "drops."

I can still remember the shock and inner laughter I experienced when one morning in Nepal the old Tibetan mystic who was teaching me about dying and reincarnation said:

"In Tibetan Buddhism we say that everyone comes into this life from another with two 'tigle,' two 'drops,' one enfolded in the other. The larger one is called 'the lifetime indestructible drop' and the inner one 'the eternal indestructible drop.' The larger one develops during a particular life but dies at death; the smaller one transmigrates from life to life until enlightenment.

"The highest level of stable evolution in any given life," he went on, "saturates and penetrates the 'eternal indestructible drop' and is carried into this life. It is carried not usually as a specific memory or set of memories but as what might be called a mood of adaptation, a fundamental 'inclination' of the whole personality."

Involution and Evolution

What I also learned from my study with the Tibetans is that every larger "lifetime indestructible drop" carries within it the memory of the experience of the "white light" Shantih spoke of—of what is

called in Tibetan Buddhism "the clear light of emptiness." It not
only carries this memory of Origin but also, to be "enclosed" at all
within the human being, has had itself to undergo a process of
involution—from being one with the "white light" or "clear
emptiness" to uniting first with the psyche that forms in the inter-
mediary realms between death and rebirth and then with the body
itself created in the process of birth into this life.

What this means, in plain language, is that "enfolded" within
the "lifetime indestructible drop" or, if you like, the "soul," is the
whole intricate and extraordinary process by which the light of Divine Consciousness becomes first psyche or spirit and then matter.

The journey to Origin, then, the path of evolution that leads to
conscious repossession of Divine Consciousness, involves an
unfolding of what is "enfolded" within the inner tigle. Each of the
different levels of consciousness has to be reentered in the *opposite*
order; the identification with what some Buddhist commentators
call the "gross bodymind" has to be transcended through an identification with the "subtle" levels of the psyche, and this in turn
has to be transcended by a full realization of identity with the Divine Consciousness in nondual awareness.

This is the clearest, most precise, and scientific explanation of
what happens in the journey of return to Origin that I have come
across; it manages to convey both its difficulty and also the reason
it can be undertaken at all; its complete "code" of your life is as
much a part of our whole being as our DNA.

How Inner Evolution Unfolds

Understanding and accepting this explanation of reincarnation
and how it actually "works" brings us to two linked conclusions
about how the mystical journey back to Origin actually unfolds,
and must unfold if it is to be full and complete.

The first is that for the complete "unfolding" of what is "enfolded," all the different "steps" of awareness have to be attained
and made "solid" before being transcended: Although we may

have experiences from a level other than the one we are currently on—for example, while still largely identified with the "bodymind" we can have flashes of nondual consciousness—these do not in any way constitute a complete achieved possession of the further level of awareness; the entire being has to be "shifted" to the new level for it to be permanently attained and for it to be able to be transcended. As Aurobindo put it: "You have to climb the stairs and rest your feet firmly on each step to reach the summit."

In this connection, the Sufis make a vital distinction between what they call "states" and what they call "stations." "States" are inner experiences that, while they may be marvelous and revelatory, come and go; "stations" are achieved and permanent levels of awareness that necessitate a complete reorganization of the experiencing self and show that it has completed another stage in its unfolding into Divine Unity. The journey back to Origin can be completed only "station" by "station": There are no shortcuts.

The second conclusion about how the path of return unfolds, builds on, and enriches the first is implied in the model of enfoldment to begin with. This is that as we progress from level to level, or station to station we lose nothing of what is essential that we have learned along the way; what was our whole understanding on one station becomes an integrated part of our developing awareness on another. The journey back is like a series of ever-larger concentric circles, all dwelling, or "nesting," within each other. Nondual realization, then, is *not* as some people persist in seeing it, something "floaty" or "blissed out," but a consciousness that contains and embraces while totally transcending all other forms of awareness, able to use them all when necessary, but finally freed from any clinging identification with any of them.

Keeping constantly in mind these two linked conclusions about the nature and full unfoldment of the "enfolded" powers and capacities within us is essential because it keeps us continually realistically informed of where we actually are along the journey, and of what we must still strive to incarnate if it is to be complete.

The Journey Is "Natural"

What can never be stressed too much or meditated on too deeply is that the journey of return to Origin, the journey to our divine nature, is in its own way just as *natural,* just as inherently part of the fullness of nature and creation as growing roses in a garden or wheat in a field. One of the ways in which we have all been devastated by a society and culture addicted to materialism and to materialist explanations of everything is that everything that does not fall within the narrow confines of these explanations takes on immediately an unnatural, weird "mysterious" glow and seems unfathomable. This is especially true of our attitude toward mysticism and mystical development.

The truth of the actual experience of mystical growth when it is fed by and combined with deep knowledge is very different. While no one will or can ever know the mystery that is God (this becomes clearer and clearer as we progress), a great deal about how this mystery works in us to take us closer and closer to it *can* be known, and has been known by mystics and mystical traditions down the ages.

No one will ever finally know in all its facets and depths the force that makes a rose grow, but the different stages of the rose's growth, from a cutting to a stem to a bud to the glorious final unfolding-in-splendor, can be known, charted, humbly celebrated, and comprehended. The same is true of the growth of transcendent awareness within us; its stages have been charted in astonishingly similar terms by those in every tradition who have given their life to pursuing its full unfolding. And this unfolding, like that of the rose, obeys the laws of a nature that is fully divine in all its organic rhythms.

Karma and Consciousness

We have already explored together one of the essential "laws" of divine nature—that of reincarnation. Now we must become clear about the relationship between past karma and the consciousness with which we enter our present incarnation.

We are all born with the direction and intention of our consciousness already determined by what Hinduism and Buddhism refer to as "past karma." What we have lived, experienced, and realized in our past lives affects in different, sometimes profound, ways the direction of *this* one.

It is essential to remember, however, that karma—which means simply "the law of cause and effect"—is not something irrevocably fixed. Every choice we make, every thought we think, every action we take, "causes" new "effects" that can alter "past karma" in constantly changing and subtle ways. Just as the universe is in constant dynamic change, so are we, and so, therefore, is our destiny. The Buddha made this clear when he said: "Karma creates like an artist and composes like a dancer."

The more awake we become to our divine nature and to the laws of divine evolution, in fact, the more consciously we become the "artists" and "dancers" of our own karma, the architects of our fate in and under God. So, while the direction and intention of our consciousness at the beginning of this life may be partly, even profoundly, shaped by what we have experienced and realized in our past lives, we are in no way imprisoned by such a shaping. We have in fact taken birth again to seize the immense opportunity that birth into human consciousness provides for growth, progress, and evolution; life in this universe of time and space is not in any way our "enemy" but a medium of astonishing richness and flexibility, offering us marvelous chances of self-transformation.

This tremendous hope inherent in human birth cannot be stressed too strongly, especially since many easterners interpret karma far too mechanistically and many westerners are still deranged by notions of "original sin." Not to acknowledge the partly determining power of karma would be to deny the truth of reincarnation; to overstress it would be to limit the freedom-for-growth of the divine that is seeded in us.

As the Tibetan mystic I met in my late twenties in Ladakh, Thuksey Rinpoche, once said to me, "It is as absurd to think yourself completely a slave to your past, whatever it may have been, as it is to think yourself completely free from it. If you were a mass murderer in your last life, you will have to work out the consequences in this, or another life. But if you understand now, here, the enormous chance that spiritual development offers you, you can burn up and transform *all* your past karma and achieve liberation even in this life." And then he told me the story of Milarepa, Tibet's greatest saint, and the founder of the Drukpa Kargyupa lineage he belonged to, who had begun his life by being a black magician and serial killer and who, through intense repentance, divine grace, and long passionate inner work, became perhaps the best-loved saint of Tibet.

The Law of Forgetting, or, Amnesis

The "laws" of divine origin, reincarnation, and the effects of past karma ensure then that we enter this life as divine human beings on a vast journey through time to realize our timeless nature.

All the mystical traditions agree, however, that this life begins with a forgetting of our inherent connection to the divine, an "amnesis." In order to "unfold" in time and matter and space, it seems, the drop, or "soul," has to "forget" its Source and Origin in light and start again its whole evolutionary process, even if it enters this dimension already highly evolved.

Several explanations have been given for this; the most convincing, to my mind, is that remembering too much either of the experience of divine union in the light or of the details of past lives would greatly confuse the soul's development in *this* life. For *complete* unfolding of consciousness within matter—the aim of life—the entire process has to be begun again: a certain "masking" and self-ignorance is essential, especially in the initial stages. *Behind* this "masking" or self-ignorance, however, the divine consciousness waits for its moment of recognition; in fact, even the "masking" and "ignorance" is one of its modes.

This amnesis, or, forgetting, is not final in every case. My friend Shantih, after all, remembered details of her past life in startling detail; Tibetan mystics claim that highly evolved beings can often remember their past life clearly for the first three or four years of childhood. The Dalai Lama, it is said, as a little boy of three in this life, remembered the tutor he had had in his last one and could identify various objects that had belonged to him in his last incarnation.

Even in such cases, however, the memories of past existences fade after a while so that *this* life can be lived with total concentration, and the "unfolding" of consciousness along the path can progress from station to station, until spirit has completely flowered in matter, and the divinization of the human is complete.

The Map of the Transformation of Consciousness

Childhood, the Formation of the Ego, and the Beginnings of the Path

In childhood, many, if not most, of us have what can be called "numinous" experiences of the divine—ecstatic experiences of joy or unity, or even direct initiations into other worlds. Some of us, as I have said, may even remember past incarnations.

This numinous awareness fades fast, however, so that we can undertake the *full* journey of unfolding in this life. And while some of us may remember all our life—and be inspired by, the splendor of these experiences or memories of early childhood—it is important to remember that they are only glimpses of the awakened consciousness and not that awakening itself. The journey of unfolding has to progress through *all* the stages for the full divine consciousness to be born. While the child may be briefly initiated into unity consciousness, or bliss, its fundamental awareness is unavoidably self-centered and not other- and world-centered like the consciousness of the awakened being.

The subsequent development of ego consciousness that occurs, most psychologists agree, in gradations between the ages of five and twelve, is *not*, as some "romantic" mystical traditions have claimed, a fundamental "tragedy," the equivalent in psychological terms of the biblical fall. On the contrary, developing a healthy ego is an essential prerequisite for the full unfolding of the path. You cannot go beyond and transcend something that is not there in the first place; the ego has to be developed clearly and strongly before it can be transformed and eventually unmade and remade in divine consciousness: The full open rose needs a stem to grow on and out of.

While the development of the ego gives the unfolding person certain essential powers of discrimination and strengths of self-definition that the child's mind does not have, there is an inherent danger—that the evolving personality should identify itself completely with it and define the whole range of its possibilities within its narrow terms.

Also, very few, if any, of us develop entirely healthy egos; mostly, our ego development is conditioned by parental, social, and religious restrictions. Many of us also will be marked at an early age by various forms of trauma—whether of abuse or abandonment or other forms of psychological difficulty. In some cases this experience of trauma will be so severe that any further unfolding of the personality will be aborted; in most cases, wounds will be inflicted on the psyche around which defenses will be built like hardened scars. These in turn will come to seem essential parts of our innate character—and not "accidental traits" that a great deal of inner work can dissolve and undo.

Another problem the unfolding personality will meet in a culture like ours is that almost everything in our world celebrates the values of the ego and not of the soul; celebrates, in other words, self-centeredness and the pursuit of personal power. The prevailing worldview of our culture is almost exclusively materialist. So not only are the limited values of ego consciousness adored as the ultimate meaning of life, but real knowledge of the possibilities of awareness beyond the ego is either denied or derided.

None of this need make us despair. The Divine is extremely resourceful in its efforts to reach and transform us; the "seed" of Divine Consciousness within us is always alive, even if we are not aware of it.

Only a very few people in any time make the transition from ego consciousness to the beginnings of mystical awareness without having to pass through a sometimes prolonged period of crisis. The limitations of life within the ego and its agendas have to be experienced, sometimes painfully, for the desire to transcend them really to take root in our being. What usually happens to the modern seeker is that he or she has to pass through some loss or breakdown that reveals clearly the hollowness of all the proposed "solutions" and the emptiness of our contemporary culture's cult of power and greed. These can be anything from a sad love affair to bankruptcy to illness or even a nervous breakdown.

It is best, I believe, if this "breakdown" of ego consciousness happens young; the older you get, the harder it is to undo the habits of limited awareness. Also, it is essential not to "waste" the opportunity for further growth such a "breakdown" offers; if you let it make you bitter, scared, or desperate, its potentially transforming openings cannot occur.

If you let yourself become vulnerable and bewildered, and start to search, even half consciously, for a higher meaning to life, you will find that the Divine will start to initiate you in direct and sometimes shocking ways. One of the truths that all mystics recognize is that the Divine is looking for us with far greater intensity than we are looking for *it;* as the prophet Muhammed says in one of his sacred sayings: "Take one step toward God and God will take a thousand steps toward you."

Start to search sincerely for a higher vision, and the Divine will open for you a door into its, and your, essential truth; you will be given whatever is needed to invite you forward—a series of dreams or visions or a meeting with someone further along the Path than you are whose personality you trust and whose witness you can listen to without fear.

What begins now is the first stage of the four stages of the unfolding of Divine Consciousness, "falling in love."

Falling in Love

The beginning of the stage of "falling in love" is usually a series of vivid, overwhelming experiences of Divine Presence that overturns the seeker's understanding of the world and reveal that a wholly different dimension is present in consciousness; such illuminations are far more common than the prevailing scientific-materialist vision of things would have us believe; in my twenty years of seeking, I have met countless people who have had wonderful "openings" to divine reality.

It is important to know this for two reasons—so that you don't think that you are going mad when such experiences explode in your inmost consciousness and also so that you don't overprivilege them and exaggerate their status and importance. All the mystical traditions agree that the visions of initiation or inner experiences of bliss that may occur at this stage are only the beginnings of Divine Consciousness; they are "glimpses" only of a divine truth, love, and joy that will, if you develop and allow them to grow in you, grow infinitely.

What you have to understand, then, at this initial stage, is how little you know, how much inner work you will have to do to progress, and how open you still are to the pressures of the outside world and your still-insistent ego and its many forms of ignorance and illusion. Ramakrishna used to say that a seeker at this stage is like a young, vulnerable sapling that needs to be ringed by a fence if the "goats" are not going to nibble and destroy it.

The best way of building such a fence around your evolving divine self is by devoting yourself, as quickly and consistently as possible, to prayer, meditation, the study of spiritual and mystical texts and systems, and the cultivation of compassion, patience, humility, and generosity in all your practical choices in life and all your dealings with others. Prayer will open you up to the Divine within and around you; meditation will help you stabilize your turbulent ego and make it more and more transparent to the peace, joy, fearlessness, and bliss of your essential divine nature; the study of mystical texts and systems will inspire you and give you courage and help make your awareness of the process you are starting to be engaged in more and more precise, full, and humble. And cultivating what the Buddha called the noble virtues will enable you to begin the great work of the path of attuning your "outer" nature and your actions in every arena to your growing inner knowledge.

The first part of this wonderful stage of "falling in love" with the Divine is what is called in many mystical traditions the "honeymoon" stage. The seeker is amazed and entranced by what he or she is discovering within his or her depths; the visions and experiences that are being received have all the glory of freshness and are welcomed with rapture.

What then happens, however, is that this honeymoon period evolves, when the seeker is ready, into a period of self-purification in which the seeker strives passionately to make her being ever clearer and ever more open to the Divine. This first great purification on the Path is known in many mystical systems as the purification of the senses; in it the different physical senses of the seeker are increasingly clarified and "divinized" so that they can hold more and more of the divine experience being offered them.

This is a demanding process. It entails a tremendous inner analysis, a continual commitment to expose the ego's games by the increasing light of divine awareness; it demands a facing of past trauma and its effects on us and a lucid confrontation with all the forms of subtle self-betrayals that society conditions us to. Only if you have developed a stable practice of prayer and meditation and service, and only if you have truly aroused devotion in your heart toward the Divine, will you be able to "travel" through and endure the rigors—both physical and spiritual—of this period.

The rewards of such discipline and of the deliberate cultivation of longing for God and passion for the Divine are, however, miraculous. Slowly, as the seeker more and more devotedly faces what in himself or herself is untransformed, addicted, and still desperate, and more and more completely exposes his or her being to the divine beauty and mercy, the Divine Presence starts to install itself in increasingly steady ways, and what were visionary "glimpses" become, as all the seeker's senses become steadily more purified, a recognition of the Divine in all things.

What ends the stage of "falling in love" and attests to the "divinization" of the senses is a direct vision of the Presence of the divine light in everything. In this vision, all things are recognized as the creations of the light; the seeker also sees, beyond any shadow of a doubt, that his or her inmost consciousness, the light and the

Divine, are "not two." This is by no means a "final" awakening, but the beginning of another journey, what the Sufis call the "journey in God." The journey to God—to a definite and indubitable awareness of the Divine in and as all things—has ended; the journey of conscious divinization in and under Divine Consciousness has begun.

Engagement

In the stage of engagement, intense love for God becomes a commitment of the whole self to an increasingly conscious transformation *in* God. The ego still remains, but in a subtilized form, since its senses have been purified enough to perceive the Divine Consciousness at all times. The glory of the final experience of "falling in love" becomes a permanent "station" of awareness.

The focus, passion, seriousness, and relative clarity of being that the seeker has now attained enables the Divine within and without to expose its radiance more and more. The stage of "engagement" is always characterized by an often shattering and bewildering series of visions, ecstasies, and illuminations that tremendously expand the seeker's knowledge of his or her own identity and tremendously enhance his or her powers.

With these expansions and enhancements, however, comes a new set of difficulties and temptations. The greatest danger in the first stage of the Path is fear and bewilderment: In "engagement" the greatest danger to the seeker is inflation. The powers and revelations that will awaken in you and be given to you by the Divine in "engagement" are so vast and so astounding that they will derange you and destroy you if you do not remember at every moment what their Source is and if you do not continue to cultivate an ever-more-radical humility.

A wonderful Sufi story helps to make us aware of what is now at stake.

There was an emperor who had a slave he loved passionately and who, he believed, loved him with his whole self. But the emperor wanted to be certain. So he filled ten rooms with heaps of every kind of treasure imaginable—rubies and emeralds, strands of large black pearls, chests full of the richest cloths and rarest, most marvelously illuminated manuscripts, large leather wallets with deeds in them to houses and country estates. When the rooms were full of this treasure, and the walls of the rooms seemed to glow and radiate in the radiance of so much glory, the emperor summoned everyone in his court and all his servants and slaves and said, "Today I am releasing you all from my service. You are at perfect liberty to take anything you want from any of the rooms before you." Even the chief vizier, normally a rather austere kind of man, started to dance a jig and to cram as many jewels and house deeds under his arms as he could.

The slave whom the emperor loved, however, did not move. He stayed standing where he was, silently, his face gazing at the emperor until all the treasure was gone and only he and the emperor were left in a desert of empty rooms. The emperor said quietly, "And you who have stayed and not sought for anything for yourself, what is it you want? You can have anything you want." The slave said nothing, and then the emperor almost shouted, "What is it you want? I order you to tell me!" At last the slave said slowly, "I want you."

The emperor embraced his slave passionately and held him to his breast a long time. Then he said, "Everything I am and have is now yours always."

This wonderful and poignant story reveals that if you want the emperor's "rubies and emeralds and strands of large black pearls"—the wonder and dazzle of various mystical states and powers constantly infusing you—you can never transcend "engagement" and come into the "empty desert" of the "sacred marriage." To do that, you have to stay by the emperor's side "not seeking anything for yourself" and to want the Divine above and beyond anything it can give you or do for you or in you.

What happens at the end of "engagement," then, is a temptation or series of temptations, followed by a long ordeal. Just as Jesus was tempted by the "devil" in the desert to use all the immense, even miraculous, powers that illumination gave him in the service of fame or glory or the exploitation and domination of others, so every seeker who has attained this stage will also be tempted, and tempted finally and deeply, within the terms of his or her own temperament and gifts, to see if in the end what they want is not the truth of the Divine but their own flamboyant advancement in the eyes of the world.

The ferocity, danger, and extent of this temptation is known in all the secret traditions. These know that the stage of "engagement" can endow you with extraordinary occult powers that can tempt you to mimic the Divine before others and to perform what others in lesser states of evolution will call "miracles" but which are really displays of natural spiritual force. These occult powers are well known to include clairvoyance, telepathy, the ability to read others' minds and transmit thoughts and inner messages and appear in others' dreams, the capacity to emit or manifest divine light, and to change, shift, or in some other way transform objects, and the force to compel others to give you money, sex, or to adore and follow you slavishly. The power to do specifically "black" magic, and so to maim psychically or even physically destroy others, may also be given at this stage.

If you choose to exercise these powers in any way for your own advantage, the traditions warn, you will join the ranks of the demonic, and through your perversion of the gifts of God will forfeit not only your spiritual development but also your soul. Most of those the New Age calls "enlightened gurus" or "avatars" are not divine or divinized beings at all, but powerful and unscrupulous occult manipulators who, from the point of view of authentic mystical tradition, are not only *not* in any way enlightened but spiritually on a lower rung even than murderers or child molesters, because they have *chosen* to use the highest divine gifts for worldly power and influence.

It is essential for all seekers now to know of the existence of such occult powers and to face without illusion their almost universal use at this time by so-called gurus and masters. Such beings are not able to give others "freedom," as they so vainly proclaim, for the simple reason that they themselves are not free; how could they be if they are compelled to use occult force to secure money or fame or adulation? Most gurus of this or any time have in fact succumbed to the temptation to power that arises in the stage of "engagement."

It is fashionable in the New Age to dismiss altogether or greatly water down the power or reality of evil. This is a fatal mistake and one of the major reasons that so little authentic and transformatory spiritual progress is being made. In ultimate awareness and in the being of God, evil does not exist; in the dimension of earth life and in *all* but the final stages of the developing consciousness, the power of evil is horribly real and can wreak extreme and even fatal damage. Not to know this and keep it unwaveringly in mind as you go forward on the Path is to make yourself vulnerable to catastrophic forms of failure.

The higher you go on the Path, in fact, the farther and worse you can fall. Your *only* authentic safety as your inner powers and gnosis grow is to remain as self-aware, as humble, as awe-struck before the indescribable and boundless glory of God as possible, and as unimpressed as possible by all the new insights and revelations that are given you. As Rumi says:

Since intelligence only incites you to pride and vanity
Become a fool, so your heart stays pure.
Not a fool who wastes his life in playing the idiot
But a fool who is lost and astounded in Him.

The reward for overcoming the temptation to power is the ordeal that ends "engagement" and allows for the transition into nondual consciousness characteristic of "sacred marriage." This transition involves nothing less than what the Christian mystics have called the "mystic crucifixion" or the "dark night of the soul," what Sufi mystics have named *"fana,"* annihilation, and what in the shamanic traditions and some of the tantric systems is known as the "dismemberment of the false self." In this stage, the seeker's old self is subjected to exactly the forms of suffering and deprivation that will finally destroy it altogether. This annihilation is at once the greatest grace and the most protracted agony of the Path.

Just as at the end of the stage of "falling in love," the senses

have to be purified for them to hold the extraordinary illuminations that characterize "engagement," so at the end of "engagement" all traces that remain in the seeker of the self-referential
"ego" have to be burned away so that the divine "I" can be born in
all its splendor. This can take place, as the mystics of all traditions
tell us, only by a prolonged and precise stripping of the entire created self from the divine self. Everyone will experience this stripping as "tailored" minutely to their own personality, shadow, and
karmic formations: Every seeker will go through at this stage exactly those torments designed to annihilate most swiftly and totally his or her attachments. As Rumi wrote:

> In the last mercy of Love
> Agonies will crowd you from all directions
> To drag you into the Directionless

What is slowly born from the ashes of all the seeker's previous
"selves" is the phoenix of divine identity.

And the seeker enters the miracle of "sacred marriage," an increasingly stable awareness of "nondual" relationship with the
Godhead at all moments and in all circumstances.

Sacred Marriage

In this third stage—of "sacred marriage"—a knowledge of union
with the Godhead in the deepest part of the self is made clearer
and clearer, and an ever-steadier understanding of it is deepened
progressively. This knowledge is nothing less than a new "birth"—
the birth of the divine person. No one has described this "birth"
more accurately than Meister Eckhart:

"In this divine birth I find that God and I are the same; I am
what I was and what I shall remain, now and forever. I neither increase nor decrease, for in this birth I have become the motionless
cause of all that moves. I have won back what has always been
mine. Here, in my own soul, the greatest of all miracles has taken
place—God has returned to God."

In this "return" of "God to God," the seeker realizes that lover, Beloved, and love are all "not two," and realizes this in every conceivable way and from every conceivable angle in a graded series of supremely beautiful experiences of merging with the Divine.

The most defining characteristic of "sacred marriage" is not, however, rapture or vision but a steady "possession" of divine awareness in all states of consciousness (including deep sleep), a stable indwelling in the Divine, and a continual knowledge of innate identity that underlies every activity and every moment.

There is, however, one final temptation that occurs at this high and exalted stage—what I call "the temptation to transcendence." This temptation to transcendence is the last, subtlest, and most dangerous of all the temptations to power that appear on the journey to the Divine. What was in "engagement" the temptation to use divine occult powers to dominate and exploit others now becomes a finally seductive temptation to use the realization of divine identity as a way of "signing off" from every kind of earthly responsibility and in the name of "ultimate awareness."

The history of humanity would have been very different had nearly all the major mystical traditions not succumbed in varying degrees to this temptation. In them, the worship of transcendence has become the most powerful drug of all against the pain of being and against registering in their full atrocity the horror and injustice that mutilate human society; those who take this drug and become serenely addicted to it feel themselves immune from any need to fight existing circumstances or conditions—what are they after all but illusion; the different shiftings of a vast and unreal dream? In the name of final awakening, then, the addicts of transcendence leave the world and its beings in agony, offering as an "ultimate solution" only the opiate that has sealed them off from reality. And this is a disaster because it prevents the powers and insights of Divine Consciousness and being from entering into human reality to transform it.

What the seeker on the Direct Path needs to embrace at this exalted stage of the Path is what I call the motherhood of God. God is Mother as well as Father; the Divine who manifests the world is overwhelmingly, passionately, and "maternally" in love with all the sentient beings within it, for, as Blake wrote, "Eternity is in love with the productions of time", the eternal light in birthing the universe from itself also committed itself to the suffering of extreme and final love for all beings and things, and to profoundly humble service to all beings and things created out of Itself at every level and in every dimension.

The complete realization of your divine nature, then, must contain an embrace of the "motherhood" of God that created the creation and sustains it with infinite love, infinite humility, infinite self-sacrifice, and tireless action. This is at once a very complete and a very frightening demand, because it involves an embrace of the conditions of the world and the world nature in all its complexity, ambiguity, and potential for destructiveness. You cannot hide anymore in "transcendence"; all your awareness of the transcendent has to be employed in making you calmer and stronger and more and more committed, integrated, and humble within the whirlwind of the world. In choosing to love and be one with the motherhood of God, you choose, in fact, to embrace the suffering of struggling for the transformation of real conditions in the world and the suffering of constant labor and disappointment, even defeat; you put your entire being constantly at risk in the name of divine love and for its sake and for its victory in the real. You become a gambler for love and justice in the core of a dangerous world, and what you gamble with is your life.

The strength that this choice to embrace the motherhood of God gives you is extraordinary. Because you do not need to be adored or to have power of any kind since you know yourself one with God and fed directly by the divine powers, no system can conscript or terrify you; you are free to be completely your divine human self in the ground of your origin and so are ultimately dangerous to all the various forms of intimidation, manipulation, and control that make up the world. Because you are fearless with the knowledge of your transcendent truth-in-God, you can work tirelessly in the immanent for truth and justice and not be humiliated by insult or defeated by adversity or made hopeless by defeat. Freed by transcendent wisdom, you can dive with transcendent love into the heart of immanence, and work there with God-given energy, hope, clarity, and stamina for the establishment of what Jesus called "the Kingdom" and Aurobindo "the Supramental Creation"—a new world, a new creation, in which the highest truths of mystical meditation and nondual love will be married, in every dimension and in every arena, to the highest scientific, social, economic, and technological understanding that humanity has acquired. You become, in fact, a "birther" in and through the Divine of divine works of compassion and justice.

All the serious mystical traditions have had glimpses of the extraordinary state of loving and serving freedom that the Mother's gift of nondual consciousness makes possible. Plato's philosophers, having seen the illusion of the world return to the world to teach others about it; the Zen master after realizing that "nothing is real" returns to the "real" to help others liberate themselves; those who follow the Christ follow him beyond all the temptations of power and false transcendence into the depths of an abandoned self-donation to all beings; those who have taken the bodhisattva vow in Mahayana Buddhism pledge themselves to return to this world of pain and constriction forever until every sentient creature is finally liberated; the great Sufi mystics proclaim with one voice that those who are truly "lords" of being choose the glory of "servanthood" to work tirelessly for the salvation of all; Lao-tzu advises us: "With the truth of the great Light, work tirelessly in the world." What the Direct Path does is take all these highest illuminations and aspirations of all the mystical traditions and focus them in an overwhelming and divinely empowered sacred passion to labor, in every inner and outer way, to "birth" transformation in all conditions of world life.

Jesus' "Kingdom" and Aurobindo's "Supramental Creation" are not in any way otherworldly utopian dreams; they represent the final possibilities of the evolution of the human species, the ultimate flowering of human potential that could be affected by a marriage at the highest level and in every arena between complete mystical awareness and empowerment by love with all sciences, all arts, all aspects of political and economic reality. Through such a marriage of transcendental wisdom, divine compassion, and direct practical technological intelligence, a wholly new world is waiting to be engendered—a world in which the rhythms of nature will be secure from human greed and exploitation, in which all beings will be united in a vision of social, spiritual, and political equality and justice, and in the possibility of the highest mystical development, a world in which all beings will be offered the highest choices for their lives in an environment made safe and luminous by holy sciences of spirit and matter, a spiritualized technology, a mystically illumined academy, a music and painting and literature inspired by divine awareness. This is the kingdom of heaven on earth that all the Mother-Father's lovers see clearly in their illumined eye of contemplation; this is the new world that they all know is not a dream and not a fantasy but wholly possible if only human beings will work and love and serve passionately enough.

The Garden of Eden does not lie in our mythical past but in our potential future. To a humanity freed from all addictions, whether to the "transcendent" or the "immanent," living in dynamic sacred balance with its own nature and with nature, illumined by sacred awareness in every arena of the world, liberated from all "material" and "religious" tyrannies, and so completely and brilliantly fecund and inventive, at last, what miracles of transformation would not be possible?

Birthing

Many mystical systems—most notably those that have succumbed to the "temptation to transcendence"—end in "sacred marriage." The map of the Direct Path, however, opens onto a last, final stage—that of "birthing."

"Birthing" is about being a mystic revolutionary and a co-creator in and with God of a new integral sacred reality on the Direct Path. As Aurobindo described it, "You are to be a living, ardent tool with which the Supreme artist works, one of the instruments of His Self-manifestation—the perpetual process by which His reality is birthed into concrete expression."

The process is endless, because the love that is fueling and evolving it is endless. There are always more and more refined levels of integration of spirit and body to work for, always deeper and deeper expressions of love and justice in society and politics to labor toward. Ceaseless clarity, vigilance, discrimination, and sacred passion are required and demanded: There is no rest for the good whose eyes love has opened except in the calm eye of the whirlwind. Late one night, aged eighty-six and dying, Bede Griffiths said to me as we stroked each other's hands: "Are we just indulging ourselves in sentiment or are we using each moment and each caress to go deeper into love?"

Because there is no end to transformation, both on an inner and outer level, there is no end to striving and no end to the suffering that comes with striving and from opening to the needs and pains of others. St. Francis said it exactly: "Love suffers as a bird sings." But this suffering is not neurotic, self-absorbed, and self-obsessed; the suffering of "birthing" takes on more and more a "divine" quality; it becomes the clear heartbreak of pure love for all beings.

"The end of life is not to be happy. The end of life is not to achieve pleasure and avoid pain. The end of life is to do the will of God, come what may," said Martin Luther King, Jr. Living your life as a mystical revolutionary will provoke all kinds of dislike, rage, even hatred. You have two consolations in this; all those who have tried to birth a sacred reality before you have suffered in the same way; there is divine protection at all times and in all circumstances, even in those that seem terminal. The more you abandon yourself to the struggle for the victory of love, the more love's miracles will support, sustain, and dance around you.

Humility is the beginning, the middle, and the end of the Path. You can never be humble enough. Only God is humble enough. The more humble you become, the greater the divine transforming power that can be given you. The more humbly you are willing to do whatever is asked of you, without asking for certainty or reward, the more can be done through you and by you by God.

The rewards of "birthing" are "birthing" itself—knowing that through divine grace you are becoming more and more of an instrument of divine love and justice, feeling the Divine working more and more intimately within you, seeing and knowing the Divine inspiring more and more of your works, growing wilder and calmer, more and more heartbroken and blissful, watching the Divine manifest more and more richly and playfully in your mind and heart and soul and body and relationships and surroundings. No external glory or fame or success could ever approximate the ecstasy that such awareness will bring you or awaken in you such depths of gratitude; no external failure can ever take its joy from you.

While it may not be certain that to be a "birther of a new sacred reality" will ultimately transform our world enough, it *is* certain that only increasingly divinized humble servants of love can be of any real use now. Aspiring with all your heart and mind and body and soul to be one of them is the one authentic desire and the *one* true success.

Whatever happens to us and our world, love has already won in a dimension evil cannot understand or reach or defeat. To live in the joy of birthing divine truth and justice is to live on earth in that deathless reality. As Sheikh Ansari said:

O Lord, give me a heart
I can pour out in thanksgiving.
Give me life
So I can spend it
Working for the salvation of the world.

Two

Practicing
the Path

We call upon those who have lived on this earth
Our ancestors and our friends,
Who dreamed the best for future generations
And upon whose lives our lives are built
And with thanksgiving, we call upon them to

Teach us and show us the way.

And lastly, we call upon all that we hold most sacred
The presence and power of
The Great Spirit of love and truth
Which flows through all the universe
To be with us to

Teach us and show us the way.

CHINOOK BLESSING LITANY

Monks, what is the noble truth
about the way that goes into
the cessation of suffering?

Just this noble eightfold way,
namely, right view, right purpose,
right speech, right action, right
livelihood, right effort, right
mindfulness, and right concentration.

THE BUDDHA

FOR ANYONE TO TAKE the Direct Path happily and success-fully, two things have to come together—a disciplined, ethical, unselfish life and daily humble spiritual practice. Without the con-text of a clear and compassionate life, no amount of meditation or prayer will transform the being; without profound practice, a good life cannot flower consciously into a divine human one.

Taking the Direct Path means, then, living with acute ethical responsibility on all levels. As a Jewish mystic, Ben Gamliel, said:

> The world stands upon three things;
> Upon truth.
> Upon Peace.
> Upon justice.
> "Speak truth to the other, establish peace
> And render honest judgment in your gates" (Zechariah 8:16)

This "speaking of truth," establishing of "peace" and "justice," are the preconditions for authentic divine human life. As it is written in the Mundaka Upanishad, "The Atman [the revelation of the unity of the soul with God] is not reached by the weak, or the care-less, or those who practice wrong austerity; but the wise who strive in the right way lead their soul into the dwelling of Brahman" (the eternal reality).

In the Bhagavad Gita, Krishna defines this "striving in the right way" to Arjuna when he says:

> That one I love who is incapable of ill will
> And returns love for hatred
> Living beyond the reach of "I" and "mine"
> And of pleasure and pain, full of mercy,
> Contented, self-controlled, firm in faith,
> With all their heart and all their mind given to me—
> With such people I am in love.

All the serious mystical traditions have known that for people to live "contented, self-controlled, firm in faith" an ethical reordering of the whole of life is necessary.

What I suggest, then, is that before you undertake the eighteen practices that I am going to offer later in this section, you subject your life to profound and unillusioned scrutiny. Allow yourself one complete day of contemplation; during it, write down all your faults and all the ways in which your life still does not harmonize with your spiritual ideals and the "sacred way." Don't be easy on yourself and don't be excessively harsh with your shortcomings; try to make your assessment of where and who you are as objective as you can.

Then I suggest that for one week you do the following meditation exercise for one hour a day, either in the morning or in the evening. It is based on a Buddhist meditation, "Undertaking the Five Precepts," and I have found it extremely helpful as a way of sharpening my ethical standards and continually reminding myself of the level of self-awareness at which I must live to be consciously on the Path.

Undertaking the Five Precepts

IN BUDDHIST PRACTICE, one way to establish virtue and integrity firmly is to formally (and again and again) repeat and undertake the five precepts. These, as you will see, can easily be taken by anyone of any faith; they include in their simple affirmations the kernel of the ethical wisdom of the world. (After you have practiced them several times, you may feel you want to add one or two precepts of your own making; be as creative as you wish. You know your limitations and needs better than anyone, so choose precepts that will help you become more and more self-aware, honest, and attentive to reality.)

To begin the meditation, sit in a quiet place in your house. If you have an altar, you may wish to light a candle or offer flowers or incense. Relax your body and open your heart. When you feel you are ready, recite the following five precepts slowly and pay great inner attention to what you are saying:

I undertake the training precept of refraining from killing and harming living beings.

I undertake the training precept of refraining from stealing and taking what is not mine.

I undertake the training precept of refraining from causing harm through sexual misconduct.

> I undertake the training precept of refraining from false speech, harmful speech, gossip, and slander.
>
> I undertake the training precept of refraining from the misuse of intoxicants such as alcohol or drugs that cause carelessness or loss of awareness.

For the first two of the days of the week you are practicing "Undertaking the Five Precepts," simply meditate on them one by one as fully and as richly as you can, and make notes for yourself in a journal about what insights arise as you practice. I always find when I do this practice that I become increasingly aware of aspects of myself that are unfocused or inharmonious; just saying the precepts over and over and thinking deeply about them has the effect, I find, of making me awake to what I am *not* paying attention to enough. When I write down what I am learning about what needs to be changed in my actions, it helps me to see even more clearly what I must do.

For the next five days, during the meditation hour, take just one of the precepts and explore it in depth, opening up the whole of your life to its scrutiny.

Day One

I Undertake the Training Precept of Refraining from Killing and Harming Living Beings.

This is a precept about maintaining at all times a profound reverence for life. As you take it, repeatedly vow each time you say it out loud to consciously bring no harm in thought, work, or deed to any living creature. Then examine without fear or shame all the ways in which being the way you are does "kill" other beings—how your anger can cause suffering, or how your pride can make others feel inferior or shut out. Each time you become aware of how a part of you offends against the reverence of life that you have chosen, make a note of it and pray to the Divine to transform it in you.

Become particularly aware of any living beings in your world that you are ignoring or not caring for enough. This can include relatives, pets, even household plants. Every time you become aware of something you are *not* doing, make a commitment to do it. And not in a casual way either; I find it helpful to write down what I need to do and to add concrete suggestions, times, and methods. Think, too, of larger environmental issues as you meditate; how can you restructure your life so as to "kill" other beings or mistreat them as little as possible.

Day Two
I Undertake the Training Precept of Refraining from Stealing and Taking What Is Not Mine.

This precept deals essentially with respect for material things but can, of course, be extended to embrace anything that can be "stolen" or "misappropriated." As you take the precept again and again, saying it out loud, reflect deeply on how you may misuse the things around you, how—especially in a culture like ours—you may be encouraged to consume mindlessly. Note down all the areas where you spend too much and too selfishly; make specific detailed commitments on driving less, for example, or spending less money on useless or inessential things. Then make a commitment to act on every generous impulse that arises in you. Each day you meditate on this precept, give away a dollar to someone who truly needs it; each time you do so, pray that your anxiety about your own life and possessions and about the future be lessened so that your generosity to others can become more and more fearless.

Day Three

I Undertake the Training Precept of Refraining from Causing Harm Through Sexual Misconduct.

This is a precept about responsible and "conscious" sexuality. As you say this precept out loud again and again, remember the times you have not been responsible sexually or when you have hurt someone; face the selfishness in yourself without fear. Then try and face the *roots* of that selfishness—in secret panic or self-hatred. Call out to the Divine to heal whatever in you can cause pain to others. Try, too, to look honestly at how often sexual feelings and thoughts arise in your consciousness unconnected to any ethical or caring motivation. Whenever they do arise, make a commitment to note what particular mind states you find linked to them, such as passion, tension, loneliness, aggression, hunger for companionship, etc. Becoming more mindful will itself help you become more responsible with your sexuality and personal relations. Being more responsible will help you to "consecrate" your sexuality and its expression to the Divine in you and in your partner, and so begin an initiation into the divine possibilities of human love that will irradiate your being.

Day Four

I Undertake the Training Precept of Refraining from False Speech, Harmful Speech, Gossip, and Slander.

As you take this precept again and again, be honest with yourself about how often you have gossiped against or slandered others, how often your harsh words have caused pain. Remember particular occasions in which you know you have caused suffering and ask God for forgiveness and the transformation of those forces in you that compel you to judge or make trouble. Contemplate, too, those occasions on which slander and gossip have hurt or disturbed *your* life; recapturing these painful emotions will help you resolve more deeply to end whatever in you risks imposing them on others.

An astounding amount of harm is done in life by people who speak carelessly, meanly, or without enough thought; face this squarely and make notes about the kinds of situations in which you are tempted to indulge in "false speech, harmful speech, gossip, and slander." Sometimes, for example, you will lie to escape judgment or to impress someone; sometimes you will slander another person simply to look better than them or to flatter someone who dislikes them and whose advocacy or friendship you need. It isn't at all pleasant to go exploring the reasons we do these things, but it is essential work if we are going to become more careful and more judicious about what we say. Each time you discover another hidden motive for "false speech," make a commitment not to forget it and to transform it.

Day Five
I Undertake the Training Precept of Refraining from the Misuse of Intoxicants Such as Alcohol or Drugs That Cause Carelessness or Loss of Awareness.

During the week you do this practice refrain completely from all intoxicants and addictive substances—caffeine, wine, cigarettes, and drugs of all kinds. Examine during the day you concentrate on this precept all the different impulses you experience to use these; explore the various kinds of emptiness, panic, hunger for sensation, need for comfort or anesthesia that might prompt your various addictive behaviors. The more clearly you can see that your behavior is being controlled by different fears and hungers, the more successfully you can begin to heal the roots of those fears and hungers by real spiritual practice.

When I meditate on this precept, I also take the phrase "misuse of intoxicants" in a richer, metaphorical sense. Am I, for example, using my passion to create as an "intoxicant" to save myself suffering? Is a desire for fame or power or worldly success in any way "drugging" me from being aware of my intimate responsibility to others? Am I in any way using my mystical practices as a way to "escape" reality? I love what George Eliot once said: "The highest election known to man is to bear pain without opium," and I know that the authentic Direct Path is naked and fully alive to both the glorious and dreadful facts of the real; any "misuse of intoxicants" in however exalted or high-minded a fashion will in the end cripple the seeker or make him or her unaware of where and how he or she needs to change. Each time, then, that I uncover during this practice a new "intoxicant" that I am misusing, I note it down, and pray for it to be transformed or to be given the strength to do without it.

PRACTICING "Undertaking the Five Precepts" with this degree of self-honesty for a week is a demanding and purifying act. At the end of the week, look over everything you wrote on the first day and through the subsequent days; read your notes very carefully and then throw them away. Then, from memory, write down the essence of what you have learned in as simple a way as you possibly can. Don't forget, every time you write down a fault or a mistake or a perception of where you must change, make a specific recommendation or commitment; the Direct Path is nothing if not practical, focused, and hardheaded.

At the end of the entire practice, read a passage from one of the great mystical traditions that concretizes for you what you would most like to become, or that states most eloquently the ideal of the selfless, disciplined, supple, and sensitive life you want. The passage I find myself using most often at this stage comes from the *Tao Te Ching:*

I have three treasures
That I keep and hold.
One is mercy,
The second is frugality,

The third is not presuming
To be at the head of the world.
By reason of mercy
One can be brave.
By reason of frugality
One can be broad.
By not presuming
To be at the head of the world,
You can make your potential last.

Now if one were bold
But had no mercy
If one were broad
But were not frugal
If one went ahead
Without deference
One would die.

Those whom heaven is going to save
Are those it guards with mercy.

As I say these words at the end of this demanding and beautiful practice of "Undertaking the Five Precepts," I pray to commit my whole being to understanding ever more deeply and to living ever more authentically the "mercy," "frugality," and "humility" of which Lao-tzu is speaking. I have learned enough to know that such a fusion in the core of life of compassion, good sense about all my inner and outer resources, and real, radical, always-deepening humility are the conditions for true growth on the Direct Path; Lao-tzu's sublime words remind me of what I know and now must live without blockage or backsliding or fear.

End the practice by praying in great confidence and faith that everything you need to change yourself will be given you—all the courage, all the strength, all the trust, all the necessary insights and revelations.

Finally, dedicate the whole week's process to the liberation of all sentient beings everywhere, wishing them all happiness and illumination with the fully awakened love of your whole heart.

Eighteen Sacred Practices for Transformed Spiritual Living

WHAT I WANT TO OFFER now are eighteen spiritual exercises that I consider the most powerful of all in helping anyone to stay focused on and inspired by the Divine in the core of everyday life. They are designed to provide the seeker on the Direct Path with an array of techniques that he or she will be able to use in all life's circumstances.

Intellectual or even inward spiritual understanding of mystical truths is not enough; they must be integrated into the fabric of our every thought, emotion, motive, and action. This can be done only by spiritual practice, by a daily, constant, fervent, and humble commitment to see, through the practice of meditation, prayer, and other exercises, that we remain always in the Divine Presence as far as we can and as open as we can to divine inspiration and divine guidance.

The eighteen practices I have elected—from many different mystical traditions—have been chosen for their effectiveness and, often, for their simplicity; spiritual practice is not, as so many people tragically assume, an esoteric or elitist activity; it can be, in fact, as natural as breathing or walking or eating, and just as thoroughly part of the needs and necessities of everyday life. You can discover this healing and thrilling naturalness only through a steady commitment to realize the truth of practice for yourself; no one else can meditate or pray for you and no one but yourself can help you integrate your deepest feelings and perceptions of the nature of God with your everyday life.

What follows, then, are exercises and practices essential for anyone who wants to become aware of their "original glory"—the "original glory" of their inmost divine nature—and to remain in constantly galvanizing contact with its energy, passion, nobility, truth, wisdom, and peace. This galvanizing contact with the transcendent within and outside our embodied nature is essential to the Direct Path; from it derive continual graces of divine help, divine guidance, and divine strength. Spiritual exercise is in fact the "mother" of all our ascents and transformations on the Path; divine grace may initiate us through inner mystical experience or revelation, but it is only through daily practice that these initiations become constant possessions of consciousness, integrated into every aspect of our lives.

Let me offer a few pointers as to how these exercises can be practiced most richly and imaginatively.

First, select a calm, quiet room in your house or a calm, quiet corner of a room and set it apart just for prayer and meditation. Furnish it as you wish, with what you feel most at home; many practitioners of the Direct Path like to have an altar with statues or photos of beings who inspire them on it, or other sacred objects. What is essential is to keep the place you choose clean and consecrated to practice and to return to it every time you pray or meditate. You will find that in the end, just sitting down in your chosen place will help bring you directly into the Presence; over time, a great deal of spiritual power will accumulate there and "wait" there to empower you.

Secondly, as you do the practices, do them without expectation. By this I mean do them humbly and patiently, not demanding that they "work" immediately. Sometimes an exercise will reveal its power and transforming truth immediately; sometimes you will have to work with it for a long time before its secrets will start to be unveiled to you. Different temperaments find different kinds of exercises easy or compelling; some people find it immediately exciting to "visualize," for example, while others—the majority, perhaps—have to work at visualization before it can become second nature. For many, their initial foray into meditation is fraught with panic; their first sessions seem so troubled and hectic that they cannot believe they will ever achieve inner peace. Nearly everyone begins meditation with these fears, and for nearly everyone it is only time and dogged selfless work that prepare the real initiation into the calm that meditation brings. It is essential to remember this; a commitment to spiritual practice is a commitment to perhaps the most useful work you will ever do in your life. But it *is*, at times, and sometimes for long, demanding stretches, hard work. While you are doing the exercises that follow, remember always that they have been practiced successfully sometimes over thousands of years; if they do not seem initially to work, it may not be their "fault." Either you are not doing them with enough faith and fervor, or their "results" will appear only with patience and humility. If you were learning to write, for example, or to paint, you would not immediately expect to write like Flaubert or paint like Leonardo da Vinci; spiritual practice is in many ways the highest and most exquisitely demanding of all arts and like any art demands a great deal of selfless attention.

Third—and this I have found very important—keep, as you undertake the journey into the mystery and power of these practices, a detailed, daily "practice diary." After each session, note immediately what you feel you have learned, either about the practice itself or about your own responses—positive or negative—to it. You will find that your reactions grow deeper and richer all the time. You will also be helped by this to know which of the practices move and help and sustain and inspire you the most and in what circumstances and situations.

On the Direct Path, each seeker is his or her own "spiritual laboratory" experimenting on himself or herself with different techniques and exercises in different situations to find out which ones work and in what way. This is an exhilarating adventure, but it requires real precision and mindfulness; don't waste the wealth of practice by being "unaware" of it, or "vague" about its effects. Write down every day that you practice what you are coming to understand and what you are experiencing—even if it seems trivial or self-indulgent. At the end of a year you will find that your inner self-knowledge and your knowledge of what works for your temperament and developmental stage on the Path will have increased astonishingly.

What I hope for all who undertake these eighteen practices is that by the end of the time you devote to them you will have found at least six or seven different spiritual exercises that you have really understood and experienced with great joy and recognition; these six or seven exercises will then go on to form the inner foundation of your life on the Path and to provide endless inspiration and power.

Fourth, remember always that as a seeker on the Direct Path you are not undertaking these practices for your own liberation only; you are doing them on behalf of *all* sentient beings. You know that you cannot be truly effective as an agent of the transformation of the world until you have become yourself increasingly one with God; all your commitment, then, must be to become an ever-clearer instrument for the Divine to use for the benefit of others. It is vital to remember this at all times, since practice done purely for the self can never liberate you from your self. The best way of always remembering that you are practicing to be of true transformatory help to others is by *always* beginning your sessions by dedicating *all* of their beauty, power, and insight to the welfare of all beings throughout the universe. End in this way also and dedicate everything that you have experienced during your practice session to the freeing of all beings everywhere from every kind of misery.

I love to use in this context the beautiful Tibetan prayer:

By the power and the truth of this practice
May all beings have happiness, and the causes of happiness;
May all be free from sorrow, and the causes of sorrow
May all never be separated from the sacred happiness which is
    sorrowless:
And may all live in equanimity, without too much attachment
    and too much aversion,
And live believing in the equality of all that lives.

If this prayer seems too specifically Buddhist to you, choose another that invokes the welfare of all beings from any tradition of your choice or improvise or write your own. What is essential is not so much the words as awakening the heart before practice to compassion for all beings and to an inner determination to become divinized so as to serve with more passion and effectiveness the laws of God in the real.

Finally, I strongly suggest that you choose the same times every day for your practice sessions. Choosing the same times for prayer and meditation give a calm, spiritual order to life and show that you have given your inner evolution the priority it demands. Don't believe for a moment what your ego will often try to tell you—that you don't have time. One of the nastiest games of the "false self" is to try to persuade you that spiritual practice is a luxury or boring or that you simply do not have the time in your hectic schedule to accommodate it. This is nonsense; many of the busiest people I know—businessmen and women, politicians, nurses, doctors—find time every day to practice. So can you, whatever your circumstances. Be firm with yourself on this point; it will save you a great deal of indecision, lukewarmness, and confusion.

Traditionally the best times for meditation and prayer are said to be first thing in the morning, twilight, and late at night. My advice is to set aside two twenty-minute periods daily—one in the morning after breakfast and the other in the evening before sleep. In this way your days begin and end by the invocation of the Presence; over many years the simple act of opening and closing your day in prayer and meditation will give all your life a secret holy fullness and rhythm.

Practice 1
Practice Mindfulness Through Watching the Breath

Before I begin to explain this wonderful and powerful practice, let me make some simple remarks about meditation in general.

Remember always that meditation has nothing to do with competition or achievement and everything to do with profound, lucid relaxation. The purpose of meditation is to introduce us to what we really are, to the peace, luminous clarity, and abiding strength of our inmost divine nature and to help us gradually tame, discipline, and refine our minds so we can remain in constant contact with our essential truth.

Everything depends in life on the quality of our mind's response to what happens. As the Buddha is reported to have said in the Dhammapada:

> Everything has mind in the lead, has
> Mind in the forefront, is made by mind.
> If one speaks or acts with a corrupt
> Mind, misery will follow, as the wheel
> Of a cart follows the foot of an ox.

> Everything has mind in the lead, has mind in the
> Forefront, is made by mind. If one speaks or acts
> With a pure mind, happiness will follow
> Like a shadow that never leaves.

The aim of meditation is to help us purify and illumine the mind with the ageless light of the spirit and its clarity.

It can never be said too often, especially to westerners accustomed to think of everything important as involving strenuous and visibly exhausting effort, that what such a process involves above all is *letting go*—letting go as far as we possibly can of all our worries, thoughts, fantasies, fears, and habitual patterns of dread or longing or anticipation. The best and most liberating advice I ever received about meditation came from the Tibetan mystic Thuksey Rinpoche, whom I met twenty years ago in Ladakh. On a brilliant summer morning in the small bare room of a mountain monastery, he said to me, "Do not worry too much about techniques, such as posture, for example. Just sit as comfortably as you can on the floor or on a cushion and keep your spine as straight as possible, so the inner energy, or prana, of your body can flow through its channels. How you sit—whether you sit in the full or half lotus or in another way that suits you—is up to you. How you keep your eyes—closed or half closed—again is up to you. Just be as warm and happy and balanced and comfortable as you can. Meditation is not gymnastics; it is an art of peace, and for it to be practiced with true success you must feel as serene and as secure as possible." Then, after a pause, he smiled and said, "But there is one thing I do want you always to remember. If you do, it will help you make excellent progress very fast. When you begin to meditate, imagine that you and all your worries and fears and fantasies are like a large lump of butter left out on the ledge outside this window [he pointed to the window to his right] left out in the full warmth of a summer morning like today. Just rest in that great shining warmth, rest, rest, and melt slowly away."

This "melting slowly away" is not, of course, a melting into nothingness or somnolence; what you will find you "melt away into" if you follow Thuksey Rinpoche's advice is the alert spacious shining of your inmost nature. What does this state feel like? A great Hindu mystic, Ramana Maharshi, said to imagine a man who has been toiling all day in his fields coming home after a long day's work and sinking into his favorite chair in front of the fire. He knows he has done everything he can; there is nothing more to worry about, nothing left unattended to, and he can abandon all his worries and just rest, content simply to be.

Perhaps the greatest reward of this simplicity and this happiness at simply "being" is the mindfulness it naturally engenders. When you are peaceful in this way, your mind naturally becomes clear and aware and extraordinarily sensitive to every shifting thought and emotion while not being in any way defined by them. The more we can do so, the more aware we become of how we think, act, and are, and the more completely and lucidly we can work on ourselves to transform our habitual reactions and so free ourselves of the damage they continually create.

ONE OF THE MOST powerful ways of practicing mindfulness is also the simplest—watching the breath. The focusing of attention on the breath is perhaps the most universal of the many hundreds of meditative practices used worldwide. It is used in Buddhist and Hindu mystic practice and is central to Sufi, Christian, and Jewish traditions. In Judaism, *ruah*, the breath, means "the spirit of God that infuses the Creation"; in Christian mysticism there is a profound link between the Holy Spirit—the Source of all life—and breath. In the teaching of Buddha, and in Hinduism, the breath, or prana, is said to be the "vehicle of the mind" because it is the prana that makes our minds shift and move.

What this means in simple terms is that from humanity's earliest beginnings it was understood that breathing meditation can quiet and tame the mind, open the body, and develop a great power of holy concentration. I have been using the meditation I am about to give you for over twenty years now; I never fail to be amazed at how effective it is, and at how it works even in the most extreme and harsh emotional circumstances to bring peace and perspective. I have placed it here at the beginning of the eighteen practices because in many ways it seems to me the essential foundation of all the different kinds of practice, and one that can be done anywhere, at any time. Breath, after all, is what we live by and is everywhere free and available, like the truths of the Direct Path itself.

PRACTICE OF MINDFULNESS
BY WATCHING THE BREATH

Sit calmly in your place of prayer and meditation and imagine that all your thoughts, concerns, and worries are, as Thuksey Rinpoche said, like a "big slab of butter left out in the summer sun." Compose your being as far as you can and allow your tensions quietly to subside.

Keep your focus constantly at your nostrils, noting the passage of every breath into your lungs or out into the air in front of you.

Just keep on noting its flow in and out of your nostrils. Note the subtle and refined sensations of the breath as it comes in and out. Don't try to control it; just be aware of each in-breath and each out-breath as it passes through the nostrils, like a doorman watching each person who comes through the door.

Focus your most acute attention on how the breath feels. Don't try to imagine or visualize it in any way; don't get involved in mental commentary, analysis, or gossip. Never mistake the commentary in your mind ("Now I'm breathing in," "Now I'm breathing out") for authentic mindfulness. Mindfulness does not mean that you should think "I am doing this" or "I am doing that"; on the contrary, the moment you think "I am doing this" you have become self-conscious and you do not live in what you are doing but in your *idea* of "I am doing this or that." Authentic mindfulness is to be totally and transparently present in whatever you are doing; it never means separating ourselves from experience, but on the contrary allows us to live and sense it fully.

So, in paying attention to how the breath feels, just note the sensation of the breath exactly the way it is. You may feel it at the edge of the nostrils, or inside the nose, or on the upper lip under the nose. The sensations you feel will keep changing subtly; sometimes you will feel your breath like the light tickle of a feather, sometimes like a dull pulse, accompanied by an ache in the space between your eyes, sometimes as an intense point of pressure on your lips. There is no "right" way for the breath to feel. What you are doing is training and refining your perception so you can note exactly how the breath feels at each moment, and, through this, training and refining your powers of mindfulness in general.

Inevitably, as you try to focus your whole attention mindfully on your breath, your thoughts will become distracted. Don't worry; distractions are natural and arise because our minds are not initially clear or pure. Sometimes painful memories, traumas, humiliations, will surface. Again, don't be surprised; this is normal in such simple but profound work. The best way of dealing with these thoughts and emotions is not to allow yourself to be waylaid or diverted by them. Do not judge or condemn yourself for having them; whatever bizarre or dark shapes they take, simply try to witness them lucidly and let them go. If you keep on gently refusing to judge or "follow" them and go on letting them go, you will find they will die down and dissolve of their own accord, just as muddy water will clear in a glass if it is left alone.

There may also be external as well as internal distractions—of noise or physical aches and pains. Deal with them in the same calm and gentle way. If a noise jolts you, for example, don't let yourself be alarmed or distracted long; just return to noting your breath. If you develop an ache in your legs or back, do whatever you have to do to ease it as quickly and unobtrusively as possible and return to noting your breath.

If you find that your concentration on noting each breath wavers, don't worry either; this also is normal in all but the most experienced practitioners. I find it helpful when I am losing concentration to start counting each breath up to ten and then start again at one. Sometimes I also take a deep breath deliberately and slowly, paying special attention to its arising and falling, and then let my breathing return to its normal rate.

While doing this exercise of mindfulness, I try to stay "mindful" of its many teachings. I note how my breath is always changing and shifting, like life itself, and appearing and disappearing like the events and phenomena of reality; this helps me cultivate serenity and detachment. I note, too, as my perception grows more and more alive and transparent, how parts of my being contract and resist when I breathe in, and others open and let go; the more often I do this exercise, the more deeply I realize how connected working with the breath is with the deepest part of my psyche and emotions, and how much I have to learn from breathing more deeply, evenly, fully, and fearlessly. I note, too, how I often long to speed up, control, or in other ways "dominate" the process of breathing; and this makes me sometimes painfully aware of how much more my mind longs impatiently to "master" reality than be guided and instructed by it. At some point in every breath meditation I hear myself inwardly shouting "This is crazy, boring beyond words, why am I sitting here!" I have come over the years to smile at myself when I hear this inner shout, for I know by now that it usually precedes a sudden subtle breakthrough into spaciousness and peace; it is as if all the fury of my false self tries to sabotage this experience before it can be dissolved by it. Working with the breath is a marvelously rigorous way of becoming intimately acquainted with all the different aspects and ruses of the mind and psyche.

Go on, then, breathing and noting and refining your mindfulness until the end of the half-hour session. When you end, dedicate everything you have experienced and learned to the liberation of all sentient beings. Then make a vow to prolong the mindfulness you have been practicing through *one* of your activities during the day that follows. You could choose, for example, sitting or standing or washing the dishes or doing paperwork at the office or riding on the train to work; the activity does not matter. What matters is your commitment to perform it mindfully. Choose a different activity every day, and at the end of the day note in your practice diary what happened to you, how the activity you chose "changed" for you, and what you discovered about your habitual patterns or performing it. Gradually you will find yourself wanting to extend your mindfulness to all activities during the day, and you will find yourself acting and reacting with a wholly new lightness, precision, grace, and force.

Practice 2
Breathing in the Power, Love, and Strength of the Divine and Breathing out Your Inner Tension, Sadness, and Fear

This simple and powerful exercise has been used by Christian monastic orders since the first centuries after Christ, and by certain Taoist, Sufi, and Hindu sects. In the first practice, "Practice Mindfulness by Watching the Breath," I offered an exercise that, if done steadily, brings tremendous rewards of self-control and mental and spiritual clarity. This second practice works in a different but complementary way; instead of focusing on your powers of insight, it focuses on the omnipresence of divine grace inside and outside you; it makes you aware, if you practice it with faith, of how *available* the divine power is and how willing the Divine always is to help, succor, sustain, and inspire everyone. In this second practice you are invited to experience the breath as an infusion of divine grace, and that helps you remember that your life is at all moments a divine gift.

Ever since I was first taught this exercise by a Greek Orthodox monk on an Aegean island twenty years ago, I have found myself using it constantly, especially in times of stress and spiritual suffering or exhaustion. I have never performed it without being astonished yet again by its demonstration of the central truth of the Direct Path—that all of us have a *direct naked* relationship at all moments with the Absolute which, if we risk claiming it with the ardor and simple faith of a child, can change everything.

Sit, then, in your place of meditation; compose your being and dedicate what you are about to do to the awakening and liberation of all beings. To inspire yourself at this moment with full trust in God's mercy and passion to help you in all circumstances, read slowly a great mystical text you love especially from any of the world's traditions that awakens in you feelings of confidence and gratitude.

Now, with your whole being in a state of love and trust, start the exercise itself. Breathe in slowly, fully, and deliberately, and as you breathe in *know* that you are breathing into every part of your body, heart, soul, and mind the power, love, bliss, passion, peace, and strength of God. I find it helps me to visualize this divine in-breath as a wind of sweet healing flame that penetrates and absorbs every part of me.

Then, when you breathe out, breathe out consciously all your sadness, tension, doubt, distress, uncertainty. Breathe out, in fact, everything in you that in any way blocks or prevents you from being completely and tenderly possessed by the flame of the Presence.

Do this again and again, with as profound a concentration as possible, trying to keep your heart always fresh and alive in the fire of the inspiration you felt when you recited whatever text you chose. Above all, perform your in-and-out breathing with deep faith in your spirit; try to know the truth that illumines all the mystical traditions—that you have a right to call on God for help since God is your Father and your Mother, the infinitely kind and empowering Source of your whole being.

Often, when you do this exercise, you will be working with a particular grief or humiliation or distress that is marking your life at the time. When you breathe in, open your whole being in all its present confusion or anguish to the all-healing all-loving breath of God. You will find here that the more consciously and trustfully you open up your distress to God, the more immediately you will feel the power of the breath of grace working within you to transmute it, or give you the strength to see it in perspective. Spiritual practice is, in the deepest sense, co-creation with God, co-participation with the Grace of God; the more "active" you are in opening yourself up to Grace, the more "receptive" you will be to its transforming effects.

Sometimes your life will be relatively calm and even when you do this practice. In that case, use the practice as a way of inviting the divine power to work on the transformation of your faults. I know, for example, that one of my greatest faults is impatience. My impatience has, in the past, caused me great suffering and caused suffering to others. When I breathe in, then, I invoke the great loving detached patience of the Divine to possess my whole being; when I breathe out, I try to "expel" everything in me that resists the rigors of that sublime patience or tries to sabotage it.

I also know that many of the mistakes I have made in my life have stemmed from my pride, a pride in my own powers or "experiences." When I breathe in, then, I breathe in consciously the infinitely tender maternal *humility* of God, the humility that God's love ceaselessly shows to every sentient being, every fern and stone and lichen. I try to allow God to fill my whole mind, heart, body, and soul with the all-deranging humility of divine love; as I breathe out, I try to "dissolve" everything in me that still clings to my old proud versions of myself, everything in me that is still afraid to bow down in adoration before the Divine in all things.

The times when I have found this practice particularly powerful are those when I have been terrified of "going forward" or of confronting a difficulty my mind has made seem insurmountable. In such times I have found that breathing in God's unshakable majestic power and security and breathing out everything in me that is scared and self-piteous has helped me to steady myself. When I do the practice to overcome fear in this way, I find that it helps to sit in a consciously strong way, imagining myself a rock or a mountain; the posture I take helps the practice work more powerfully.

There are moments, too, on the Direct Path when you will be working at a deep level to infuse your entire being with the meaning and power of a particular mystical experience that has revealed to you some greater part of yourself and of God. I have found this breathing exercise especially valuable in such circumstances. What I do is try to recall the experience I am attempting to make always conscious in myself in as much of its splendor and truth as I can. Then, when I breathe in, I ask the Divine to permeate my entire self with the bliss and knowledge that was momentarily revealed to me in the "experience"; when I breathe out, I vow to "expel" from my being everything in me that consciously or unconsciously fights against this new knowledge or wishes to subvert it. Perform this with real passion and intensity, and you will discover, as I have, that this exercise has a marvelous way of helping us stabilize in ourselves the graces that the Path gives us.

When you near the end of the practice session—say, five minutes before—repeat the text you used at the beginning of the practice and bring to its repetition everything you have experienced of God's living help to you in the last half hour. This will help you make your faith and trust even stronger. Then, as in the first breathing exercise, choose one activity in the coming day that you vow to attempt to transmute by using this exercise. If, for example, you have problems with your boss at the office, make a commitment to breathe in God's compassion and strength and breathe out your resentment or fear just before you have to deal with him or her. If your relationship with your lover, husband, or wife is going through a difficult passage, pledge to use this exercise often during the time when you are with him or her. Note in your practice diary the results of the exercise; over time, you will be amazed at how effective it is.

When you have finished your recitation of the text and chosen the activity you are going to work on, dedicate everything you have experienced during your session and everything you are learning to the liberation of all beings.

Practice 3
Three Practices of Concentration

In Practice 3 we return to the clear austerity of mindfulness. Concentration and clear focus are essential on the Direct Path. So much of the misery in human life comes from our inability to stay alert and focused in and on the present; so much of our real authentic joy comes from the gift of being able to concentrate on the present with transparent attention. Especially when we begin to meditate, we experience ourselves as hopelessly, even dangerously and absurdly, scattered. Fortunately, this scatteredness is not an absolute; working humbly with age-old "concentration" techniques can help us considerably to learn how to train our attention.

Training our attention is, of course, essential not only for all our worldly activities—how can you write a good paragraph, cook a good meal, or write a helpful business memo if you can't concentrate?—but also for the success of spiritual practice. The more wholeheartedly we can plunge into practice, and the more completely we can gather all the powers of our being and focus them on the practice we are doing, the more richly it can reveal its power to us and in us.

Many people of goodwill, I have found, give up spiritual practice of any kind because they are not aware of the degree of concentration it requires. They wonder why it doesn't "work" for them when they haven't really "worked" for it. In fact, there is no human activity I know—not even writing—that demands so acute and honed a concentration. This is especially true at the beginning of any period of practice; if we haven't learned how to train our attention in simple, humble ways, we can easily become distracted and lose all creative focus.

In this third practice, then, I offer three ancient techniques for achieving what in Hinduism and Buddhism is called "one-pointedness." They are meant to be done in order; since they are each more demanding than they might initially appear, I suggest that before you begin the session, you clarify and pacify your mind as deeply as possible by doing one of the two breathing exercises you have already learned.

FIRST EXERCISE: FOCUSING UPON A PEBBLE

Find a pebble in the street or in your garden. (Any pebble will do, it doesn't have to be special in any way, or especially beautiful.) Place it in front of you against a white cloth, which will help it to stand out sharply. Now just gaze at it one-pointedly, letting your awareness neither stray from it nor identify with it.

Inevitably, of course, your attention will stray at times. Sustaining several minutes of concentration on any one object requires a great mastery of the will. When your attention does stray, be gently ruthless with yourself and bring it back immediately to the pebble. You will find at times that your whole being will resist this exercise, finding it ridiculous or pointless; don't give in to the false logic of your mind's laziness. Continue to gaze at the pebble.

You will find that as you do this exercise day in and day out for a month with the same pebble, you will discover the miracle of what a medieval Christian called the *haecceitas*, the "thisness" of things. You will discover the uniqueness and dense presence of the pebble, its astonishing dense stability. You will discover, too, that as your concentration increases so will your admiration and love for the pebble, and your sense of its miracle. What began perhaps as an exercise will by the end of the month have revealed itself as a form of prayer to the Divine Presence in all things.

SECOND EXERCISE: FOCUSING ON AN IMAGE OF A SAINT OR TEACHER OR PERSON WHOSE SPIRITUAL ATTAINMENT YOU ADMIRE

Taking the Direct Path does not, of course, mean that you no longer admire or revere anyone else's spiritual attainment; what it *does* mean is that you never deify anyone and always recognize that what you are admiring and revering in others is also latent in yourself. Concentrating, then, on the image or photo of a particular spiritual figure or teacher you love in this sane and complete way can help you evoke in yourself the qualities you admire in him or her.

In doing this practice over the years, I have used many images and figures—Jesus, Ramakrishna, Rumi, the Virgin, the Buddha. Recently I have found myself using the photograph I keep on my desk of my dead father; his goodness and dignity radiate from it, and when I concentrate on it I feel everything I loved in him penetrate and infuse me and awaken in me the qualities of calm, strength, and truthfulness I admired in him.

The simplest way of doing this exercise is to place on the white cloth before you an upright image of the teacher, saint, or friend you have chosen. Practice mindful breathing for a minute or two so as to empty your mind of all its memories and preconceptions about the person whose image you have chosen. Then just gaze one-pointedly at the image, keeping your whole heart and mind trained on it and watch and witness the thoughts, feelings, and insights that arise in you. Do not, however, allow any of these thoughts, feelings, or insights to sidetrack you from your work for keeping a clear focus on the image. When your attention strays, be gently ruthless with yourself as before and bring it back to the image in front of you.

If the image you have chosen is, for example, a portrait of Rumi or Jesus or the Virgin, gaze deeply into the portrait's eyes. You will find this a very effective way of stilling the mind and opening it to peace and joy. Try to keep your gaze as even and sustained and focused as possible and blink as little as possible; this way your whole being will be filled with the silence of profound concentration.

This is a very powerful exercise because it works not only with the mind's power of attention but also with the heart's deepest feelings at the same time, fusing both and bringing both to a pitch of pure, clear intensity.

THIRD EXERCISE: FOCUSING ON A CANDLE FLAME

This exercise is used in nearly all the mystical traditions I am familiar with as an excellent way in which to train attention. As a child in India I used to calm myself and dream myself into other magical worlds and dimensions by lighting a candle in a dark room and staring at it for a long time; when I lived in Paris thirty years later in a small, fifth-floor converted maid's flat, I found myself starting most evenings by this simplest of meditations. Now I frequently use it as a preparation for beginning to write, especially on sacred matters; its power to concentrate, awaken, and hallow the mind is astonishing.

Place a candle on a white cloth in front of you. Turn off the lights in your room and draw the curtains and shutters so there is as little light as possible. Then light the candle. For the best and clearest meditation, sit about three or four feet away from the candle.

Just gaze at the candle flame for two or three minutes. As in all previous exercises of mindfulness, when you find your attention wandering, bring it back to paying total attention to the flame. You will discover that as you do so, you will find yourself becoming more and more absorbed by the flame, until you "enter" it with your mind and "become" it.

When you feel yourself as deeply as one with the flame, suddenly blow it out and close your eyes. Now watch as the afterimage of the flame begins to form itself more and more distinctly on the inside of your eyelids. Savor the mystery of what was—or seemed to be—"outside" your eyes now forming "within" them. Repeat the same absorption you had trained on the "real" flame with this afterimage; allow your mind to "enter" it and "become" it.

WHEN THE THREE EXERCISES are completed, rest a little in clear peace. Then, as always before, dedicate everything you have learned and experienced to the liberation of all sentient beings.

During the day that follows, make a point of concentrating on at least three different objects with the same focused intensity as in the meditation. Before you go to the office in the morning, you might look at one of the flowers in your garden for a full minute; if you are on a walk in the afternoon, stop and look at the way the light moves in the trees lining the street, or at a hedge. Note in your practice diary what discoveries you make both about the objects themselves and the nature of your own mind. At the end of the period you dedicate to this practice, read through several times what you have written; you will be moved at how much you have learned about the power of attention to increase concentration, insight, respect, and love for what surrounds you. You will find that through concentration you will "see" everything with a more detached clarity, and that that clarity will awaken awe and love for what normally you do not notice or notice only with the banality of rushed perception. Slowly you will come to know what Gerard Manley Hopkins meant when he wrote in his diary about a solitary bluebell he had observed in an Oxford meadow: "I know the beauty of our Lord by it."

Practice 4
A Practice of Gratitude

Practice 3, "Three Practices of Concentration," aimed at training the concentration of the mind and at developing and enhancing that lucid, pure awareness that blossoms in the mind's stillness: Practice 4, "A Practice of Gratitude," focuses on training the heart and on developing that sacred ecstasy that flowers from a grateful adoration of the Divine and its gifts.

For the seeker on the Direct Path it is essential to learn how to awaken and sustain gratitude, for gratitude is the key to many of the highest, most noble, and most transformatory sacred emotions. A heart tuned constantly to be grateful comes to revere the Divine in the whole of existence and slowly to recognize the unity of the Presence behind all diverse appearances. A heart trained always to be grateful will also grow more and more humble; it will be fearless in its recognition of how everything it loves, needs, and celebrates streams in a never-ending river of grace from God. The nineteenth-century Hindu mystic Ramakrishna used to say often: "You can see how evolved someone is from how grateful they are for all the gifts of God." After his own first initiation into the omnipresence of the Divine Mother in the Kali temple at Dak-shineswar, when Ramakrishna saw the altar, the image of the goddess, the oil marks on the floor and the temple cat as shimmering manifestations of the fire of Divine Consciousness, he rushed out into the temple courtyard, saw a basket full of marigolds, started to dance wildly, flinging the marigolds in all the four directions. As we cultivate a grateful heart, we come to understand more and more intensely Ramakrishna's passion of celebration, and why he wanted to honor the Divine in all manifestation. Gratitude is the gift of, and the door to, revelation, the gift of, and the door to, humility, the way to adoration and its supremely transforming prize.

In the Jewish mystical system of cabala, one of the central aspects of the mystic's life is called "the raising of holy sparks." This comes from the teaching of a master mystic, Isaac Luria, known as Ari the Lion, who lived in the sixteenth century in the city of Safed. He wrote: "There is no sphere of existence, including organic and inorganic nature, that is not full of holy sparks which are mixed in with the husks [*kelippot* in Hebrew] and need to be separated from them and lifted up."

Isaac Luria and the school of cabalistic mysticism that flowered from his astonishing and sublime theories recognized that every particle in our universe, every structure, and every being is a shell or husk that contains "holy sparks." The task of the seeker, especially the seeker on the Direct Path, which aims at the creation of the sacred marriage on earth, is to release each spark from the shell and raise it up.

The way the cabala suggest the seeker do this is through acts of lovingkindness, being in harmony with the universe, and through higher awareness. One of the most potent forms of lovingkindness, harmony, and awareness is gratitude. Each act of gratitude symbolically both recognizes the Divine in a thing or event *and* consecrates that thing or event, "raising the spark" within it. Through continual gratitude, then, we not only *realize* the glory of God's continual action within creation and within the most intimate details of our lives; we also participate in the great work of the divinization of the whole of life and of the whole of the universe that is the guiding master plan of divine evolution.

Seeing gratitude in both a receptive and a sacredly active way
helps us prepare for all the kinds of heart-work in the practices
that follow. When we learn to open the heart and to live from the
vision and passion of the sacred heart in reality, we not only "re-
spond" fully to what Sufi mystics calls the *kibriya*, or the glory of
God, we also become ourselves "radioactive" fields of transformation, agents of holy change in ourselves and our surroundings.
This becomes more and more thrilling knowledge as the Path pro-
gresses and the alchemical results of all kinds of heart-work become apparent. Perhaps the greatest astonishment that awaits the
seeker is the discovery that she is, under and in God, given divine
powers to transform the world around her—divine powers that are,
however, given only to those vessels that have made themselves
empty through grateful abandonment to God's will and humility.

Let us now turn to the practice itself.

Sit down in your chosen place and compose your being. Then,
with great focused reverence, place one flower on the altar in front
of you. Any flower will do, but it helps if the flower you choose is
one you find especially beautiful. The flower in this exercise sym-
bolizes both the beauty of the creation and the beauty of the heart
open without any inhibition or fear to receive it.

Meditate silently on the flower, gazing at it as far as possible
with unblinking eyes, allowing every detail of its form to arouse
wonder and awe.

When your mind is calm and filled with love and starting to
open like the flower in front of you, offer up thanks for every part
of your being. Begin with your body; thank God for having a body
in which to experience the wonders and raptures of the spirit and
to witness the glory of the creation. Then thank God for your
heart, the heart which he has graced you the power to worship him
with and so to live in the joy of adoration. Then thank God for
your mind, the mind with which you can interpret the heart's visions and serve its transforming values in experience. Then, finally, and with awe and wonder, thank God for having a soul that
God has given you to stay always connected directly with himself.

Each time you thank the Divine for each part of your being, try
to find new aspects of each to celebrate and to be grateful for. For

instance, you can focus on different sections of the body; one day you might thank God for your hands, and explore in meditation all the joys they give you and make possible, from eating to caressing to writing to making love; on another day you might express your gratitude for your skin or your feet or your mouth. And when you thank God for your heart and mind and soul, try to explore each day different facets of their operation. On one day you might, for instance, celebrate your heart's passion; on another, its God-given power of compassion. One day you might celebrate your mind's clarity, another its visionary capacity. On one day you might offer up your wonder at the very fact of your soul's existence; on another you might choose to be grateful for the experiences of its existence that God has given you in mystical revelation. Remember always, as you thank God for your being, that *all* the gifts of your being are God-given; constantly keeping aware of this will drain the exercise of any self-flattery or narcissism and focus your whole self on the wonder of God's living Presence in you.

Now, having thanked God for your being, turn to the Divine and in your own words thank God for your life and for the chance to realize, savor, and serve the Divine in life. Look carefully over the course of your day and enumerate to yourself everything you have to be grateful for in it—from the way your sandwich tasted at lunch to the kindness of the cashier at the grocery store to the beauty of a child's laughter you heard on the train and the splendor of the late light as you walked home from the station. Choose one special incident or sight or moment of quiet revelation and note it in your practice diary, writing two or three lines about how it made you feel and what you noticed about yourself and your relationship to God through it. I find it helpful when I do this exercise to meditate on two marvelous lines of Rumi's.

> Whatever inspires the mind is of the perfume of My Beloved
> Whatever fires the heart is a ray from my Friend.

Turning these lines over constantly in my heart helps me remember that everything kind and beautiful or any moving experience comes in the end directly from God; every small joy I experience during every day is, in the end, yet one more sign of the One Presence that permeates all things. Remembering this trains the mind and heart to recognize unity behind multiplicity, to see the Beloved in every flower and fall of light, hear the Beloved in every sound and bird's cry, taste the Beloved in every peach and omelet, hold the Beloved in every child or cat or dog or bowl of fruit. The cashier's warm smile as she hands you your bag of groceries is God's smile; your cat purrs on your lap with God's purr; the river laughs in the light with God's laughter. What the practice of gratitude opens up to in fact is the mystical revelation of the "holy sparks" hidden in the "husks of everything"; by recognizing, saluting, and praising this revelation you "release" the "sparks" and help return them consciously to their place at the sacred center of the universe.

Slowly, this practice of gratitude will begin to transform your consciousness so you start to detect Divine Presence and divine mercy all around you. Seeing Presence and mercy all around you will in time tremendously lessen your fear and suffering, for it will make you aware of the maternal protection of God and of how the entire universe and all of life is constantly giving you signs of God's glory, beauty, and love. Practicing gratitude not only heals you of vanity and pride; it also heals you of the fear, grief, and almost pathological insecurity that the false self's passion for separation breeds.

At the end of the practice, stand up, move nine or ten feet backward and slowly, consciously, prostrate your entire body before the altar, offering up your being, your life, and the entire universe to the Divine in a final act of gratitude, and dedicate the energy of your meditation to the "raising of holy sparks" in everyone and everything.

Practice 5
The Practice of the Mantra

What you need above all on the Direct Path are simple, clear, powerful practices that work fast to put you into direct contact with the Divine in whatever circumstances you find yourself. In my experience, one of the most effective mystical practices in making possible—even ensuring—this direct contact is that of the mantra. Since I first discovered twenty years ago in India the astonishing power of the mantra to protect, ennoble, calm, inspire, and transform the whole being, practicing mantra has become the foundation of my inner life. I have drawn on the power of mantra to help me stay joyful, concentrated, and creative during periods of illness and suffering both mental and physical; I have drawn on it constantly, day in and day out, for passion, wisdom, strength, divine guidance, and peace of soul and have never been disappointed.

A mantra is a spiritual formula, a combination of sacred syllables transmitted from age to age in a religious tradition that forms a nucleus of spiritual power. In nearly all the major mystical systems of the world—the Sufi, Hindu, and the Buddhist in particular—maintaining a fervent, continual, focused inner recitation of a mantra is seen as the fastest and most immediately transformatory way of transcending the surface mind and entering the depths of the spirit where the mystery of the Presence is always alive.

Since earliest times, mystics have discovered that repeating a simple sacred phrase or single word or holy name of God with one-pointed passion and concentration in the depths of the heart unifies all the faculties of being and gathers them together in the indwelling presence of the Divine—and in an almost miraculously potent and quick way.

The word mantra is derived from the Sanskrit *man,* "mind," and *trai,* "protect"; *trai* also echoes within itself the word *tri*—"to cross." A mantra, then, is something that protects the mind and enables it to cross the sea of phenomenal existence with all its deceptions and illusions.

True mantras are not simply sacred syllables sanctified by tradition and many ages of religious devotion; they are, as the Buddhists and Hindus remind us, *embodiments* of the truth in sound and so supremely effective in helping us to embody the truth within our lives. According to the Upanishads, the original dwelling place of the mantra was the Parma Akasha, or primeval ether, the eternal and immutable substratum of the universe, out of which, it is said, in the uttering of the primal sound, the universe was created. Mantras existed in this ether and were directly received by the ancient rishis, or seers, who translated them into an audible and sacredly *empowered* pattern of rhythm and words. Each syllable of an authentic mantra, then, is impregnated with living divine power that streams directly from its source in the Absolute; each syllable condenses spiritual truth with immense intensity and vibrates—not poetically but actually and literally—with the blessing of the primal word of the Divine.

Reciting or chanting an authentic mantra, then, *activates* this accumulated power within the seeker's own being. Since the mind, as many mystical systems point out, rides on the subtle energy of the breath (which in turn moves through and purifies the subtle channels of the body), when you recite or chant a mantra, what you are in fact doing is charging your breath and energy with its divine energy, and so working *directly* with divine energy on your mind, heart, and subtle body. The more you practice mantra, the more clearly you will become aware of how this astonishingly simple and powerful system works; if you persist in your practice, you will come to a time when you want to laugh out loud and clap your hands for joy that so easy a way of living in the Presence could be available to all humankind.

You will find, in fact, that keeping up a constant practice of mantra works to refine your entire being. Through it, you can come to relax your body and open it to divine sweetness, peace, and joy and discover that real health is far more than an absence of disease but a living, vibrant possession of the divine energy in every limb, breath, and movement. Through it, you will come to know how to refine and toughen your will, which will help you free yourself from addictions that may have kept you enslaved for years; there is no more powerful way to dehypnotize the mind from its old hungers, projections, and fantasies than working on it with mantra. Through the constant practice of mantra, you will gain access to reserves of courage, patience, passion, and compassion you never imagined you had and you will learn how to give and receive love from a position of divine trust, confidence, and faith. In the end you will discover what all those who have persisted in this practice discover—that mantra has transformed your entire consciousness by permeating it with the strength and energy of the Presence. These are tremendous claims; you have only to practice to discover them to be real and to discover for yourself the radiance of what Gandhi meant when he wrote: "The mantra becomes one's staff of life and carries you through every ordeal. It is not repeated for the sake of repetition but for the sake of purification, as an aid to effort. It is no empty repetition, for each repetition has a new meaning, carrying you nearer and nearer to God."

I think it is essential to choose a mantra that has been sanctified by centuries or even millennia of use; its power will be immeasurably enhanced by the longing and passionate devotion of the millions of seekers who have employed it. What I am going to offer now are five different mantras from different mystical traditions; select one that moves you and then stick to it throughout the practice. In general, it is best to stay with one mantra, most especially at the beginning of the Path; later on you may find yourself wanting to work with several for different purposes. Even then you will usually find yourself returning in times of stress or acute need to your root mantra, the one that has always accompanied and fueled your journey.

The five mantras I want to offer here are: *Ribbono shel olam,* which means in Hebrew "Lord of the universe" and is tremendously effective in awakening the entire being to rapture and awe at the divine majesty; *Maranatha,* which means in Aramaic "O Lord, come" and was the mantra used perhaps by the disciples and certainly by the Desert Fathers to invoke the full splendor of the Christ-consciousness within and without; *Om namah shivayah,* which means in Sanskrit "All hail to the Holy name of Shiva" and summons and celebrates the immense purificatory power of the "masculine" transcendent power of the Godhead (known as Shiva in Hinduism); *Om mani padme hum* (pronounced "Om mani peme hung"), which is the great mantra of Avalokiteshvara, the Buddha of compassion and means "All hail to the jewel at the heart of the lotus"—all hail, in other words, to that enlightened love-consciousness that waits to be uncovered and lived at the core of our being; *Allahu Akbar,* which in Arabic means "God is great" and is used in Sufi mysticism as a way of remaining always in contact with the glory of the One Beloved.

At the very beginning of this practice, then, recite each of these mantras to yourself, noting very carefully their effects on you. As you recite, meditate in your heart on the *meaning* of the mantra; that will help you discover, too, which one resonates most intensely with what you yourself know and experience of the Divine most vividly. If, for example, your most familiar experience of God is as a majesty beyond you that continually possesses and exalts you, then working with the Hebrew or Sufi mantras may be the most powerful for you; if your relationship with the Divine is more usually tender and devotional, you might find that *Maranatha* will help you most; if you most often experience the Divine as an *inner* presence, then working with *Om mani padme hum,* with its invocation of that inner presence, might be most effective.

Once you have chosen the mantra you will work with, begin the practice.

Sit down in your chosen meditation place; dedicate your practice, as always, to the liberation of all beings everywhere. Then—and this I find is very powerful—pray to all those other beings who have used the mantra you have chosen before you to infuse you with its sacred truth. By praying like this, you will be consciously pacing yourself in a living brilliant stream of adoration that has persisted over centuries and making yourself available to its power.

Now, with your heart open and devoted and inspired, begin the practice of the mantra.

In Hindu mantra practice, there are four main ways of practicing mantra: *Vaikhali japa* (saying the mantra aloud); *Upamsu japa* (whispering the mantra); *Likhita japa* (writing the mantra down); and *Manasika japa* (internal mental repetition). The fourth is the most powerful, but the others are effective also and can be used in many different circumstances. So I suggest that during your practice period, devote separate sessions to each of the different ways of reciting.

In the first set of sessions, say the mantra out loud. Say it slowly, richly, with all the passion and tenderness and longing you can muster, savoring each syllable and focusing your entire being on the sacred meaning of the words you are using. Don't worry at all, however, about pronunciation. God will hear you however well or badly you pronounce the words if your motivation is sincere.

In the second set of sessions, just whisper the mantra. This can be a very emotional and moving experience; your practice can seem like a kind of mystical pillow talk to the Presence who is, as the Upanishads say, "closer to you than your jugular vein." Whispering the mantra can bring you, if you let it, to an almost miraculous sense of the *intimacy* of the Divine with your every need, thought, and movement. My advice for this week is that when you whisper your mantra, do so with your head bowed in adoration and your two hands placed on your heart-center in the middle of your chest. This, you will find, will dramatically increase your powers of devotion and the tender revelations of divine friendship that it can bring.

When you come to the practice of the third set of sessions—writing the mantra down—perform the practice on pieces of large white paper you have already sprinkled with holy water or consecrated with the ash from an incense stick burned in honor of God. When you come to write out the mantra, do so with infinite care, concern, and devotion; the number of times you write out the mantra is not as important as the motivation with which you write it. Make every letter of every word as clear and graceful as you can; as you write out the mantra, believe and know that by manifesting it in the written word, you are helping the power contained within it to become actively embodied. As you write, then, imagine the mantra being "written" forever in the inmost part of your heart; every time you write it down with this intention, you will experience its deepening in your being. In other words, believe and know that the *exterior* writing you are performing is effecting an *interior* transformation of your essence into the essence of the mantra. When you have finished the practice, put all the pieces of paper in a box under your altar; the power of your accumulated "written" devotion will protect and inspire you.

By the time you arrive at the fourth set of sessions, you will discover with joy that you are longing just to repeat the mantra silently within your heart. The previous three sets of practice sessions will have acquainted you so completely with the different powers of the mantra that you will now long to take it in silence into your inmost depths. Practice with passion and adoration and you will come to know what the great Indian mystic Kabir meant when he wrote:

> The true diamond is the Lord's name, the mantra;
> Seek it, find it within your heart;
> Outside, it is present everywhere;
> Within, it fills every pot.

At later stages of this practice, you will discover that the power of the mantra will unlock for you the visionary center at the center of your forehead, prepare the great opening of the heart-center, and initiate you directly into the great sound of the universe—the *shabd*. Don't expect too much, however, in your first month of practice; it usually takes several years of constant practice for these mystical phenomena to manifest themselves. If you do, however, start to hear at moments a high whirring sound like the sound of electrical wires or distant bees, do not be alarmed; this is the beginning of the experience of the Shabd.

At the end of the half hour of practice, dedicate everything you have learned and experienced to the liberation of every sentient being. Then make a commitment to keep repeating the mantra as far as possible throughout the day. You will discover if you do that there is no more wonderful or faster way of entering the Presence than by saying the mantra—whether you are walking or shopping, cleaning the floor, washing the dishes, or attending to office work. You can repeat the mantra before you eat to remind you that all gifts come from God; repeating it, too, before going to sleep can purify your dreams and ensure you a restful and restorative night.

Throughout the month, keep a careful note of what you are experiencing. Experiment; if you find yourself, for example, growing bored or impatient or angry during your day, return to work on the negative emotion you are living by working on it with the mantra. You will discover that using the mantra in this way can tremendously effect your level of cheerfulness and creativity and inspiration. Within us all is a limitless sea of divine energy, peace, truth, and power that the mantra provides direct access to. Practice daily, constantly, humbly, and with imagination, and you will discover just how literally and marvelously true this is.

Practice 6
Chanting

Chanting is one of the most effective and exhilarating ways of raising your entire being into receptivity and joy and has been used in different but profoundly connected ways by all the major mystical traditions. Ancient Hindu rishis developed intricate chants to "embody" mantras in waves of transformatory sacred sound; Sufi mystics have set passages from the Koran or love poems by Rumi or Hafiz to chantlike melodies that immediately exalt both listener and practitioner; many Christian monastic orders—notably, of course, the Carmelite, Cistercian, and Benedictine—have kept alive the tradition of Gregorian chant and its power to open the whole psyche to the vibratory peace of the Infinite.

You don't have to have a strong singing voice or musical talent to discover the power of chanting for yourself. You can derive a great deal of comfort and inspiration by chanting in simple ways that have strength and beauty and dignity.

The rewards of developing the simple practice of chanting are many. You will find that chanting in the middle of an emotional or spiritual crisis can be as effective as mantra in clearing the atmosphere of the heart and mind. Many different kinds of emotional disturbances can be soothed with wonderful swiftness and efficiency by chanting; I use it especially when I am feeling impatient or blocked in creative inspiration. Chanting can tremendously enhance our feelings of devotion to the Divine also; opening up the throat-center through chanting opens up also the visionary center in the Third Eye and the heart-center, and connects them all by a living, vibrant energy that is inextricably related to the energy of divine love. To learn how to chant can be for many people their first experience of pouring out their being in adoration of God; the joy, even ecstasy, that such an experience brings can lead them into deeper and deeper revelation of the transformatory power of devotion.

For the purposes of this set of practices, I am going to concentrate on two extremely simple but extremely powerful chants; *om* and *ma*.

THE *OM* CHANT

Sit in your chosen place and, as always, dedicate the practice you are about to do to the liberation of all sentient beings. Then meditate silently on the divine significance of the sacred syllable *om*.

The importance that was attached to the word in ancient India can be seen from the following quotation from the Chandogya Upanishad:

> *Om* is the essence of essences, the highest, the eighth rung,
>   venerated above all that human beings hold holy.
> *Om* is the self of all.
> With the word *om* we say "I agree"
> And with *om* we fulfill desires.
> With *om*, we recite, we give direction,
> We sing aloud the honor of that Word
> The key to the three kinds of knowledge.

A similar passage is found in the Mandukya Upanishad:

> The mantra [*om*] is the bow, the aspirant
> Is the arrow, and the Lord the target.
> Now draw the bowstring of meditation
> And hitting the target be one with Him.

As Lama Govinda tells us in his *Foundations of Tibetan Mysticism* "the sound-values of *om* and their symbolic interpretation [in the Upanishads] are described in the following manner: O is a combination of "A" and "U"; the whole syllable . . . consists of three elements . . . A-U-M. Since *om* is the expression of the highest faculty of consciousness, these three elements are explained accordingly as three planes of consciousness: "A" as the waking consciousness (*jagrat*), "U" as the dream-consciousness (*svapna*), and "M" as the consciousness during deep sleep (*susupti*). *Om* as a whole represents the all-encompassing cosmic consciousness (*turiya*) on the fourth plane, beyond words and concepts—the consciousness of the fourth dimension.

When you come to chant *om*, then, believe and know that you are chanting the most sacred syllable of all, one that corresponds to the most intimate and holy sound of the cosmos. Believe and know that you are chanting at one and the same time the sound of your own inmost divine consciousness, the "sound" that the entire creation is always resonating to, and the "sound" that the Godhead "makes" when and as it creates reality. A sweet old Hindu priest in Tanjore once told me before we chanted *om* together in the twilight in one of the halls of the Shiva temple: "Always remember that when you chant 'om' you are yourself one vibrating note of the always-silent and always-sounding *om* sounding *om* back to Itself; if you chant in this all-embracing way, you will very soon come to have an experience of nonduality." The truth of what I was told on that evening has been revealed to me in many, many subsequent meditations and will undoubtedly be revealed to you if you approach this practice with sincerity, knowledge, and real devotion.

Let us return to the actual practice now. When you have spent a few minutes meditating, as I suggested, on the sacred significance of *om*, start slowly to chant it. Use one of the lower notes in your voice register; *om* should never be chanted too high, because chanting it too high diminishes its power. Find and hold a note not too far away from the natural note your speaking voice makes when it is speaking tenderly and raptly.

Don't vary the note as you chant *om* again and again. Try always and sound the *om* with the same amount of breath and vocal power. You will find if you do that the repetition of the same sonorous pitch and sound will calm your whole being and make it receptive to spiritual joy. It will also encourage a kind of "selfless-ness" that makes the cosmic dimensions of *om* more accessible; if you are concentrating even slightly on how you sound or on the "beauty" of the sound, its full transformatory power will be diluted by your self-consciousness.

Om (A-U-M) should be chanted in three parts, with equal time given to each part. Traditionally, *ah* is chanted in the region of the navel, *oo* in the sternum, and *mm* in the throat.

When you come to chant the last syllable, *mm,* with closed lips, you will become aware of how millions of cells have been awakened in your body by the sacred syllable. After each chanted *om,* savor the ringing silence that follows and the marvelously joyful way your whole being resonates to it. At the end of the practice session, chant four long slow *oms,* directing your intention to each of the four directions of the universe and saying silently:

> By the power of this *om* may all creatures to the East of me be
>   liberated
> By the power of this *om* may all creatures to the West be
>   liberated
> By the power of this *om* may all creatures to the South be
>   liberated
> By the power of this *om* may all creatures to the North be
>   liberated

As the last sacred act of the practice, believe and know that your chanting of *om* during the session has transformed your entire body, speech, mind, and heart into an *om,* silently sounding together with the *om* of the universe and radiating divine light throughout the cosmos. Rest in the great joy and peace that this recognition brings.

THE CHANT OF *MA*

The syllable *ma* has been used in the East for millennia to symbolize the concentrated power and glory and love of the divine Mother aspect of God. Chanting it with devotion and passion has an extraordinary power to invoke the Presence of the Mother aspect of God and to connect the seeker with its inmost Presence within herself.

The first sessions have been devoted to chanting *om*, the sound of the Godhead. Now you are to chant *ma*, the sacred infinite sound of the Mother aspect of the Godhead, that final and all-embracing love of the Mother that permeates the creation at every level and draws every sentient being in the creation always to its breast.

While you should chant *om* as "impersonally" as possible, so as to enter most completely into the Godhead's divine calm and wide splendor (and their presence within your own consciousness), I recommend chanting *ma* softly and with great tender emotion. The Mother aspect of God, after all, has a fervent and intimate love for all creation.

Begin this part of the practice of chanting by sounding *ma* in a quiet, soft, low, long-drawn-out way. Every time you chant *ma*, you should meditate inwardly on another aspect of the Mother's being and your relationship with it. This will enable you to make every time you chant the sacred syllable a different inner experience. Sometimes you will find yourself chanting with longing to feel the Mother's love; sometimes you will chant with awe at her grandeur and at her vast, all-creative and all-destructive power; sometimes the way you chant will be infused with holy gratitude for everything that she has given and gives you; sometimes when chanting *ma* you will find yourself wanting to send its healing and transforming blessing to people in pain that you know, or to parts of the world where wars or natural disasters are occurring. Vary each time you chant the sacred syllable of the Mother and you will come to know and experience in each of the chanting sessions something more of her infinite variety and of the infinite variety of your nondual relationship with her.

Try devoting half of your time this month to chanting *om* and half to chanting *ma* with a pause for silent meditation in between. You will find that if you have been chanting with one-pointed sincerity, you will now, by combining the two forms of chant, be able to experience both the infinity of the Godhead and her tender, all-encompassing, all-penetrating love.

You will be in effect "marrying" your deepest insights into the transcendent aspect of God with your deepest feelings for the immanent Mother aspects of the Divine, which will ultimately help you contact the Father and Mother aspects of your own inner divinity and aid you in their intense sacred fusion.

Practice 7
Practice of Simple Meditation

In his great work *Fukanzazengi,* the fourteenth-century Zen master Dogen wrote: "Truth is perfect and complete in itself. It has always existed. It is not something to be attained since not one of your steps lead away from it."

Dogen goes on: "Do not follow the ideas of others, but learn to listen to the voice within yourself. The practice of meditation is not a method of the attainment of realization—it is enlightenment itself. Your search among books, word upon word, may lead you to the depths of knowledge, but is not the way to receive the reflection of your true self. When you have thrown off your ideas as to mind and body, the original truth willfully appears."

To sit in meditation, then, is to invite the discovery of your essential self beyond the mind. In the practice of simple meditation, we drop below the surface of consciousness and become concentrated on one thing and one thing alone; our authentic identity.

To discover what Dogen calls the "original truth" within us is to know ourselves linked to every other sentient being and thing in the universe. When we plummet deep into our real nature, the boundaries that separate us from the rest of the world start to disappear. The duality of subject and object, I and other, knower and known, starts to dissolve; gradually, we are opened to a bare, naked, transcendental way of knowing that over time becomes a force of clear love that connects us effortlessly, naturally, and transparently to all things.

Meditation is the way of entering into communion with this innermost force of peace and love within ourselves; the deeper the contact we make with this force, the more transformed our lives and everything in them become.

The practice of simple meditation I am now going to offer is one of the most crucial on the Direct Path. By introducing you to your essential nature, it will gradually help you liberate yourself from all negative conditionings and emotions, inspire you to choose joy and peace of mind at all moments—even in the worst circumstances—and initiate you into your fundamental strengths that time and loss cannot rubble.

This cannot be a fast process—do not expect immediate results. As a Tibetan adept once said to me, "Meditation is not some 'Star Wars' magic pill; it is like the waterfall near my village in Tibet, falling for years on the rocks before they are worn away." Commit yourself to it, however, practice it day in and day out calmly, with no expectation and no grandiose hankering after any kind of visionary experience or sudden mystical "breakthrough," and you will soon notice the beginnings of small changes in yourself—the growth of detachment, of compassion, of patience—which will encourage you to continue.

Above all, as I have said before, do not approach meditation as a strenuous, competitive activity. Meditation is not about achieving anything. The truth of your essential nature is not something you have to "win" or "earn": It is a God-given grace of nondual connection with all things. What you most need to discover or recognize is a steady alert calm, a grace of lucid relaxation.

There was once a monk called Shrona, studying meditation with one of the Buddha's closest disciples. He found that he could not discover the right frame of mind. He tried hard to concentrate, and only gave himself a headache. Then he decided he would try relaxing his mind—but only fell asleep. In the end, he appealed to the Buddha for help. The Buddha knew that Shrona had been a famous musician before he became a monk and so asked him:

"When you were a vina player how did you coax the finest sound from your vina? Was it when the strings were very tight or when they were slack and loose?"

"Neither," Shrona replied. "When they had the right tension, neither too taut nor too slack."

"Well," said the Buddha. "It's exactly the same with your mind."

What you need, then, for successful meditation is a delicate balance of alertness and relaxation, one-pointed lucidity and spacious peace of spirit. Dogen informs us: "To actualize the blessing of meditation you should practice with pure intention and firm determination. Do not dwell in thoughts of good or bad. Just relax and forget that you are meditating. Do not desire realization since that will keep you confused. The human mind has absolute freedom within its true nature. You can attain your freedom intuitively. Do not work for freedom, rather allow the practice itself to be liberation."

Before you begin your practice of simple meditation, write out in large letters on a piece of paper that wonderful last remark of Dogen's: "Do not work for freedom, rather allow the practice itself to be liberation." Look at it every time you sit down to meditate and it will help you poise your being.

Let us now begin the practice. Sit in your chosen place and dedicate your meditation to the liberation of all sentient beings.

Meditation is, in fact, an act of service to others; you know that if you are a happy, more peaceful, and integrated being, the lives of all those who come into contact with you will be subtly altered and the effects of your growing transformation will be felt beyond even your immediate circle throughout the cosmos, because all beings everywhere are connected in the web of the real. Make your initial dedication of the practice as rich and heartfelt as possible; you will find the more intimately and imaginatively you commit yourself to the adventure of meditation out of compassion for others, the more determination you will find in yourself to continue.

Dogen's advice on how to proceed is, as always with him, wonderfully concise and to the point: "Hold your body straight without leaning to the left or right, forward or backward. Your ears should be in line with your shoulders, and your nose in a straight line with your navel. Keep your tongue at the roof of your mouth and close your lips. Keep your eyes slightly open, and breathe through your nostrils. Before you begin to meditate take several slow, deep breaths. Hold your body erect, allowing your breathing to become normal again."

The posture that Dogen recommends is classic, easy, and the one I myself practice. If you can sit in a full lotus position, do so, but don't worry if you can't. Just sit on your meditation cushion in as relaxed and painless a way as you can manage. Your aim is to sit in the most peaceful way you can, so that you can, as far as possible, "forget" the body and dive deeper and deeper into your essential nature.

Sitting erect and calm, then, just be as natural and spacious as possible. If your thoughts start to run riot, don't imagine that you are "failing" in your meditation; in fact, you are "succeeding." Since you are becoming quieter, you are becoming more aware of the circus that is your mind.

In the ancient Tibetan meditation instructions, it is said that at the beginning thoughts will arrive on top of another, uninterruptedly, like a steep mountain waterfall. Gradually, as you persist, these thoughts will become like water in a deep, narrow gorge, then a vast river winding its way down to the ocean. Finally the mind will become like a vast still sea, ruffled by only the occasional ripple or wave.

The best way to treat the thoughts and emotions that arise in meditation is with spacious compassion. Your thoughts and emotions, after all, are your family, the family of your mind. A great Tibetan practitioner, Dudjom Rinpoche, used to say, "Be like an old man, watching a child play."

In the stress of life we are often conflicted as to how to deal with our negative, difficult, troubling emotions. In the calm spaciousness of meditation, we can start to view these emotions with detachment. Slowly this practice of detachment, of not identifying or judging the thoughts and emotions that arise, will change the whole atmosphere of our mind by making us aware of the peace and calm within us that thoughts and emotions cannot qualify or destroy. Then the pain that our negative fantasies and passions bring us will be defused; we will no longer feel so scared by, or vulnerable to, their power.

So during your meditation session, practice letting whatever thoughts and emotions come up to rise and settle like waves in the sea. Whatever you find yourself thinking—however weird, "irrelevant," or trivial or even "scandalous"—do not identify with your thought but "watch" it rise and settle, without any constraint. Don't grasp at it, or avoid it, or flinch from it, or feed or indulge it; don't cling to it and don't attempt to solidify it or trace its origin or understand its "truth." Don't either follow thoughts or invite them. Thuksey Rinpoche used to say when he taught meditation: "Be like the sea gazing at its own waves, or the sky gazing at the clouds passing through it."

One of the greatest rewards of meditation is coming to cultivate, know, and possess at will what Dogen called "awareness that does not think." In the fierce stress of life, this "choiceless awareness" will keep us sober, calm, poised, free from the conditionings of the past; it will act, in fact, as a kind of "mirror" within us, always exposing to us where we are unbalanced or crazed or simply repeating in the present the patterns of thought or emotion left in us by past trauma or humiliation. The more "aware" we become of the presence within us, of this "awareness that does not think" at all moments, the more awake, sensitive, spontaneous, and supple we become and the more integrated with Divine Reality.

Eventually you will discover, if you practice meditation "with pure intention and firm determination" that you will be able when life presents you with great pain or difficulty to "see" the pain or difficulty from a position of peaceful detachment; this will not dissolve either one but will enable you to remain creative within them, free from their worst ravages, and constantly subtly in contact with that divine part of you that is never stained by them.

As you come to the end of your session, make a commitment to try to taste the freedom of this "awareness that does not think" at moments throughout your day. One excellent technique for "integrating" the truth of meditation with everyday life is to take what Sogyal Rinpoche calls "meditation minutes"—meditation periods of one minute each, taken at odd moments of "dead time" during the day. Doing this will help you sustain "this state" through all the demands of your routine.

At the end of the session, dedicate everything you have learned and felt to the liberation of all sentient beings. Do this as you d[i] the initial dedication with deep, heartfelt joy and compassion, knowing that through the law of interdependence, your dedication of your meditation will now inevitably infuse the universe with illumination.

It is very important not to come out of meditation too quickly. Allow a period of three or four minutes to allow the peace of the practice of meditation to infuse your life. Dudjom Rinpoche used to say, "Don't jump and rush off, but mingle your mindfulness with everyday life. Be like a man who's fractured his skull, always careful in case someone will touch him."

What really matters is not just the practice of sitting but far more the state of mind you find yourself in afterward. You should try to prolong this calm, spacious state throughout the entire day. Bring its awareness to everything you do, from riding the bus to shopping to going to the bathroom to making a meal, and you will gradually discover the joy of being completely present in all your actions, without any of the distractions of the false self to stop you being there. And then you will be naturally embodying the transcendent in all you think, do, and are.

Practice 8
The Practice of Self-Inquiry: Who Am I?

In many spiritual traditions, repeatedly asking yourself the question "Who am I?" or a variation of it, such as, "Who is carrying this body?" is the central practice that is offered for awakening. Zen masters have recommended it in China and Japan; Mahayana Buddhist practitioners of Dzogchen know it as *rushen*, analytic contemplation that uses the mind to destroy dualism; certain Sufi sects employ it with breathing and mantra exercises to bring seekers to a knowledge of their true nature; an ancient Hindu sage, Vasistha, wrote: "This inquiry 'Who am I?' is the quest of the Self and is said to be the fire that burns up the seed of the poisonous growth of conceptual thought."

...dvocate in modern times of this practice was the ...c Ramana Maharshi, who made it the founda- ...ing. The following conversation, which took place ...en the swami and one of his most devoted followers, ...nam Pillai, makes clear the spiritual and metaphysical ...of "self-inquiry":

S.P.	Swami, who am I? And how is salvation to be attained?
SRI RAMANA	By incessant inward inquiry, "Who am I?" you will know yourself and thereby attain salvation.
S.P.	Who am I?
SRI R	The real I or Self is not the body, or any of the five senses, nor the sense-objects nor the organs of action, nor the prana [breath or vital force] nor the mind, nor even the deep sleep state where there is no cognizance of these.
S.P.	If I am none of these what else am I?
SRI R	After rejecting each of these, and saying "This I am not," that which alone remains is the "I" and that is Consciousness.

Another great modern Indian mystic who attained illumination through the process of self-inquiry was the wonderful cigarette-smoking mystic of Bombay, Nisargadatta Maharaj, whose book *I Am That* is one of the greatest testimonies to mystical freedom ever compiled. Again and again he would repeat, "Give up all questions except one—Who am I? After all, the only fact you are sure of is that you *are*. The 'I am this' is not certain; the 'I am' is. The impersonal is real, the personal appears and disappears. 'I am' is the Supreme Being, 'I am this' is the person. The person is relative and the Pure Being is fundamental."

Nisargadatta Maharaj's emphasis in the practice was slightly different from that of Ramana Maharshi. Whereas the maharshi emphasized cutting away all false thoughts of ego, mind, and body to arrive at the Supreme Consciousness of what is forever behind them, Nisargadatta Maharaj would always stress the power of meditating directly on the "I am." He would say to those who came to visit him: "Give all your attention to the level on which 'I am' is timelessly present, to focus mind on pure being. By focusing the mind on 'I am,' I am so-and-so dissolves."

Both Ramana Maharshi and Nisargadatta Maharaj stressed how intensely committed the seeker who wishes to uncover his or her Self through this method has to be. Ramana Maharshi frequently referred to this practice of self-inquiry (*vichara*) as the "ultimate austerity" because it demanded constant vigilance and a continual, even violent, effort of will has to be sustained if vichara is to yield its supreme secret. Nisargadatta Maharaj said in *I Am That,* "What matters supremely is sincerity, is earnestness. See the urgent need of being free of this unnecessary self-identification with a bundle of memories and habits. Resolutely reject what you are not till the real Self emerges in its glorious nothingness, not-a-thing ness."

Realize, then, when you begin your adventure into this practice that you are undertaking something at once supremely simple and extremely demanding. You will need all your powers of focus, concentration, and will and to summon up all your desires really to change the way you think and live, all your passion to know the truth about the divine self you essentially are.

When you do the practice, try, too, to keep the mind always in the heart-center. This heart-center (the *hiranyagarbha,* as it is called) is the seat of the consciousness of the self. As Ramana Maharshi reminds us: "When the mind that is subtle goes out through the brain and the sense-organs, the gross names and forms appear; when it stays in the heart the names and forms disappear. Not letting the mind go but retaining it in the Heart is what is called 'inwardness,' letting the mind go out of the Heart is known as 'externalization.' When the mind stays in the Heart the 'I' which is the source of all thoughts will go and the Self which ever exists will shine."

Sit down, now, in your chosen meditation place and dedicate your session to all sentient beings. Begin to focus in your heart-center and pray that through your practice of self-inquiry *all* sentient beings might be brought closer to their realization of the self and so freed from the illusions of separateness and death.

Begin now the practice of self-inquiry, trying to keep alive and vibrant your concentration in the heart. Ask yourself a series of clear, probing questions. Are you your body? Are you your sex or sexuality or family name or nationality or profession or reputation? Are you your age or your complexion or even the thoughts that come dancing in and out of your mind or your emotions? Are you your spiritual experiences that are so revelatory but which inevitably arise and then pass away?

Go deeply and fully into each question, and you will find that you are none of these things. Eliminate calmly, then, all the conventional answers you or our society give to try to define who you are. After each elimination, I find it helpful and inspiring to say inwardly, "No, I am *not* that." I find that just the act of saying what I am *not* can bring me closer to the mystery of who I *am*.

Once you have formally and inexorably eliminated in this way all the false answers to the question "Who am I?" don't in any way try to force or invoke or conjure up an answer, either conceptually or even experientially. Anything you force will be false to the true experience they will arise of itself when you are ready. Just continue holding on to the thought and question "Who am I?"

When Pillai asked Ramana Maharshi "What is the means for constantly holding on to the thought 'Who am I?'" he replied, "When other thoughts arise, one should not pursue them but should inquire, 'To whom did they arise?' The answer that would emerge would be, 'To me.' Therefore, upon if one inquires 'Who am I?' the mind will go back to its source; and the thought that will arise will become quiescent. With repeated practice in this manner, the mind will develop the skill to stay in its source."

Whenever any thought or emotion arises during the practice, just ask yourself "Who is feeling this?" or "Who is thinking this?" Don't follow or entertain or grasp in any way the thought or feeling; every time a thought or feeling arises, just return inexorably to the question so as to drive home again and again that it is your "I" that is the source of all passing emotions and thoughts.

This is hard, sometimes even grueling work, but its rewards are magnificent. The more you keep on concentrating not on thoughts and feelings but on who they are "arising" in, the more you will be reminded of your core-consciousness, the stiller your mind and emotions will become, and the more your consciousness will begin to merge consciously in the self. The key, as Ramana Maharshi keeps telling us, is to let the mind develop the skill to stay in its source, the heart; the more the mind can stay in the heart, the more the heart's essential awareness can permeate the mind and through it the perception of everything.

The point of this practice of self-inquiry is not to confine it to a practice session but to employ it as uninterruptedly as possible also during ordinary life. So, as you find yourself coming to the end of your session, make a vow to keep asking the question "Who am I?" throughout the day, to keep asking, "Who are these feelings and thoughts arising in?" to trying to return at every possible moment your mind to its heart-source. You will find that although this is a demanding practice, it will tremendously help you to become clearer, calmer, more fearless in your life; over many years of practice you will undoubtedly grow more and more aware of your essential divine self, and then everything you do or experience will be more rich and strong and beautiful. You will come to know what Nisargadatta Maharaj meant when he said, "Beyond happiness there is pure intensity, inexhaustible energy, the ecstasy of giving from a perennial source."

At the end of the practice, rest in whatever you have come to experience of the conscious bliss-presence of the self. Finally, with gratitude and joy, dedicate the practice to the self-realization of *all* sentient beings.

Practice 9
Become Buddha or Christ

This practice is a directed visualization. In directed visualizations the seeker summons into her mind a mental image on which she can meditate. What visualization of this kind does is harness the mental power that is usually dissipated in fantasies, daydreams, and imaginings by directing it to a holy image. The power of this method—which is used with particular intensity in Taoism, Tibetan Buddhism, Hinduism, and certain forms of Christian mysticism—is that it enables the practitioner to evoke and discover the qualities of the imaged being within herself.

When you practice a visualization method seriously, you soon discover that what you are imagining and focusing on—the creation of your own spiritual imagination—reflects deep laws, powers, and possibilities of your own being; what you are meditating on, in fact, is the highest imaginable version and emanation of yourself. As you come to know and experience this more and more, the visualization becomes more and more powerful, until it becomes an almost instantaneous way of connecting with and summoning the force of your own innermost divine identity.

I have called the practice "Become Buddha or Christ" because those two great beings tend to be the inner archetypes that the majority of people work with. But if you feel a special link to the Mother, you can, of course, work with an image of her, from any religious system. I myself have often done this practice with either the Virgin, Kali, or Tara as the divine being I am invoking; in every case the effect was revelatory and opened myself up to more knowledge of my "mother" within in different aspects of her tenderness, ferocity, and power.

Begin by sitting down in your chosen place and breathing in and out consciously for two or three minutes to calm your mind.

Imagine now that your heart-center—which is located in the middle of your chest, an inch or two to the right—has a nose. Breathe deeply in and out of this area until it begins to feel warm and expanded. Then rise up to the center in the middle of your throat and start to breathe in and out of this center until it begins to feel vibrant. Now take the breath up to the center of spiritual vision—the Third Eye—between your eyes and again breathe in and out from here until you feel warm or a slight tingling. Then take the breath up to the crown center on the top of your head and imagine that you are breathing in and out vertically. Then, to complete this first part of the exercise, return your awareness and your breath into your heart-center. By then you should be able to feel vividly and precisely the living connection between your heart and head centers and to savor the flow of soft, sweet, fiery energy between them.

Now return your awareness to your heart-center in the middle of your chest. Visualize that the sacred figure you have chosen to work with—the Buddha or Christ or the Mother or any other saint or mystic you love or any other holy person whom you have met or read of—is sitting there, tiny, glowing with tender compassion and divine light. Whoever you have chosen radiates with intense force, equanimity, compassion, and all-embracing, all-enduring love.

As you breathe quietly and slowly in and out, imagine with all your powers of faith that the sacred figure you have chosen starts to glow brighter and brighter and to expand. Follow this amazing radiant expansion with your breath and with the clarity and flow of your focused attention, "feeding" the sacred figure with the power of your devotion and your breath until he or she fills your entire heart-center.

At this point, pause for a few minutes and savor the miracle of this Divine Presence alive and marvelously, palpably vibrant within you. Silently invoke everything you know of the sacred image's powers and qualities into your life. If I am doing this exercise with an inner image of the Buddha, for example, I invoke as profoundly as I can the Buddha's vast poise, grandeur of mind, and equanimity of spirit and pray to the Divine to fill me with them. If I am working with an inner image of Jesus, I invoke as richly and deeply as I can Jesus' fearless courage and his wild and holy passion for justice, and pray to the Father-Mother to irradiate my entire self with them. When I work with an image of the Mother, I usually at this point read out a text or poem associated with the image of the Mother I have chosen and by meditating passionately on its invocations and images learn to articulate what qualities of the Mother I most need to be infused with through divine grace.

What this sacred pause in the middle of the practice allows you to do is to summon one-pointedly your full attention on the sacred image you are working with and to saturate your whole spiritual imagination with his or her beauty, truth, and power. If it helps to say a mantra associated with the figure in question, do so. When I am using the inner image of Christ, I often employ the mantra *Maranatha,* "O Lord, come," asking the cosmic Christ to possess and illuminate my whole being. If I am working with the inner image of Tara, I will use a shortened version of the Tara mantra—*Om Tara*—repeating it again and again with tender devotion as I evoke different aspects, qualities, and powers of the savioress. If I am trying to imbue my being with the radiance of the Buddha, I might use either *Om mani padme hum* or *Om gate gate paragate parasamgate Bodhi svaha* (the glorious mantra that ends the Sutra of Supreme Wisdom and that seems when you recite it slowly to articulate and make present the sublime peace of Nirvana).

Keep on breathing slowly in and out and know that as you keep breathing you are filling the sacred figure in your heart-center with brilliant life. He or she keeps on expanding and expanding slowly, dazzlingly, inexorably, until your sacred image has taken over every single part of your body, from the top of your head to the end of your fingertips and the end of your toes. Imagine this divine "invasion" as steadily and thoroughly as you can. When it is complete, rest in the certainty that you and the one you have chosen to meditate on are now one. Allow yourself to feel in all its splendor the passion, strength, truth, and dignity of this oneness, its grandeur and unshakable security.

You are now the one you have chosen to meditate on—the Buddha or the Christ or Tara or Mary. As that one, now, in full confidence and loving wonder, begin to breathe into your now-divine heart, drawing in light with each breath and transmuting it into love in your heart. Imagine your heart growing more and more brilliant as you keep breathing in and out until it is a blazing diamond radiating pure dazzling white light.

Now start to emanate that brilliant diamond light in a stream from the Third Eye between your eyebrows. Keep breathing in more and more light into your always-more-brilliant heart-center, and as you do so, keep sending out a steady stream of brilliant light from your Third Eye. Let that stream become a continuous dazzling river that pours out of your forehead to gradually engulf and dissolve first your own body, then the cushions you are sitting on and the altar in front of you, then the entire room around you, and then, in ever-widening circles, your house, the town you are in, the country, and on and on until the entire universe lies bathed in a sea of splendor that keeps growing vaster and vaster from its source in your forehead. As this marvelous experience grows, let all awareness of your body become, as it naturally will if you are doing this exercise with authentic concentration, fainter and fainter. Come to see and know that all you are now is a diamond-heart-on-fire and a Third Eye pouring that fire out in all directions.

The work of the practice is now almost done. Slowly, delicately, with wonder and reverence, start to draw into your heart-center until the sacred image you have chosen fills it. As the diamond-body contracts, it will become even more brilliant, leaving you with a burning radiance in your heart-center for the rest of the day.

Make a vow to approach everything you do or experience during the day with the wisdom and compassion of this burning radiance and dedicate every illumination and joy that the practice has given you to the liberation of all sentient beings.

Practice 10
Invoking the Presence and
Force of the Divine Mother

The constant invocation of the grace, power, joy, presence, and force of the Divine Mother is crucial to the truth and to the transformatory effectiveness of the Direct Path. The virtues of the Direct Path—tenderness, supple sensitivity, peacefulness, generosity, charity toward all embodied creatures, a steady passion to serve all beings—are primarily those of the Mother aspect of the Godhead. The aim of the Direct Path—to infuse becoming with the transcendent truth and powers of being so that all the levels of human life become divinized and "earth" is transformed into "heaven"—cannot be realized without conscious, loving, patient, and continual cooperation with the force of the Mother. As Aurobindo, the great Indian mystic, wrote: "There is nothing that is impossible to Her who is the conscious power and universal Goddess all-creative from eternity and armed with the Spirit's omnipotence. All knowledge, all strength, all triumph and victory, all skill and works are in her hands and they are full of the treasures and the fruit of all perfections and powers."

Nothing is more essential on the Direct Path than developing a practice of invoking the Presence and Force of the Divine Mother in such a way that the whole of your being becomes increasingly open and devoted to her. As Aurobindo wrote: "There is a force which accompanies the growth of the new consciousness and at once grows with it and helps it to come about and perfect itself. This force is the Yoga-Shakti [Yoga is Sanskrit for religious discipline that creates union, and Shakti is the Sanskrit for the power force of the Mother]."

In this practice I shall concentrate on invoking a descent of the Mother's Force; it has been my experience, as it was of Aurobindo, that this is the most usual and powerful way she has of working. The Direct Path, I have found, goes much faster, more smoothly, more comprehensively, and with a far greater richness of integration of heart and mind, body and soul, "earth" and "heaven," immanent and transcendent, when the Mother's Force is allowed to keep up as uninterrupted a descent as possible. The more the white diamond-light of the Mother can be invoked in all its properties and powers to descend into every aspect of our being, the more completely and integrally will the Mother be able to work within us.

The great Mother-mystics of all cultures—from Lao-tzu to St. Francis to Ramakrishna and, of course, Aurobindo himself—have been unanimous in their claim that the best and surest way of securing this uninterrupted "descent" of the Force of the Mother is by keeping the whole self in a state of receptivity, peace, and calm aspiration. The more peaceful we are, the more open to her we can be; the gentler and less ego ridden our demands on her are, the more she can accomplish in us whatever she needs. Aurobindo writes: "Allow a quiet and steady will to progress and be settled in you . . . Cultivate a state of inner rest, not of straining, of quiet opening."

When this peace is established, the descent can begin in continual uninterrupted force. The Force usually descends into the head and liberates the inner mind centers; then it descends into the heart-center, liberating fully the psychic and emotional being. It then descends into the navel, freeing the inner vital, and into what in the Hindu system is known as the *Muladhara* (the root-center, which is found in the perineum at the base of the spine). When it has reached the Muladhara, it liberates the inner physical being. One by one, as it descends, the Force of the Mother unknots and unties and dissolves and releases all the difficulties that prevent all the centers of the psychophysical being from being open to the Divine in rich mutual harmony; it also progressively divinizes heart and mind, body and soul together, taking up the whole of our nature part by part and dealing with it, rejecting what has to be rejected, sublimating what has to be sublimated, creating what has to be created. It integrates, harmonizes, establishes a new rhythm in the nature.

The first part of the practice I am offering here is devoted to opening the heart-center in profound, tender adoration to the Mother. The more easily you come to awaken this state within you, the more you will be able to call on the Mother's Force in every circumstance. It is vital to keep always alive in the heart a calm, tender, and gentle yearning for more and more of the Mother's grace, love, and transforming power. This, you will find, enables the Mother to give us more and more and allows her Force direct access to what in us needs changing.

Sit down, then, in your chosen place and dedicate the practice you are about to perform in the Mother's name to the transformation of the earth into her living garden of love and justice and divine freedom. Imagine for a few minutes what such a world would be like—where the forests would be growing again and the vanishing of innumerable species halted and the whole of civic and political life dedicated not to the controlling of billions by fantasy and greed but to a liberation of soul force in every human being. Allow your sense both of the catastrophe that we are living and of the extraordinary possibility of transformation open to us to grow together until your whole being yearns for the establishment of the Mother's truth in all institutions, activities, relationships, and arenas.

Then choose which aspect of which "image" of the Mother you want to invoke. The Divine Mother has many names and images; select which one—Kali, Tara, the Tao, Kuan-Yin, Gaia, Mary—you wish to work with. If you prefer to work with the Mother beyond name or form, that, of course, is fine. I myself work increasingly with images of the Virgin, especially in her aspect of the Black Madonna. Whichever aspect or name of the Mother you are working with, conjure it up with great devotion and power. If you are not using an image, invoke a Presence of brilliant diamond-white light and know that in that brilliant light are all the saving, invigorating, and healing powers of the Divine Mother.

There is a prayer I always use at this point in the practice that I would like to share with you. It was originally created by the great Indian mystic Ramakrishna, who lived in Bengal in the nineteenth century and single-handedly gave to the world the *full* undogmatic path of the Mother: He showed in his extraordinarily passionate, eloquent, and pure-souled life just how far a human being can progress when he or she hands his whole being over to the Mother. Ramakrishna's prayer contains, I believe, a final wisdom and final clarity about what is essential; its power to purify the mind and spirit and to remind the seeker of that holy devotion that must always be kept alive in the heart are almost miraculous. Here is the prayer:

> O Mother, here is Your ignorance, here is Your knowledge
> Take them both and give me only pure love for You.
> Here is Your holiness, here is Your unholiness—
> Take them both and give me only pure love for You.
> Here is Your virtue, and here is Your sin
> Here is Your good and here is Your evil
> Take them both and give me only pure love for You.
> Here is Your dharma, here is Your adharma;
> Take them both and give me only pure love for You.

Dharma means "law" or "right action"; *adharma* is its opposite.

Say the prayer of Ramakrishna out loud three times, very slowly, in a deep, soft, reverent voice, savoring each phrase, bringing the full power of your sacred memory and imagination to bear on feeling as intensely as possible what it would be like to live in "pure love" beyond all the dualities that keep life conflicted. I find it helps me to place my open right hand on my heart-center, and to bow my head; placing my hand on my heart-center helps me to center my whole being there, and bowing my head helps me to remember the majesty and glory and infinite tender beauty of the one I am praying to.

After you have said the prayer out loud three times, say it again very slowly, as before, but silently this time and in the depths of the heart-center, summoning as you do so every memory of every sacred experience of the Mother's help or guidance or love that you have ever had. Know that she is listening; know that she loves you infinitely and wants the entire integral flowing of your whole being in freedom and truth; know that she longs to grace you with the "pure love" you are asking her for, because, just as you long for union with her, so she longs for union with you, her always-beloved, eternally adored unique and holy child. If you pray this prayer with this kind of sacred fervor, you will find your entire being become infused with divine tenderness. Very often people tell me when they come to this part of the practice, they start to cry; they come into connection for a few moments with the full depth of the passion of longing for the Mother that is in every human being. Allow these holy tears, without exaggerating or "milking" them; they are a sign that your psychic being is awakening in all its wondering vulnerable sensitivity and direct connection with divine love.

When you have finished your inward recitation of the prayer and have filled your heart with devotion for the Mother, lie back and gaze up at the ceiling of your meditation room and project onto it the "image" of the Mother you have chosen to work with. If you are not working with any image but simply with the diamond-white light of the Mother's Force, imagine that light as a star or a round brimming circle.

Keeping constantly alive in your imagination the projected image or star or circle you have now evoked, start to talk to the Mother directly within your heart. Ask her for whatever you feel you need at the moment, for whatever you feel you most need to be able to go forward into her transformation. If you are feeling discouraged, ask for her great courage. If you are feeling lazy, ask for her stamina. If you are sick, ask for healing. If you decide you do not want to ask for anything specific but simply want to give over to her your whole being for her to do with it as she wants, offer yourself again and again to her.

As you ask for what you want, or simply offer yourself to her again and again, imagine that from the image or star or circle you have projected on the ceiling come waves of brilliant white light that entirely carpet your whole body and enter into its every cell and pore. The more ardently you ask or offer yourself, the more brilliant the light becomes and the more torrential its descent of white fire. Know that this light is entering every one of your psychospiritual centers and opening and integrating them.

Bliss, calm, joy, peace, and certainty will now be alive in your body, heart, mind, and soul. Imagine now that the divine light of the Mother has transformed you into a diamond agent of her transformation of the world, has made you in fact a diamond emitting brilliant white light yourself. Send that divine light in the name of the Mother and of her longing to see her justice and love reign on earth to all the four directions.

Make a vow to keep calling down the Mother's Force in the days ahead, as constantly as possible throughout the day, whatever you are doing. Wherever you are, remember to imagine her force entering your body from the top of your head and continually sweeping through it to "wash" it clean of any difficulty or distress and to harmonize your psychospiritual centers. This simple abbreviation of the longer practice given here will help you activate the Mother's Force in all the different aspects of your life and keep you always remembering her. Keep notes in your practice diary on how the Force works in you and on what you discover about how you can increase or "block" its working.

As Aurobindo reminds us all, "In your work and acts you must do the same as in your concentration. Open to the Mother, put all of them under Her guidance. Call in the peace, the supporting power, the protection, and in order that they may work reject all wrong influences that might come in their way by creating wrong, careless, or unconscious movements. Follow this principle and your whole being will become one, under one rule, in the peace and sheltering power and Light."

Practice 11
Conversation with God

As a child in India, I found talking to God quite normal and natural. Then, in my teens and early twenties, I underwent a prolonged and painful loss of faith. I doubted everything, myself most of all, and the exhilarating ease of my early communication with the Divine vanished.

Now, in my late forties, after twenty years of seeking and sustained inner experience, I am still trying to recapture and deepen the simplicity I had as a child. I know beyond any doubt that God exists and that God is in all things. At times, however, life becomes so hard that I feel estranged from God or unable to speak directly with him.

It is in difficult times like these that I practice the beautiful exercise I am going to give here; I find that its power to unlock the heart and loosen the spirit is extraordinary.

First of all, I make a solemn commitment to spend a half hour a day for, say, a week "speaking with God." I try to set aside the same time each day and make sure that I am not interrupted in any way.

I begin the exercise by taking several deep, slow breaths to steady my mind. Then, as a way of easing into a conversation with the Divine, I repeat one of the names of God from one of the mystical traditions.

Sometimes I say *Ribbonon shel olam,* "Master of the universe" in Hebrew; sometimes I just repeat "Allah, Allah"; sometimes I use the name of Jesus or Mary. Whichever name I choose, I repeat it again and again, with as much adoration and heartfelt devotion as I can muster until my mind and heart start to be filled with love of God.

Usually this works and I can begin speaking quite easily with God of what is happening to me or those I love. There are times, however, when beginning the conversation at all, even after repeating the name, is very difficult. The old Jewish scholar at Oxford who taught me this form of prayer and meditation told me something that I have never forgotten. He said, "Even the greatest rabbis sometimes found it hard to speak to God immediately and directly. If they found the going difficult, do you know what they did? They would use the difficulty itself as a way of starting the conversation." I asked him to explain what he meant. "It is very simple," he said. "Just tell God how much you want to speak with him simply and directly. Explain to him that it is hard for you to find something to say and ask for God's help to find the words to speak to him with. Discuss the problem with him as you would with me or with any good friend whom you know wants only your very best. You will find that once you have begun the conversation, you'll find it easy to continue."

My friend went on. "Don't give in to your feelings of estrangement or distance. Talk with God about how you feel lost or sad or fearful or distant. Ask God to help you, to bring you closer to him. You will find this very effective."

My old Jewish friend gave me another hint which I have found invaluable. He told me, "Don't think you have to sparkle with God. It is impossible to bore God. Sometimes the best way of using this exercise to come closer to God is to *repeat* the same conversation day in and day out with God. I have found that I have spiritual problems that recur, and I suspect that everyone is the same way. What I do then when I talk to God is to take one of these problems—say my difficulty with always trusting him—and *talk* to him about it again and again. By talking to God repeatedly about this problem, I find that I slowly become wiser about it, or am given direct inner help with it."

I have followed my friend's pieces of advice repeatedly, and they have helped me. I found also that if you do this practice with true sincerity, it can often end in an extremely powerful experience of the Divine Presence. By speaking nakedly with God, you can open yourself up so completely to the Divine that you feel it within and without you. Sometimes, too, I have found I have been given direct inner answers to my problems and clear guidance. Usually, however, the "answers" or "guidance" came more gradually—often in the course of an event or incident during the day that revealed the nature of the problem I was dealing with and its possible solution. Once you start speaking to God in this way, God "answers" very fast, and usually through something in life itself.

If I had to apply one adjective to this practice, it would be "strengthening." Conversing with God in this way *strengthens* you. It strengthens you because it gives you the detachment to see yourself from the position of the Divine and not your own ego; in talking of your problems to and with God, you will slowly be led to see them from a more detached and serene perspective and the wisdom to understand something of their purpose will be given you.

Conversing with God also strengthens you in another way; it makes you feel, after practicing seriously for some time, as if you were *partners* with God. Very often, when I am writing a book, I talk to God about the problems I am having or the inspiration I need to go on; that makes me feel as if God is my partner in my work, my constant helper. A doctor I know speaks to God in this way about all his most difficult cases and believes strongly that by so doing he draws the Divine into the process of healing directly. A wonderful woman friend of mine, a real estate agent who spends a great deal of her time trying to raise loans for poor people, tells me that she always lays out before God exactly what the difficulties are in any given case and asks for direct and precise intervention; the results are often extraordinary.

One word of warning: Conversing with God is a very powerful exercise and can uncover deep unsolved problems. All kinds of memories and anguishes can surface, especially if you are talking with God about serious and long-standing difficulties in your life. Do not be afraid when this happens; it can be a sign that the exercise is "working" by making you conscious of the suffering in you that drives or blocks you. What I find most useful at such moments is to do a simple deep-breathing exercise; with each in-breath I breathe in divine healing, with each out-breath I breathe out and offer to God whatever fear or anguish I am feeling. I do this as often as is necessary to feel relatively calm again and then continue the conversation. Often you will find that when you resume it, your conversation with God will be even deeper and more intimate because of the suffering it has awakened and allowed you to begin to notice and heal.

Practice 12
Using a Great Mystical Passage or Prayer as a Focus for Meditation

When I was eighteen, I spent eight months hitchhiking around Italy. At the time, I was waiting to go up to Oxford and thought that I wanted to be an art historian. So I visited all the great artistic centers of Florence, Rome, Naples, and Venice. Then one day in early May I found myself in Assisi, where St. Francis had lived and died. Nothing I had seen prepared me for the impact of Giotto's paintings of the life of St. Francis in the basilica; their grave, exalted purity dazzled me. I decided to stay to contemplate them for a week and slept out in the ruins of an old castle, surrounded by the rough, fragrant hills of Tuscany in spring.

I can still remember the sunlit afternoon when, sitting in a field of yellow and blue wildflowers, I first read the Prayer of St. Francis. Every word pierced me with the freshness of Giotto's vision and of that high and noble Tuscan landscape:

> Lord, make me an instrument of thy peace
> Where there is hatred, let me sow love.
> Where there is injury, pardon
> Where there is doubt, faith
> Where there is despair, hope
> Where there is darkness, light
> Where there is sadness, joy.
>
> O Divine Master, grant that I may not so much seek
> To be consoled as to console,

To be understood as to understand,
To be loved as to love:
For it is in giving that we receive,
It is in pardoning that we are pardoned,
It is in dying to self that we are born to eternal life.

I remember that afternoon, reading the prayer over and over, savoring every word, how astonished I was at its spiritual truth and beauty. The more I contemplated the prayer and the holy passions behind it, the deeper my joy became until I, the sunlit afternoon, and the wind moving in the brilliant flowers seemed to become one vast sustained movement of adoration within the being of God.

The practice I give here is one that is used in all the great mystical systems because of its great power to transform the personality.

Choose and memorize a mystical passage or prayer that deeply moves you and that enshrines for you a noble, inspiring spiritual ideal; then, sitting calmly in meditation, say it over and over again to yourself very slowly, bringing your mind home to its words whenever it begins to stray. Do this for about a half hour at a time and you will find that your mind and heart will be made joyful and peaceful and that, over time, your entire being will come to correspond more and more with the strengths and virtues the passage celebrates. All mystical systems know that we become what we think; this exercise is a wonderful way of saturating the mindstream with holy truth and passion.

As you have probably guessed, the passage I use when I practice this exercise is the Prayer of St. Francis. That afternoon thirty years ago initiated me into its mystic power, and everything I have learned since on my search has only deepened my amazement at its depth. It seems to me a prayer that transcends tradition or any particular religion; in a very few, utterly stripped and simple phrases, it condenses the deepest wisdom of the Direct Path in all its heroism and selfless compassion. Over the years I have shared it with seekers of all kinds—Hindus, Sufis, Tibetan Buddhists; they have all recognized the transmuting power of the holy inspiration that still sings along its lines. One young Tibetan priest I met in Ladakh translated it into Tibetan and started to use it every day in his morning prayers to the Buddha of Compassion; a Hindu devotee of Shiva I know uses it every morning in her prayers to the "Lord of Love."

Let us, then, for the purpose of explaining how this practice proceeds, use the St. Francis prayer as our text.

Begin by sitting calmly in your place of meditation and then breathing in and out deeply to steady your mind. If you have any incense, light a stick of it so the whole atmosphere around you can become fragrant. Sometimes it helps in order to enter the spirit of adoration and dedication of the prayer to place your hand over your heart and repeat the name of God gently and with fervor.

When you feel ready, read the entire prayer slowly once through, savoring each word and trying to enter as deeply as you can the inmost meaning of each phrase. When you have done so, rest a little in the sacred emotion such a reading will arouse.

I find it helpful at this moment to pray to God to open me still more deeply to the holy passion of the prayer. Often I say something like "May the love speaking this prayer open me completely to itself!" or "Remove all fear from my mind and heart so it can go fearlessly into the fire of absolute love!"

Then, slowly, I start to say inwardly the first line: "Lord, make me an instrument of thy peace." I try to dwell richly on each phrase; what does it mean to say "Lord, *make* me," for example? What *is* an "instrument of peace," and what has to be given up in oneself to become one? Why does St. Francis seem to stress the holiness of peace above all other aspects of the spiritual life? What is "thy peace"? To each inner question I try to bring the totality of everything that I have understood about these questions from my search and from my own experience and from the experience of others.

Very often my mind starts to wander almost immediately. Something about the power and beauty of this prayer scares it profoundly. I think this is a prayer that breathes in each phrase the kind of sacred selflessness that terrifies the ego. I try to be compassionate to my mind and its need to evade the seriousness of the prayer's attentions, but I also try not to let it wander too far. As soon as I catch it wandering, I bring it back to the line of the prayer it was contemplating before it started to wander. This can be difficult work, but it is worth it. It trains the attention and over time allows the sacred power of the prayer to infuse the mind and spirit at profound levels.

Slowly and with as much sacred concentration as I can muster, I go through the prayer phrase by phrase, trying to bring everything I know and long for to my inner reading of it. Then, after a brief pause, I return to the beginning. In the course of a half hour's meditation, it is rare that I will find myself saying the prayer in this way more than twelve or thirteen times; I find that if I practice with sufficient devotion and sincerity, the prayer draws me into the passionate silence of the heart that it was created from. To enter and become one with this silence is the true goal of all prayer. So, when this silence arrives, I stop speaking the words of the prayer inwardly and continue only when my mind starts getting restive.

At the end of the practice, I find it helpful to recite slowly the entire prayer once more, steadily and slowly, dedicating my whole being to its force and power. Then, as the final act of the exercise, I dedicate whatever insights and sacred emotions saying the prayer has aroused in me to the awakening of all sentient beings.

One way I find helpful to make this dedication at the end real and vivid is to imagine that saying it sends in God's name dazzling white light in all directions, light that will heal, save, inspire, and embolden all those it invisibly touches.

Practice 13
Practicing the Presence of the Beloved:
A Sufi Heart Practice

Keeping the heart always in a state of sacred openness and calmly passionate devotion to God is perhaps the hardest task on the Direct Path. So much in life menaces the heart's truth; we easily become dulled by daily chores and worries, and the many sufferings that eat at us in the course of our lives can all too easily dishearten us. This is why the seeker on the Direct Path needs a strong heart practice that he or she can do regularly and steadily, one that will always remind the seeker of the truth of his or her inmost connection in love to all things and beings and to the Beloved.

Of all the great mystical traditions, it is perhaps the Sufi tradition—that of the mystical core of Islam—that has most intensely stressed the heart as the way to true vision and divine life. In one of his sacred sayings, Muhammed proclaimed, "The heart of the believer is the place of the revelation of God. The heart of the believer is the throne of God. The heart of the believer is the mirror of God." Rumi wrote, "Adore and love Him with your whole being, and He will reveal to you that each thing in the universe is a vessel full to the brim with wisdom and beauty. Each thing he will show you is one drop from the boundless river of his infinite beauty."

To know the truth of what Muhammed and Rumi are telling us, you have to work to open the heart to love and to keep it open to the powerful presence of the Beloved at all times, whatever happens. Slowly you will discover that as you do, your heart will become the "place of revelation" and the "mirror" in which the glory of the creation will always be shining. Keeping your heart always open and aflame with adoration and devotion will make it the conduit of divine vision, the source of direct divine guidance, and the site of an always-expanding initiation into the splendor of God and the creation. This is not poetry; this is an exact scientific description of what happens on the mystical journey.

What I give now is a form of the heart practice that many mystics in the Sufi tradition have used for centuries. Fifteen years ago I read of it when I was living in a ramshackle hotel in New Delhi; I withdrew for a week to my room and did nothing but eat, sleep, and try to open to this practice. Its astonishing power became clear to me during that week; the ecstasy I experienced and the many marvelous visionary insights that were graced me through it assured me that it would be one of the most important practices I would ever encounter. Since then I have turned to it very often, particularly in moments of heartbreak or tremendous stress in which I have found its power to keep me open to love despite the suffering or depression or anger I was in nothing short of miraculous.

Since the entire purpose of the practice is to awaken the dynamic power of love within the heart, it is best, I find, to begin it by trying to inspire yourself with a beautiful short mystical text or poem that enshrines for you the relationship between the heart and God. As the supreme poet of divine love, Rumi is always a marvelous helper here. I often begin this practice by reading over and over these words from Rumi's "Table-talke":

> Wherever you may be, in whatever situation or circumstance you may find yourself, strive always to be a lover, and a passionate lover. Once you possess your heart in love, you will always be a lover, in the tomb, at the Resurrection, and in Paradise forever and ever.

I try to bring to my reading everything that I have experienced of divine love and of its eternal power; I try, too, to remember from my own life examples of this love flaming out in the lives of people I have known. I think of my Tibetan mentor Thuksey Rinpoche's glorious leonine face laughing with joy as he spoke to me of the Buddha of compassion; I think of Bede Griffiths on his deathbed holding the faces of the people visiting him and crying with happiness; I think of a great friend of mine in my youth, Anne Pennington, who was a professor of Slavic studies at Oxford and whose profound kindness radiated through everything she did from the way she set the table to the way she lingered in a doorway when saying good-bye to her guests. And as I think of these wonderful beings who loved me and believed in me, I pledge myself inwardly to carry on their passion to live and be the truth of love in action at the heart of life.

Then, when love is beginning to be awake within me, I pray to the Beloved and ask his help for the practice to be as powerful as possible. I have learned over many years of practice that I am not the one who loves in me; it is the Beloved's own love that loves the Beloved through me. A human being on his or her own is not strong enough to stand the intensity and glory and power of divine love in the heart; only the Divine in us can stand them. By praying to the Beloved to inspire me at the beginning of the practice, I am really also praying for the strength to bear the presence of his love within me.

Sometimes at this moment I follow the advice of an Indian Sufi I met in Benares. He told me: "At the beginning of the heart practice it is often useful to place your two hands over your heart and repeat with tender passion 'Beloved Beloved' on and on until your whole being becomes on fire with love." Sitting by the Ganges in the late twilight, we both put our hands over our heart and murmured "Beloved Beloved" to the small stars that were starting to appear and to the red-gold water flowing before us. Very soon I felt a flame flare through my chest; it was so hot, it was almost painful. I turned to my friend to tell him, and he smiled and said, "You didn't really believe me, did you? Too simple for your Oxford brain, perhaps. But it works, doesn't it?" It does work. Try it. You will be amazed and inspired.

Now it is time to enter the practice itself. With your heart open and the power of the Beloved invoked with devotion, breathe calmly and deeply and go into that place within yourself which is solitary, peaceful, and still. This is the "virgin" space in the heart that no afflictions can destroy and no other loves can exploit.

As you enter it more and more profoundly, you will discover that from it an endless longing for the Divine keeps streaming. This longing is the heart's wild hunger to be always in direct connection with the love of the Beloved; it is this longing that is the force that will open the heart more and more to the Beloved's passion, empty it more and more profoundly so the Beloved can pour into it his sacred dynamic fire. Allow it to grow in you and become increasingly passionate and intense.

As you do so, imagine yourself seated in, immersed in, and surrounded by a sea of light. This light is the light of the heart of the Beloved; it is the light that is always manifesting all the universes. It is consciousness, bliss, knowledge; all divine powers, in fact, are one in its brilliance. It is all around you, above you, beneath you; its waves stretch away infinitely in all directions.

Savor and rejoice in the glory and power of the light of the heart, and know that in the deepest part of your being you are one with them. Now, with your heart aflame with awe and exultation, allow this light to penetrate slowly and completely your whole being with its fire. Feel that fire enter your head, your neck, your arms, the inmost part of your chest, your genitals, your legs. Feel that not one part of your being—spiritual or physical—is outside this love fire, not one toe or fingertip. Even the tiniest hair on your arms or legs is alight with it. Slowly, as you allow the light to penetrate your every part, surrender your inmost soul to the fire and imagine it rushing into the deepest depths of your heart and soul, burning down any barriers between you and it as it does so.

You are now seated in the fire of the heart, one in all your physical and spiritual being with its light. Inevitably, thoughts, memories, and emotions of various kinds will arise. Do not identify with any of them. As they arise, imagine that you reach out and grab hold of each of them with tremendous force and drown them directly in the sea of love that surrounds you and that you now are. The more fiercely you imagine yourself drowning your thoughts and feelings in the sea of light, the more profoundly you will come to feel one with the light and its power.

At this stage you will experience for yourself that the feeling and force of love is infinitely more dynamic than the thinking process. If you practice your immersion in the light sea with total sincerity and focus, all thoughts, memories, and emotions will gradually disappear. Nothing will remain. You, your heart, your mind, will become one vast, shining emptiness.

Rest as long as you can in the vast, shining emptiness you are. As you begin to "surface" into ordinary consciousness, dedicate the joy and gratitude you feel to the transformation of all beings throughout the universe.

Practice 14
Purifying and Strengthening the Heart
(Adapted from a Tibetan Heart Practice)

This wonderful practice is one of the treasures of the Tibetan Buddhist tradition. The adept who taught it to me in Ladakh told me: "I wish I could teach it to everyone on the earth! It would save hundreds of millions of lives! As a Tibetan who lived through the fall and destruction of my country and has had to endure exile, my life has been filled with various kinds of ordeal. This practice has never failed to lift my heart and strengthen my will."

My Tibetan friend's enthusiasm delighted and infected me, and I began to do the heart practice very seriously that I now give. I had thought his claims for it exaggerated; when I came to practice it during my own times of ordeal, however, I found that its power to sustain and infuse me with hope was extraordinary.

When my father lay dying, he was sometimes afraid more for how my mother would live on without him than for himself. One day I asked him if he would let me teach him a practice I had learned from the Tibetans. Immediately, he said he would, and together we did the practice I give here. He said nothing to me but looked much calmer and happier. Later he told my mother, "During the practice Andrew taught me, I saw and felt the love of Jesus." Hearing that was one of the happiest moments of my life and gave me the deepest kind of confirmation that my desire to bring the wealth of the mystical traditions' actual practices to everyone, whatever their faith or religious background, was not only not a fantasy or illusion, but directly useful.

Begin the practice by imagining yourself in a landscape you associate with peace and joy. The Tibetan who taught me this heart exercise used to stress how important it was to imagine yourself in a place that was already linked in your mind to happiness; he said that he would always picture himself in the monastery in the mountains where he had spent many serene years as a child. "Just thinking of the light on the mountains calms my spirit." I myself, when I do this exercise, nearly always choose to imagine myself on a beach I love in South India, where I have often spent afternoons and evenings in meditation with nothing but the wind in the couch grass for company. Sometimes I imagine myself in a field in Maui, overlooking the ocean of wildflowers and scented with their perfume; for me that field as I saw it first in the red late-afternoon light will always be an image of the earthly paradise.

Choose, then, a place where you have felt close to God and your heart's own truest joy, and imagine yourself sitting quietly and peacefully in it. Allow the full beauty of the place to penetrate and inspire your every sense. Recall its scents and colors, its light, the contours of its perfection. Remember as richly and comprehensively as you can exactly how that place you have chosen made you feel when you were actually in it, how full of hope and gratitude. Allow the inner security you once felt in the place to infuse your whole being.

When you are beginning to feel the charm of the place you have chosen start to work deeply upon you, imagine and invoke in a cloudless and brilliant blue sky in front of you that representation of the Divine that most moves you and with whom you feel most identified. This figure could be Jesus or the Buddha, Mary or Kali or Tara. The name and form of the divine being you choose is not as important as your deep love for him or her and your faith in his or her truth, power, goodness, and unconditional love for you. If for some reason you cannot or do not want to imagine any one divine form in this context, don't worry; invoke the Divine as a sun or blazing star or as a cloud of light. Whatever form or image you invoke, make sure that you do so as vividly as possible and that you feel with your inmost being that through whatever form or image you have chosen the Divine is appearing just for you to show you the boundless love it has for you.

I find that it helps considerably at this moment to start to pray tenderly to whatever figure I have chosen. I find the simplest prayers work the best. I usually say something like "Thank you, my Beloved, for coming to me, for appearing to me when I asked you to. I am deeply and finally grateful. Open to me the treasure house of your heart, make me alive in truth and love."

When your heart is completely open to the figure in the sky in front of you, start to speak inwardly to him or her. Speak without shame or fear, as if to your parent or closest friend or brother or sister. Don't edit your words or try to make them startling or eloquent; the divine figure in front of you knows already what is in your heart and wants you only to express yourself as honestly as possible. Speak out of the depths of whatever you are going through at the moment; don't try to conceal any of the darkness of what you might be enduring. If you have been abandoned by someone you love and feel bitter and tormented, allow yourself to explore that bitterness and torment. Pour out to the Beloved the sadness of your battered heart. If you are sick and afraid of dying, for example, express your anguish and your fear even if it brings you to tears. It is essential that you pour out whatever is in you in a sacred atmosphere and before the One who you know loves you with unconditional tenderness and wants only your full growth and healing.

You don't have to wait to be in extreme situations to find this heart practice helpful. You can share your ordinary troubles also with the Divine. I have used this heart exercise to explore my worry over money, my fear of aging, my fears over the publication of a new book, my sorrow at the crazy or wounding behavior of friends, my difficulty in writing this and other books. The Tibetan friend who taught it to me begged me not to treat this exercise as if it were something "exalted" and "only for sublime occasions." "The Buddha wants to help you to wash up with more joy," he laughed. "The Buddha wants to help you keep your temper in a shop queue!" I have found, in fact, that doing this exercise regularly has helped me be honest about my annoying small habits and problems and to ask for guidance for them. When I ask with authentic sincerity, the answer always comes, sooner or later, and the guidance is always given.

I have found, too, that the more I trust the Divine with small difficulties, the more I can trust him when the great crises break over my head. What is essential is to develop a habit of trusting and opening up to God, a habit of asking for guidance. The stronger this habit becomes, the easier it becomes in real difficulties to remain open to divine love and its empowering strengths and directions.

Speak, then, with total sincerity to the figure you have invoked to the sky in front of you about whatever is worrying you and whatever you feel you need help with. Imagine now that as you speak, the image or form you have chosen to represent the Divine begins to emit strongly a stream of radiant white light. Know that this divine light has infinite transforming and healing power and cannot be stopped in its effectiveness by any obstacles whatever. Know this, believe this with profound faith, and pray passionately to this light to enter you and possess you and infuse you and purify you of all blocks, difficulties, karmic obstacles, all illness of soul or body.

As you pray, the form or image in front of you becomes more and more brilliant with light. Now the light enters you through the top of your head, and pours in pulsing, warm, sweet, blissful waves down the full length of your body. Let the divine light wash you completely. Keep calling out for help and guidance for whatever difficulty you wish to resolve or torment you long to heal. The light will go on getting brighter and brighter as you go on trusting it enough to call out to it and soon will be falling in great cataracts of power through your body. Each time the light pours through you in this vast wave of blessing, offer up to it one more grief or worry or dark impulse for healing and transformation.

As the peace and solace this practice is bringing you deepen, allow yourself to relax as completely as you can into the bliss and protection of the Divine Presence. Allow yourself to feel how deeply and precisely you are loved.

As you feel yourself melting away more and more in the presence of the form or image you have chosen, imagine that you leave the ground where you are sitting and "float up" quietly to where the figure or image you have chosen is standing in the sky. Now embrace the presence or image. If you have chosen Christ or Mary or the Buddha as your divine form, for example, imagine that you rest against his or her breast in a simple and naked embrace, and rest in its peace.

When you feel yourself returning to ordinary consciousness, don't do anything hurriedly. Try to allow whatever you have to do after the practice to be permeated by the ease it has given you. As you begin to go about your life, say a prayer for all suffering beings everywhere and wish them healing and sacred joy and the knowledge that you have been given of the unconditional love and support of God.

In your practice period you should allow the whole exercise to unfold gradually. During the day, however, you can use a shortened version of it to remind yourself constantly of divine help and guidance. The more seriously you practice the "long" version, the easier it will become to transport yourself immediately into this heart exercise's sacred atmosphere. Nowadays I find myself using this exercise all the time—when walking to shopping, or waiting for a telephone call, even during the commercials on TV or in the bath. Through it I try to keep in constant ordinary contact with the Divine, constantly open to the Presence in all activities and states of mind.

Practice 15
Expanding the Circle of Love
(Adapted from the Jewish Tradition)

The last two heart practices—those derived from the Sufi and Tibetan traditions—enable the seeker to establish and sustain an intense inward and trusting relationship with the Divine. The heart practice I give now is designed to *expand* that heart-awareness to include and embrace in love all beings, to "expand the circle of love."

At the heart of the mystical wisdom of all the great traditions is a living knowledge that all things in all dimensions and worlds are inseparably connected. I was once sitting with a physicist friend of mine who is also a mystic at a café in Paris; she leaned forward, raised her coffee cup, smiled mischievously, and said, "Isn't it astonishing to imagine that just the small action I have just made—of raising my coffee cup here with you in the Café Flore on a gorgeous summer morning—has repercussions on Betelgeuse?" For a moment as she spoke I seemed to "see" every object in the world around us connected to every other by millions of invisible shining silken filaments whose relationships shifted with each breath, each gust of warm wind, each cough, every gesture by the bored, supercilious waiter flitting between tables. I knew that what I was "seeing" was not fanciful but a partial revelation of the real and indissoluble interconnections between all things; the silken filaments stretched far beyond the café to vanish into the street and the sky. For a moment I could see myself connected by them to the farthest and most far-flung stars, to the emptiest and darkest reaches of space.

How delicate, tender, and responsible we would be if a living knowledge of interconnection always infused our thoughts and actions! With what lucid gentleness we would be compelled to act at all moments, knowing that everything we do—even the smallest actions—have such infinite consequences! A Jewish mystic, Moses de Leon, wrote: "Everything is linked with everything else down to the highest and lowest rung on the chain, and the true essence of God is above as well as below, in the heavens and on the earth and nothing else exists outside of Him."

It is one thing to begin to understand this as a concept with the mind; it is quite another to *live* it as a constant all-demanding and all-revealing experience. The only way to begin to do so is to *practice* this consciousness of interconnection again and again so that it gradually becomes more conscious and normal to us. The rewards of such practice are nothing less than coming to live in the divine atmosphere of love itself, coming to see each human face as one of our own faces and as one of the faces of God and each sentient being as holy. At the end of his life St. Francis was so finally aware of the interbeing of all things that it is said even the worms on the paths in the hills around Assisi kindled in him infinite love. I know that even if I cannot yet live so high and all-embracing a love, it exists and is the one eternal reality. The moments when I have entered its atmosphere are the only ones in which I believe I have lived completely.

Having a heart practice, then, in which we can train ourselves to focus more and more of our inmost sacred imagination on experiencing this interconnected love for all beings is essential on the Direct Path. The one that I share with you now was given to me by a wonderful old Jewish mystic, Abraham Pagis, I met when I visited Israel nearly twenty years ago. We met quite by chance, on a brilliant spring morning in Jerusalem, immediately liked each other, and spent a long, rambling day wandering around the Arab quarter and talking about God. When evening fell, he took me to his small book-lined house on the outskirts of the city to meet his wife, and there, holding my hands in his, he said he wanted to give me a gift that would help me all my life; the gift he gave me was the ancient cabalistic meditation I now give you. I have seen it written out in other books but never in a form as rich, glowing, and compassionate as the one he transmitted to me that evening. Perhaps a lifetime of inner practice had drawn my friend to elaborate it in his own way; perhaps what he had added came from direct divine transmission. I will never know. What I do know is that the practice he taught me has again and again allowed me to awaken my compassion toward others and to deepen immeasurably my inner awareness of the unity of all beings in God.

The most important thing about the practice of "expanding the circle of your heart" is to let it unfold calmly and thoroughly and at its own pace. So at the very beginning, breathe deeply and focus and calm and steady your mind. Try to let every worry or concern melt away from you and inwardly consecrate yourself to a holy desire to experience fully your interbeing with all things and creatures in the great unity of Divine Consciousness. Ask the Divine in whatever form you love it most to grace you through the practice a deeper knowledge of your oneness with the entire universe and everything in it, so that you can become, in St. Francis's words, "an instrument of peace."

Now imagine that you are seated at the center of a large circle; grouped silently all around you are your parents, relations, and close friends. Conjure them all up, one by one, steadily, precisely, and honestly. Do not mask to yourself the dark or unpleasant aspects of any of their characters; allow yourself to experience each of them in their human fullness, in all the ambiguous richness of their personality. Acknowledge, as you do, the shadows in yourself, your own difficulties of temperament, your own problems. Do so without fear or shame and with a calm, forgiving compassion. As each person comes into your mind, say inwardly something like "Let us be one in love!" Try with your whole being to extend to everyone who appears in your mind love and recognition and forgiveness.

Now, slowly and painstakingly, extend the circle to include first your colleagues and coworkers, then your acquaintances, and then everyone you have ever seen or met. All kinds of faces and beings will arise in your heart-mind; welcome them all, try to recognize them all as faces of the One and different faces of your own inmost truth. Sometimes you may find yourself meeting a deep resistance within yourself to welcoming a particular person and acknowledging your oneness-in-God with him or her. Don't mask this resistance; be honest about it, then offer it consciously to the Divine to be transformed into divine detachment. If someone particularly enrages or disturbs you, ask God to see him for a moment with God's own unconditional love; even if your feeling for him does not immediately change, asking like this again and again will slowly breed in you greater wisdom and help you separate the innate compassion of your enlightened nature from the reactivity of your ego.

Now imagine that your circle widens still farther to include everyone you haven't yet met in your town or city. Then welcome into the circle everyone in the entire world. At this moment in the practice I find it helpful to remember images I have seen on television of people sick or struggling or reeling from some disaster; immediately I find my heart opens to embrace them and all those suffering like them.

By this stage of "Expanding the Circle of Love," you have included—and symbolically declared your inner oneness with—the whole human race.

Now turn the attention of your heart to the animal kingdom. Animals are everywhere abused and tortured by us, used in horrible experiments, slaughtered for the pleasure of our table, treated as fifth-class citizens in a world that many of them have inhabited for a far longer period than ourselves. Coming to embrace the animal kingdom in love is essential in the Direct Path; how can we work together to try to preserve the planet from environmental holocaust if we do not truly know the presence of Divine Spirit in every deer, tiger, dolphin, and whale?

Abraham Pagis told me that the best way he had found to extend love in meditation toward the whole animal kingdom was to begin by choosing one particular example of it that we love. He himself had a large, lazy black cat whom he adored and called Shekinah, after the name in Jewish mysticism for the divine feminine. "Choose one animal you love to symbolize the whole animal kingdom," he said, "and then slowly invoke other animals of all kinds, including birds, and the tiniest insects and fishes."

This part of the meditation can provide a marvelous opportunity to celebrate the diversity of nature. Increasingly, I include in this stage as many as possible of those species that are now endangered, naming them and trying to visualize them clearly in all their force and beauty: I find this stiffens my resolve to fight against environmental degradation by making what is happening directly personal. In every species that is destroyed, a part of each one of us is also destroyed. Doing this part of the meditation with focus and sincerity can help make that not just a concept or a piece of poetry but a living truth.

You are now surrounded in the circle you have created by everyone in the world and all the world's sentient creatures. Now you must do something very sacred and important; you must calmly remove yourself from the center of the circle. Choose a being or animal you want to sit or stand near and visualize yourself beside that individual or animal in the circle. The center of the circle is now empty. Dedicate this emptiness to God, and as you do so, pray that you will always be aware of what you now know—that you are just one in the vast, interconnected circle of being, permeated by God, that stretches around the universe.

Abraham warned me that at this moment I might, if I was really doing this practice seriously, experience some fear or panic. "To feel acutely your inmost connection with everything that lives," he said, "can be a shocking, even menacing experience; all normal boundaries of what you have called your 'self' are threatened, and the pain that all sentient beings endure becomes inescapably vivid to you in all its fierce, and sometimes frightening, particulars. If fears arise, don't be surprised. Know that they are arising because you are coming into contact with the demanding truth of the heart, dedicate them to the Divine, and ask for direct grace to transform them into lasting awareness and passionate and active compassion."

Standing beside the being or animal you have chosen, then, allow yourself time to savor the presence of divine power at the center of the circle and the unshakable holy strength of your link to billions of other beings. Allow your mind and heart time to contemplate as deeply as they can whatever emotions, visionary thoughts, and practical solutions may arise in you. Then, with great humility and reverence, imagining your hands raised in prayer, return yourself to the center of the circle, and turn around slowly, bowing in all directions to all beings.

The person who began the meditation at the center and the one who now returns to the center and bows in all directions are two very different people. You must imagine now that your experience of interconnection and your prayer to have all your fears of inmost intimacy with all beings transformed have changed you completely. You are now a "diamond being," an enlightened lover of God and the creation, one with the One in all Its manifestations. Because of the holy power you have gained from the meditation and from the direct operation through it of divine grace, you are now able to radiate brilliant white light from your open heart in all the four directions. Think of your heart as a flame-crystal within the larger crystal of your transformed body and let its light flow out vibrantly in all directions, sanctifying, blessing, and helping all beings throughout the cosmos.

Finally, with great joy and gratitude, dedicate everything that you have done and experienced in the meditation to the awakening of all beings to their oneness-in-God and rest in the serene peace that true love and true knowledge are bringing to you, and radiating from you.

Practice 16
The Practice of Tonglen, Giving and Receiving

Staying receptive to the extraordinary depth of suffering in the world is an extremely demanding process—especially in an age as dangerous and tormented as ours—and one that menaces the false self's passion for denial and hunger for comfort at every turn. Terror of feeling and the primitive desire to wall ourselves off from our own pain and that of others are two of the strongest sources of all the cruelty, confusion, and injustice of the world; working to eliminate them in ourselves is crucial to our own liberation and to that of others.

Tonglen—the practice of giving and receiving—is one of Tibetan Buddhism's most precious gifts to the world. It is a very holy and very powerful practice that can help anyone who does it stay open to, and expand, his or her innate tendency to be compassionate. The great mystics of all traditions remind us that at the core of all of our natures is a divine capacity for love; Tonglen helps us discover, sustain, expand, and develop this capacity until it becomes the ruling force of our whole being. Learning how strong your own inner power of love and compassion really is and then how transformative and healing it can be both for you and others brings great spiritual joy and determination.

The informing principle to Tonglen is simple; in the course of the practice you "take on" the pain, terror, and sadness of others and then "give out" all peace, all love, all help, all possible forms of healing. As you breathe in, you breathe in all suffering; as you breathe out, you breathe out all peace.

There is nothing to fear; the pain, terror, and sadness you take on in this practice will not destroy you. On the contrary, by determining calmly and consciously to take on the sufferings of others, you will wear away your attachment to your false self, the false self that is the source of all our aggression, illusion, and ignorance and that protects itself by self-absorbed hardheartedness and denial. By constantly intending to open up to and embrace and transmute the pain of others, you will be constantly wearing away everything in you that considers yourself "alone," "separate," "uninvolved," and so will be uncovering evermore clearly your true divine nature and developing at ever greater depth and passion its sacred heart-force. Every time you do this practice, then, with a sincere intention to help another person or group of people who are in pain, you will also be offering up your own separate false self for transformation and so taking a step forward toward your own liberation from illusion. The greatest mystics of all traditions remind us that progress along the Path is best gauged by growth selflessness and humility. As a Tibetan mystic, Shantideva, wrot

> The childish work for their own benefit
> The Buddhas work for the benefit of others
> Just look at the difference between them!

You will find, as I have, that if you make the practice of Tonglen your own, you will experience more and more clearly the depths of your own compassion and innate generosity, the compassion and generosity that are normal to your divine nature. You will come to realize that far from being too fragile to bear the pain of the world—one of the most effective fictions of the false self—you are in fact far more able than you ever imagined to confront without fear or illusion what is really happening to yourself and others and the natural world, and far more powerful an agent of healing than you ever suspected.

Before you begin to do the practice of Tonglen itself, I advise you to follow the Tibetan mystics' advice and sit for five or ten minutes in calm silence. The calmer and more inwardly peaceful you are, the stronger you will feel when it comes to confronting your own or others' suffering.

I find it very powerful at the beginning of Tonglen practice to imagine that I am staring out across a still and sunlit ocean or up into the boundless blue depths of a spring sky; doing this, I find, immediately expands my mind and makes it more spacious. I find it helpful also to pray to all those awakened beings, such as Jesus, Rumi, and the Buddha, who have made the practice of compassion the core of their message: I pray to them all to come and help me claim, live, and enact the truth of the divine compassion within me, and within all beings.

Now, with mind and heart composed, begin the practice of giving and taking by doing Tonglen on yourself. One highly effective way of doing this is to practice seated before a large mirror in which you can see yourself clearly. Let the person in the mirror— let's call him or her A—be your karmic biographical self, with all its sadnesses, doubts, fears, and difficulties; the person gazing into the mirror—B—is your eternal self already free, already liberated, whose essence is spacious and all-embracing love.

Gaze now with the eyes of your eternal free self at what I call "the wreck in the mirror": gaze without fear or shame and see clearly in A's face all of A's loneliness, worry, panic, and grief. Note everything calmly, compassionately, without judgment. Allow the symbolic atmosphere of what you are doing to instruct and awaken you; remind yourself that the biographical self is the *reflection* in the "mirror of life" of a far more powerful and spacious *eternal self* who cannot be destroyed or broken. Allow the full beauty of this knowledge to infuse your whole being with joy and faith.

Now imagine that all the fears and desolations your biographical self is harboring within itself issues from the stomach of your image in the mirror in the form of a ball of hot, black, grimy smoke. Visualize this ball of thickly swirling black smoke clearly. Then, as you breathe in, breathe in the black ball into the fully open heart-center of your eternal self and imagine it dissolving away completely there, as smoke would in a cloudless shining blue sky. Then, on the out-breath, breathe back at your biographical self in the mirror all the peace, bliss, strength, and healing power of your eternal self.

Make sure that your in-breaths and out-breaths are equally deep and long. Breathe in the black ball of smoke from the stomach of your biographical self; pause and imagine it dissolving in the boundless blue sky of your eternal heart-mind; then breathe out as deeply and fully as you breathed in, consciously and with great focus sending out to your biographical self as you do so all you know of the faith and radiance of your own divine truth.

If you do this whole process nine times calmly and confidently, you will be amazed at how much better and more grounded you will feel. You will now be ready to turn to the second part of the practice.

In this second part of giving and taking, you will be doing Tonglen for someone else. Select a person who you know is in psychological or physical pain. Imagine him or her clearly in your heart's eye and meditate as richly and sensitively as you can on all the difficulties he or she must be experiencing and all the grief and fear that is being undergone. If the person you have chosen is someone for whom you have sometimes conflicted or ambiguous feelings, don't be surprised if these surface and try to block your compassion toward him; offer these feelings when they arise for transformation. You can even, as I often do, perform a kind of mini-Tonglen on them; accept and own and then breathe the difficult feelings in, and then breathe out to yourself the compassion of your innate nature.

Now imagine that all the psychological or physical anguish of the person you have chosen issues out of her stomach in the concentrated form of a hot, black, grimy ball of smoke. As you breathe in, breathe in that black ball of hot smoke, and as you breathe out, breathe out to the person all the peace, strength, happiness, and bliss of your innate love nature.

Something a young Tibetan practitioner once told me has helped me immensely in this stage of the practice. He said: "Never be afraid that if you breathe in someone's pain that it will somehow 'get stuck' in you. Remember that there is nowhere in you for it to get stuck; in your essence, you are the boundless space of Buddha-consciousness." Reminding myself of what he told me has prevented me time and time again from involuntarily closing down to the being I have chosen to practice for. He also told me to imagine that as I breathed out, the blessing my out-breath sends the person I have chosen doesn't "end" with him or her but travels on and on throughout the universe. "All acts of true compassion," he said, "are infinite both in their origin and in their effect. Imagine that your out-breath cleanses, purifies, and blesses not only the person you have chosen, but the whole cosmos." As you breathe out, then, imagine with great faith that the person you have chosen is completely irradiated with grace and healed of everything that afflicts her. It helps here to see in your heart's eye the person you have chosen smiling or laughing or dancing with joy and health. Imagine that the blessing of her joy and health is contagious and spreads invisibly through all things everywhere, illumining them all with divine light.

Now, in the third part of the practice, turn in your heart to confront the suffering of the whole planet. Imagine the animals dying in the burning forests, the whales, dolphins, and sea lions suffering from pollution, the women and children murdered or maimed in wars, the monotonous horror of the lives of the desperately poor in Calcutta, Khartoum, Mexico City, and in the slums of American cities. Imagine the full danger the planet faces from environmental destruction of all kinds, and the possibility of nuclear annihilation that still exists even after the "end" of the Cold War. Try with all the force of the Divine within you to face without illusion or false consolation all the aspects of the agony that the entire planet is now going through—an agony that is demanding from each of us a passionate commitment to transform ourselves to be of real help.

Imagine now that the entire earth gives off a ball of hot, black, grimy smoke in which all these horrors are concentrated. Imagine, too, that the divine self you are now is as vast as the universe. Take that vast black ball of agony into your heart and dissolve it in its sky-pure transparence. Breathe in the earth's black smoke; pause as it dissolves utterly in your skylike heart; breathe out the divine light and bliss and strength of your divine self and imagine the whole earth bathed in its all-healing glory. Do this nine times slowly with total concentration.

Your intention to transmute all the suffering of all sentient beings and of the whole earth has transformed you now into a diamond being whose body, heart, mind, and spirit are transparent and on fire with brilliant white divine light. Send this light with its all-transforming powers in all the four directions, and know with faith and joy that it will do wonders and effect great secret healings.

As you keep sending out the brilliant white light from your diamond body, make a vow to do something specific for the world. Don't vow to do something grandiose and impossible; vow to do something you really *can* do. Mother Teresa once said: "We cannot do great thing, but we can do small things with great love." Vow to do something small with great love. A woman I know who did this practice once vowed to clean up the bus stop down the road from her apartment once a week. Another man told me that after doing Tonglen the first time, he vowed to cook one meal a week for the homeless shelter in his town, and stuck to his decision for over a decade. A teenager I taught this practice to in San Francisco vowed to dedicate three hours a week to feeding the abandoned cats and dogs who lived in a park near his school: Four years later, he has found homes for many of them.

A vow is a sacred responsibility, so don't make it lightly. And when you make it, stand by it. Even the "smallest" vow, you will find, can be transforming if you honor it.

One vow I have often made at the end of Tonglen practice is to go on doing Tonglen at odd moments throughout the day for anyone I see who looks miserable or in need. This is simple and very moving and nourishing to do. If you are on a bus and see someone looking lonely or desperate, just take a minute and breathe in their pain and breathe out to him or her your joy and inner peace. If you see on the evening news a person who moves you by his distress, just breathe it in and breathe out to him love and strength. Once you start practicing like this, you will find you will derive great joy from feeling so connected to others; your heart will go on opening until that marvelous moment when it has opened so continually and completely and with such faith and abandon that it can never close again, and then, as the Tibetans say, "Your whole life will be Tonglen."

Practice 17
The Practice of Lovingkindness (Metta)

The practice of metta—the Pali word for "lovingkindness"—was first taught by the Buddha himself two thousand five hundred years ago as a supremely rich and powerful way of cultivating a generous heart. "Without a generous heart," the Buddha said, "there can be no true spiritual life." As the Buddha said in the Dhammapada:

The thought manifests as the word:
The word manifests as the deed;
The deed manifests as into habit;

And habit hardens into character.
So watch the thought and its ways with care
And let it spring from love
Born out of concern for all beings.

Interestingly, the Buddha first taught this extraordinarily powerful practice as an antidote to fear. The story goes that the Buddha
sent a group of monks to meditate in a forest that was occupied by
tree spirits. These spirits were furious at the intrusion of the
monks into their private kingdom and tried to scare them off by
appearing as ghouls, smelling disgustingly and uttering spine-
curdling shrieks. The monks became so terrified that they ran
back to the Buddha and begged him to send them to a different
forest for their retreat. The Buddha replied, "You will go back to
the same forest you have just run from, but I will give you all the
protection you will need." Then he taught them the metta practice.
The monks returned to the forest, practiced metta, and, it is said,
the tree spirits were so profoundly moved by the waves of compassionate energy that flowed from their presence and filled the forest
that they decided to care for and serve the monks in all ways.

Whether or not this story is true, it makes the profound point
that lovingkindness can penetrate and transform a mind deranged
by fear, and also that fear cannot swerve a mind filled with the wisdom, peace, and joy of lovingkindness from its deepest truth. The
antidote to the panic that so often possesses and disturbs us in ordinary life is a mind open to love for all beings. The Buddha said,
"Rapture is the gateway to nirvana"; the practice of metta, if done
sincerely, opens us to the inner lavishness of our true nature, a lavishness that nothing can destroy, not even the fiercest afflictions.

Those who undertake the Direct Path make a commitment to
serve all beings in the heart of reality and to work for justice in the
world. Nothing is more demanding or more potentially dispiriting;
the world can often be cruel to those who want to live the laws of
compassion and justice within it. The patience that is needed to be
able to bear whatever ordeals necessarily arise and not to lose hope
has to be rooted, I have found, in a constant commitment to remember the inner sacredness of others, whatever they may say or do.

Working for justice and transformation in the world involves risking being hurt continually by incomprehension, betrayal, or fierce, sometimes ruthless, opposition. If you allow your inner pain or panic to overwhelm you, you will never be effective for long. Practicing metta for all beings—including those who betray and wound you—becomes an essential form of soul hygiene, an essential way of staying strong and open to the vivid energies of divine love. Martin Luther King once wrote, "Nothing can destroy a person who refuses, whatever is done to him, to hate back." Keeping the heart in a state of divine compassion is the clue to continued inspired action within the world, and to going on hoping calmly—and working calmly—in the middle of what can sometimes seem like hopeless and savage chaos.

To begin the sacred practice of metta, then, sit calmly and let your body and mind relax as richly and deeply as possible. Try to let go of all your hopes, fears, and agendas, and enter the purity of the present moment.

I find it very helpful and inspiring at this stage to say a prayer I have adapted from a saying of the Buddha:

Even as a mother watches over and protects her child, her only child, so with a boundless mind may I cherish all living beings, radiating friendliness over the entire world, above, below, and all around without limit! May I cultivate a boundless good toward the whole world uncramped and free from ill will or enmity!

Then I start the Metta practice itself that unfolds traditionally in carefully graded stages. I find that respecting the different stages adds tremendously to the overall power of the practice; it may seem mechanical at first, but its inner logic and effectiveness will, I assure you, become clear over time.

In the first stage, as in the Tonglen practice given earlier, you begin by directing lovingkindness toward yourself. You begin with yourself because without having compassion for yourself, it is almost impossible to have compassion for others. The method you use to do this is to recite inwardly the following phrases:

May I be free from danger
May I have mental happiness
May I have physical happiness
May I have ease of well-being

You may discover as you repeat these phrases that you find it hard to feel that you deserve such freedom. Our habits of self-contempt and self-hatred run deep. Very often, this initial prayer will uncover many of the blocks and feelings of unworthiness that prevent us from loving ourselves. If this happens, continue to breathe deeply and calmly, looking at whatever "information" arises from your meditation without fear or judgment. It can also help here to imagine someone who loves you very much—say, a mother or grandmother or school friend or mentor; remembering and invoking their love for you will help you uncover the appropriateness of loving yourself. You can also imagine how the Buddha or Christ or Mary, for example, might look at you; invoking their gaze of unconditional compassion will help you uncover your own compassion for yourself.

Repeat the four phrases quietly, softly, and with calm feeling, opening up your whole being to their blessing. If you wish to alter the words and ask for specific things that you need, don't hesitate to do so. At times when I have physical pain or financial worry, I pray for them to be eased; at times when I feel exhausted or menaced by despair, I pray to be inspired. Rooting what you pray for in the actual conditions and demands of your life can greatly deepen your awakening of compassion for yourself and your belief in compassion's healing power.

When you feel sincerely that your lovingkindness for yourself is vivid and warm, turn to direct metta to someone who has been a benefactor to you. Reflect that just as you want to be happy and healthy and free from all forms of illusion and suffering, so does everyone else. Evoke your benefactor—a mentor, or someone who has helped you in your work or life—with deep gratitude and recite the same four phrases slowly and reverently for him or her.

Now you are ready to proceed to the third stage of the metta practice. Choose to direct metta toward a beloved friend, someone whose heart and loyalty you are sure of. Recall the depth and beauty of your friendship and let your entire being be warmed by grateful memories of what it has brought you. Then, as before, recite the four phrases with prayerful tenderness for the person you have chosen.

By now, after concentrating on sending lovingkindness to yourself, a benefactor, and a beloved friend, your sense of your own inner abundance and power of love should be strong and secure: You are ready to turn to direct unconditional lovingkindness toward those who have hurt you or even tried to destroy you.

The Buddha advises us to begin this crucial and transforming stage of the practice by first selecting as the object of our lovingkindness someone who we feel "neutral" toward. In this way we prepare ourselves gradually for opening our heart toward someone who has wounded us.

Choose, then, to recite the four phrases for someone you have no particular feelings for, say, a cashier at the supermarket or a bus driver on a route you take regularly. Invoke the person you choose calmly and do the practice for him or her. One of the startling things I have found is that very often when I see the person afterward for whom I have chosen to practice, I feel a quite extraordinary warmth for them! Just thinking of someone in this charged and holy context can awaken real love for them.

Now you are ready to direct lovingkindness even to someone who has truly wanted to harm you. The wonder of the metta practice at this stage is that if you really succeed in evoking genuine compassion for someone who has wounded you, you will taste the freedom and sublime beauty of the force of unconditional love at the core of your inner divine nature. You will come to know you have within you the calm love power of a Buddha or a Christ, and that knowledge will slowly liberate you from the need to cling to any feelings of anger or bitterness that may still remain from past distress.

Of course, in practice, evoking genuine compassion for an "enemy" can be hard and painful. I find that certain simple techniques help me here. Sometimes I imagine the person I have chosen as a vulnerable small child; sometimes I try to focus on

ne good point in their character or in my past relation with
them—on a gift for music or writing they may have, or on a past
kindness; sometimes I try to imagine what may have happened to
them to make them the way they are.

Reciting the four phrases of the metta practice for an "enemy"
has enormous power. I try to perform this stage even more
methodically and slowly than all the others, offering up for transformation as I pray for my "enemy" all my own bitter or angry
feelings. If thinking of someone who has wounded me makes it
impossible not to continue being bitter and angry, I find it useful
to ask myself, "Who is really suffering from this rage? Who is really
being afflicted by this bitterness?" Such questions are immediately sobering; clearly it is not my "enemy" who is being effected
but myself; I am the victim who needs to be released. Years ago a
Burmese meditation teacher informed me that it was helpful to repeat at this stage of the practice: "Out of compassion for myself,
let me let go of all these feelings of anger and resentment forever!"
She added, "The great peace that will follow is a taste of final liberation." The times that I have tasted this "great peace" at this stage
of the metta meditation have been among the most moving and
fruitful of my life: just remembering them, I find, helps me to try
to restore balance in difficulty.

After reciting the four phrases for your enemy and truly with
your whole heart directing metta toward him or her, now, as the
closing act of the practice, direct a stream of lovingkindness toward the whole world in all directions. Rest in the bliss, peace, joy,
and unshakable strength of unconditional compassion and dedicate all the merits of your practice to the liberation of all sentient
beings everywhere.

It is essential not to limit your practice of metta to your practice period. You can, in fact, do metta everywhere—on buses,
trains, planes, in traffic jams, in lines, walking to the store. You
will find that if you practice Metta secretly wherever you find yourself, you will start to experience a marvelous sense of connection
with others and that your essential unity with all beings will become more and more a deeply felt reality. You will find, too, that
knowing and living this essential unity with others more and more

will slowly free you from all fear and bring peace, depth, and calm to your life.

Practice 18
Birthing the Divine Child in the Mother

This practice—which I have adapted from an ancient Hindu tantric practice—introduces anyone who performs it with focused devotion to an illumined wholeness of being and an integration of heart, mind, body, and soul that the Mother aspect of God is trying to birth in all of us. It will help you reach out to the Divine Child within that many mystical traditions inform us is our inmost sacred identity. It is this integrated and unified being in whom all the ancient dichotomies between mind and heart, body and soul, "transcendence" and "immanence" have been fully overcome through the healing power of an overwhelming realization of unity and balance that is, I believe, the goal of the Direct Path and the hope for a future humanity.

The holy Indian woman who taught me this practice twenty years ago in Benares told me: "Always begin it by as deep a meditation as you can manage on what it would be like to live as a fully empowered divine child of the Father-Mother. Imagine with the full powers of your sacred imagination exactly what it might be like to live a life in which heart, mind, body, and soul were all experienced as different facets of one sacred unity. Try to imagine what a great healing of all fears and false division such an experience would bring you and how finally it would illumine every thought and emotion and action. Try to imagine what an energy of joyful, integrated creativity such a living knowledge of unity would flood your whole life with."

"Then," she added, "when you have inspired yourself with a vision of the fully active, passionate, creative, healed, and balanced divine child you long with every cell of your entire being to become, invoke as fervently as you can the direct aid of the Mother aspect of God, the Divine Mother, in all her glory of light power, to come and transform you. This is very important; for the practice to be as powerful as it can be, you must begin it by this fervent, passionate, and wholehearted invocation of the light power of the Divine Mother. If you call on her with the force of your whole being, she cannot refuse to come to you immediately and you will feel a new strength and sense of purpose start to flood not only your mind and spirit but also your body."

Begin the practice, then, by imagining the wonderful new powers and energies that becoming the divine child will bring you, and by invoking with one-pointed passion, the light power of the Divine Mother.

After this period of intense and focused meditation, start the following visualization with perfect faith that it can and will act as an instrument of the birthing powers of the Divine Mother. Know that it can and will, if you do it regularly, birth more and more completely in you the divine child you essentially are and liberate you from all concepts, inherited prejudices, and psychological and physical imbalances that prevent you from attaining effortless trust and effortless being-in-her.

Imagine now the Divine Mother, in whatever form you worship her most readily, standing in the shining air above your head with her palms outspread. Imagine whatever form of her you have chosen—Kali or Durga or the Virgin of Guadalupe—surrounded by blazing golden light and smiling with joy and compassion. Imagine now that from her outspread palms above your head starts to pour a living glittering stream of soft golden light. Know that this golden light has within it every power of divine love, every power of gnosis, healing, and integration. Know this with your whole being and surrender everything you are to its operation in calm and perfect trust.

I find that it sometimes helps me at this stage to say again and again inwardly "O light of the Mother, heal me and transform me, illumine my mind and open my heart! Heal my body of its fears of separation! Integrate completely my heart with my mind, my body with my soul, and bring me whole and joyful into the blaze of your Presence!" The more devotedly I can invoke the healing and transforming powers of the light, the more powerfully I feel its operation.

Now allow the stream of living golden light from the outspread palm of the Divine Mother to enter your body through the spiritual center that is in the crown of your head. It is this center, the Hindus and Buddhists tell us, that connects us most immediately to the transcendent.

Let the golden light now pour into and fill your head. As it does so, pray particularly for your powers of vision and understanding of the sacred to be awakened and strengthened. Many people will find that they feel at this stage a kind of tickling or pressure between the eyebrows—this is the light starting to awaken what in eastern mystical tradition is called the Ajna Chakra, or Third Eye, the spiritual eye that is located at the center of the forehead, which is opened slowly through prayer, meditation, and service and which, when completely open, sees the divine light dancing in reality directly and knows the whole universe as the living dance of light consciousness.

Now invite the light reverently down into your throat. In the eastern mystical systems, the spiritual center in the throat "controls" communication of every kind. Allow the golden light now to open that center as strong sunlight opens a shy red rose. Imagine the red rose of effortless communication of truth and love opening in your throat, slowly but certainly, as the divine sunlight of the Mother's light is trained on it.

Your head and your throat are now gently on fire. Take that golden fire down into and along your shoulders and along your arms to the very tips of your fingers, imagining as you do so that every cell in that part of your body awakens to its essential divine strength and life.

Now take the golden light of the Mother down into your heart-center that is about an inch to the right of the middle of your chest. The fully awakened heart is the core and guide of your divine human being; awakening its boundless love and all-embracing skylike charity is the most crucial aspect of the birth you are allowing the Mother to prepare in you. So as you take the golden light of the Mother down into your heart, pray to the Mother to open your heart completely and to reveal the whole universe blazing in its subtle fire, and to keep your heart open in her forever. As you do so, start to feel how your light-opened heart, through her grace, aligns head and emotion, mind and psyche, your physical and your spiritual being. Pray for this supreme sacred balance of heart and mind, soul and body, "heaven" and "earth," inner and outer, masculine and feminine to become ever deeper and ever richer in you, and to inspire in you ever more profound realizations of the truth of unity.

By opening your vision, communication, and heart-centers through the grace of the Mother's golden light, you have now begun the birth of the divine child in you and established yourself in the living presence of divine love. Relish this ecstatic and blissful Presence and call out to it inwardly with words of welcoming adoration. Knowing the child is being consciously born in you, thank and adore the birthing Mother with all the ecstasy of your awakened sacred heart.

Now with full faith, trust, and confidence, take the golden light down into the rest of your body, "marrying" it and all of its conscious and subconscious movements, hungers, passions, and desires with the love power of the light.

To make this "wedding" of the rest of the body with the awakened heart-light as rich and complete as possible, it is best to perform it in stages.

First, take the golden light down into your belly, allowing it to become "pregnant" with the light's full strength and sweetness. In the belly there is a spiritual center that ensures balance in the deepest sense by grounding illumination in the real. As you take the golden light into the belly, pray to it to mature and deepen this earthing and grounding power so that you can incarnate in all your emotions, acts, and thoughts more and more of the Mother's love and force.

Confident that you are established in sacred balance and in divine love, fearlessly lower the full force of the Mother's light into your genital area. So much of human ignorance and violence and suffering comes from sexual wounding and from the millennia of sex and body hatred imposed on us by most of the world's religions. The Mother, however, wants *all* of our instincts to be consecrated to God and on the Direct Path is preparing for her children a way to a sanctified sexuality, a sexuality that provides a direct way of delighting in the divine energies that engender and sustain the creation and a direct initiation into the mysteries of divine human love. So, as you lower golden light into your genital area, pray to the Mother to remove all your guilt and shame, all the fears and blocks in you that prevent you from acknowledging the intrinsic holiness of your sexual nature, and from consecrating it. Ask the Mother to transform your sexual nature into an instrument of divine human love, not by repressing your physical desires but by divinizing them.

One very powerful way of "imagining" this divinization of sexuality is to picture the genitals before the light enters them as a dull gray-black crystal. As the light floods them, imagine this gray-black crystal starting to blaze with golden brilliance. Sustain the meditation until you can visualize the whole genital area as one soft, radiant blaze of crystalline golden light.

Now continue taking the light of the Mother even farther down—down the thighs, through the kneecaps, down the backs of the legs, and down through the ankles to the ends of the toes. In many of the eastern mystical systems the spiritual centers that govern the life of the subconscious are hidden in the lower part of your body. Pray to the Mother to clarify, purify, and divinize all the secret movements of your subconscious to help you make all its darkness conscious, and to open up all the traumas, humiliations, and fears that are hidden there to the direct light of divine healing.

Every part of your body—heart, mind, and soul—is now alight with the golden fire light of the Divine Mother. Harmoniously and blissfully relish the power of electric balance that streams in you and from you. Let your entire body-soul-heart-mind blaze in praise of the Mother who has birthed you into your whole and healed, transformed human divine being.

Now, in the final movement of the practice, slowly and with tremendous joy take the golden light back up through every center, one by one, blessing each one with its healing power again.

Pray as the light enters each center from the bottom upward, slowly, one after the other, that all remaining obscurities and blocks in your divine human nature be removed forever.

Let the light travel back into your head and then sit on top of your crown center like a large pulsing fireball. Balance it there for one long, calm moment. Then, concentrating your entire being in one huge inward shout of ecstatic joy, drop the fireball above your crown center deep into your sacred heart and let it explode there like a bomb of light, sending golden light in vast pulsing waves of healing bliss in all directions.

Imagine as your heart explodes that it is a birthing supernova of divine fire and that radiation from its birth is now expanding and extending throughout the universe.

Rest calmly and humbly in this birthing power that has now been born in you through the Mother's grace and your cooperation with it.

Three

Embodiment and Integration

O friend, understand the body
Is like the ocean
Rich with hidden treasures.

KABIR

Radiant in His Light
We awaken as the Beloved
In every part of our body.

ST. SIMEON THE THEOLOGIAN

When the soul and body marry,
they birth the philosopher's stone.

MEDIEVAL ALCHEMICAL TEXT

The Spirit shall look out through Matter's gaze
And Matter shall reveal the Spirit's face . . .
And all the earth become a single life.

SRI AUROBINDO IN SAVITRI

The Sacred Body

PERHAPS THE MOST important clue to the embodiment and integration of mystical consciousness with all aspects of life is to understand, revere, and celebrate the inherent sacredness of your body. Knowing that your body is sacred in itself and as a temple of the spirit and instrument of your divine self leads to several inter-linked and transformatory initiations in the heart of ordinary existence; it makes you grateful for the blessing of being alive, conscious that all life is the glowing manifestation of spirit, aware of the holiness of other human and sentient beings, and more and more dazzledly alert at all moments to the divine splendor of creation.

These interlinked initiations in turn lead to an inward transformation that over time comes to reflect itself in every thought, action, and choice and to heal all false divisions between "body" and "soul," "physical" and "spiritual," "self" and "other." Being conscious of the sacredness of the body slowly turns the whole of life into an experience of feast and celebration; every walk or meal or deep sleep or joy at a flower or a beautiful face becomes a form of praise and prayer. Being conscious of the holiness of the bodies of other human and sentient beings makes you instinctively more sensitive and protective toward them in every way and breeds what Buddha called "a loving harmlessness" in the core of your being. To see, know, and feel through understanding the sacredness of your own body the sacredness of the entire creation—from the smallest dancing flea to the gray whale and the Himalayas—awakens a holy passion for God in all forms of life, and a practical resolution to do everything in your power to protect and guard nature from humanity's greed and ignorance.

Being initiated into this sacredness of the flesh, of human life and relationships, and of the creation, is not only essential to the highest and richest realization of the Divine; it is now essential to the survival of the human race. If we do not, separately and together, awaken to the glory of who we are and where we are and summon all our powers to protect our divine inheritance as human beings, we will continue in our coma of denial of the sacredness of the world and destroy nature and ourselves.

In a deep sense, our contemporary crisis is a crisis of the body. Our inability to bless our own holiness and to see the infinite beauty of our own and others' bodies and to see what Blake called "eternity in a grain of sand" has blinded us to the light that lives in each of our cells and in each being and thing that surround us. Our belief in a mechanical vision of nature has made us unable to see what Rumi and St. Francis and the mystics of every age and every tradition know to be true both of ourselves and of the beings and things that ring us around and accompany us on our journey through time—that "all atoms are drunk on Perfection and are singing 'Glory be to God! Glory be to God!' " as Rumi said. We have come to the moment when we must either fall in love with the divine meaning of our lives and of the world or conspire unconsciously to annihilate both, when we must consent to the initiation of "embodiment and integration" or die out.

It is far easier to talk or write or read about such an initiation and the transformation that springs from it than it is to live them. If you are going to take the Direct Path to God, however, you are committed to living them, because the aim of the Direct Path is nothing less than the sanctification and divinization of the whole of life in all its aspects, the "embodiment and integration" of the light and its power with matter in all its forms, the birth of a healed and whole humanity at one with God and life and creation.

I had no real idea of what it meant to live the sacred life of the body until one terrible morning six summers ago I woke up with a piercing pain in the small of my back, unable to move. I had been out dancing the night before at a party given to celebrate the end of a Rumi class I had been offering at the California Institute of Integral Studies; I must have joined too enthusiastically in the "African" dancing (only in California!). At first I thought that with treatment and care, the pain in my back would go away after a few weeks; in fact, however, I would have acute constant back pain for almost three and a half years.

I now count those three and a half years of suffering one of the greatest graces I have received. They forced me to rethink my entire relationship with my body and so with the bodies of others and with the creation. To start to heal myself I had to restructure my physical life and to understand exactly how and why I had been neglecting my body and its sacredness for years.

A Native American healer I met a few months later helped me enormously by suggesting to me that I write down for myself the "history" of my relationship with my body. She said with a sad smile, "You will discover a lot of grief, humiliation, and abuse. We all do." And she was right. As I meditated on how I had lived for forty years with my body, I uncovered three different levels of physical self-contempt. The exercise the Native American healer had suggested was a very humbling one, especially for someone who considered he had already had a mystical "awakening" and thought he understood a great deal about the holiness of the creation and of the body. But to visualize your own body blazing in divine light is, I'm afraid, only the beginning of the recovery of its sacredness; you also have to *unlearn,* and unlearn as thoroughly and completely as you can, all the inherited ways and assumed patterns of bodily self-hatred you have been adhering to, often without knowing it.

The first level of physical self-hatred I uncovered in myself was cultural. I am English, after all, brought up in the Spartan and semi-sadistic atmosphere of English private education. The message about the body I received as a child was, your body is a machine to be treated harshly, with furious discipline. To be sick was to be weak; to listen to the sufferings of the body was to be a "sissy" or "patsy" or "spastic"; to be demonstrative of any "physical" feelings at all, in fact, was to be vulnerable to mockery. I was not an athletic child either, but studious, slightly effeminate, round-shouldered, and plump; from early on in my life I considered myself unattractive. In my "history" I found myself writing, "The pain in your back is all that pain about your body that you repressed and deliberately didn't listen to for so many years coming up now to be attended to, heard, and healed."

I discussed this "cultural" level of self-hatred with my friends in America and Europe. Even those who had been athletes and beautiful from an early age agreed with me that they had been taught to treat their bodies as machines and had been forced to grow "deaf" to their own physical selves. Several of my American male friends said in real rage, "How can I begin to deal with my body and its needs? I have to work seventy hours a week just to stay afloat. If I started to care about my health and stopped endlessly whipping myself and beating myself up, I'd fall behind." I was shocked to find myself identifying intimately with what they said; as a writer, teacher, traveler, spiritual seeker, and nomad, I had been "whipping and beating" my body for years in a desperate attempt to "make my way" and "keep up," and as a result of an unconscious addiction to transcendence. I had even learned—as they had—to take a certain stoic pride in how much I could "forget" my body: to remember it would be to slow down and so to fail in a world that valued only continual achievement and success.

The second kind of physical self-oppression I discovered in myself was sexual. Nearly all of us grew up with the message that sex is in some sense dirty and sinful and that our physical appetites are shameful. Uncovering the different depths of harm that such taboos have done you is one of the most grueling tasks an adult can undertake, but it is vital if you are ever going to have the chance to live a consecrated and sacred physical life. What I discovered as I investigated my past was that I had been driven to despise my body as the source of difficult sexual hungers very early on, and that painful emotional experience in my twenties had only confirmed this self-contempt. Not only did I "despise" my body because it was sexual (and so the source of grief and loneliness), I also projected back onto my body all the sorrow and confusion my heart and mind had felt as an adult as I tried—mostly unsuccessfully—to negotiate the shoals of "sophisticated" sexual life. I made my body the source of sexual pain and the scapegoat for sexual and emotional failure and so unconsciously could not help wanting to "drop" or punish it.

The obsessive sexualization of almost every aspect of our culture has made us all, I believe, profoundly insecure. As a famous young actress once said to me with a desperation so extreme it was almost comic, "Who can ever be thin or sexy or alluring enough for long enough? Who can always stay twenty-four? Who can keep up with all the different styles of 'beauty' changed twice a year?" It isn't only actresses who live haunted by the fear of growing old and unattractive; the natural fear all human beings have of being discarded as they age is infinitely expanded by our contemporary obsession with youth and physical beauty. How can we not fear and despise the body that is the source of so much anxiety and distress?

The third level of physical self-hatred I uncovered in myself was religious. Until I methodically and as fearlessly as possible started to analyze the different "religious" messages that I had been given about my body, I had never even begun to understand just how oppressive they were. I came to see how it wasn't simply my Judeo-Christian heritage of original sin that had given me the unconscious notion that my body was something ugly, sad, and disposable but also everything I had ever read in the great Sufi, Buddhist, and Hindu mystical texts that described the body as an irredeemable source of fantasy and illusion. I came to see just how damaging the cult of transcendence in *all* the patriarchal religions has been to any healthy awareness of the physical; in their rage to abandon *this* world and its messy, awkward reality, the patriarchal traditions have devalued the sacredness of creation and cut off our inner access to it.

For years I had been studying and trying to uncover and love the sacred feminine aspect of God; I now understood the necessity of the recovery of the feminine as sacred with a passion and hunger I had never experienced before. Unless I saw and knew my body as sacred in itself, how could I gain any balanced understanding of its role in life? If I didn't love and honor and revere my own body, how could I really love, honor, and revere the bodies of others and so be a guardian and steward of the creation?

The horrible constant pain in my back reminded me of everything I had neglected, ignored, betrayed, and turned away from. I wrote: "It is as if the Mother aspect of God is constantly saying to me in and through this pain, 'I will go on as long as you do not recognize me in *all* the different aspects of your life.'" I was compelled to face that behind my passion for the Mother had hidden an unacknowledged passion to be *free* of my body. I had loved the "transcendent" Mother—or what I imagined her to be—but been too vain, self-absorbed, scared, and careless to worship her in all her holy practical particulars. The pain in my back was her way of forcing me to pay attention to everything I had tried, unconsciously and unsuccessfully, to "transcend" and evade.

As so often happens on the Direct Path, great mistakes, if acknowledged and attended to, can lead to awakening. In my long journey of physical self-healing I have come to celebrate and revere the physical aspects of life in a way and with an intensity I never could before.

The first gift extreme back pain gave me was, paradoxically, gratitude. The suffering I was in made me acutely aware of how good and kind my body had been to me through many pain-free years, even as I largely ignored it. I found myself, for the first time, consciously noting all the things my body's generosity had allowed me to do—the journeys it had helped me take, inner and outer, the labors it had patiently sustained, the joys on so many levels that it had made so easily and unself-consciously available to me.

The second gift back pain gave me was a sense of my own mortality. There is nothing like constant acute pain to remind you that you are dying. As I allowed this knowledge, through prayer and meditation and suffering, to permeate my awareness, everything began to change; every peach or banana I ate tasted sweeter, each fall of sunlight seemed more brilliant, every evening spent with Eryk richer and more precious. One part of my being stayed plunged in anguish; the other tasted the joy of existence with passion it had never known before. Years before, an old woman I loved in Sri Lanka told me on our last evening together, "One day you will know you are dying and then every time you look out at the garden or up at a bird flashing between the trees your heart will catch in wonder." At last I knew what she meant.

With this growing and pervasive sense of mortality came also a great and more intimate compassion for others' sufferings. Having any form of constant physical ailment makes you far more sensitive to all the others who suffer as you do; until I had back pain I had no idea how many people suffer from it. Now I see its sad work everywhere, in post office lines, on buses, on airplanes. My sensitivity to physical pain and handicaps of all kinds has grown in a way I could never have imagined before I was sick myself. To embrace your own body is to embrace time and death and fragility not only in yourself but in everyone; from such an embrace comes, slowly, an increasing and increasingly nondual and unconditional love for all sentient beings.

It isn't only your sense of the heartbreak of things that grows when you embrace the fragile holiness of the body; you also come to appreciate far more deeply the ordinary decency and courage of all beings. The patience of the pregnant cashier at the supermarket moves you; the gaiety of the old singer at the dinner party becomes suddenly marvelous and poignant when you realize she knows she doesn't have long to live; the workman wearing out his health and back to feed his family fills you with sad admiration. Your growing acceptance of the mortality of your own body makes you far more aware of the ordinary heroism of others, and this breeds respect, compassion, and a subtle sense of universal solidarity.

Perhaps the greatest gift my back pain has given me is that it has started to make me my own mother. It took me many years of study, meditation, and inner experience before the very simple realization dawned on me that the whole point of loving the Mother aspect of God was to learn to be a nurturer to yourself and others and that acting in this way was one of the greatest keys to integrating God with life. This realization came to me one day in San Francisco as I was undressing in great pain to take a hot bath. I heard an inner voice say, "Bathe yourself as if you were Me bathing you;

treat yourself as if you were Me." With dim happy memories of my own mother bathing me as a child to guide me, I proceeded to soap and clean my body as if I were the Mother bathing her beloved child. I had *seen* the divinity of my body before in mystical experience; now I *knew* it in unconditional love. For the first time, I began to understand in a visceral way what it would be to treat myself and others with profound maternal care; deepening and extending this knowledge in the core of life has become the center of my practice. Nothing could be less flattering to either the personal or "transcendental" self, and nothing could help you more to start to embody and integrate the holy with your daily existence.

What these years of physical suffering and healing have taught me is the necessity of what James Hillman so wonderfully calls in *The Soul Code* "growing down." As Hillman writes: "To plant a foot firmly on earth—that is the ultimate achievement and a far later stage of growth than anything that happens in your head. No wonder the faithful revere the Buddha's footprint in Sri Lanka. It shows he was truly in the world. He had really grown down." What I know now is that you cannot "grow down" in this mysterious and holy way until you have known and embraced the sacredness of the body and paid the price for that knowledge by working to free yourselves from all the inherited cultural, sexual, and religious assumptions that teach you physical self-contempt. Nor can you grow down, either, except by opening to the vast poignant love for all living and dying sacred beings that comes to you when you bless life's holiness, a love that allows for no transcendental escape, no otherworldly solutions, but has to be lived at the heart of the real. Both this knowledge of the body's sacredness and the love that soars from it will bring with them new and sometimes disturbing forms of suffering and outrage; they will also birth a far richer and more deeply compassionate life, a life that has at last grown down enough to be really transformatory.

What these years of physical suffering and healing have also taught me is the accuracy of the divine vision of the ancient Chinese and European alchemists, who for thousands of years, often in secret, tried to discover a way of transfiguring the whole of life into its divine truth, without denying either the holiness of matter or the primacy of spirit.

What both major alchemical traditions inform us is that there are three stages in the turning of life to divine gold. In the first stage, the seeker comes to learn through *separating* spirit from body the primacy and glory and power and divine identity of the spirit. This first stage corresponds to what is often described as enlightenment in many of the other mystical traditions. The alchemists do not end here, however. In the second stage of their scheme, the seeker has to go on, now, to *marry* his or her now conscious spirit with the body and all its thoughts, actions, and appetites. This increasingly precise and revelatory marriage naturally gives birth to the third and final stage, that of a sacred union between the adept's inner being and the one world of divine reality. In this final stage, a wholly new kind of divine human being starts to appear, a child of the wedding of heaven and earth, matter and spirit. In European alchemy, this new divine human being is identified with the resurrected Christ, the Christ awake in transcendent consciousness in a transfigured body. In Chinese alchemy, this child of the sacred marriage between soul and body is called a "golden immortal"—someone who through marrying the spirit with matter has become one not only with the source of creation but with every aspect of the creation itself and so empowered to work in healing bliss in all its dimensions. In modern times, the greatest prophet of this marriage between soul and body and its revolutionary potential was Aurobindo, who understood that it provided the key to the future evolution of humanity.

This marriage of soul to body and body to soul that the alchemists have described to us is the hardest, most intricate, and demanding—and least flattering—of all spiritual work. It demands constant surrender to the wisdom of the sacred feminine—to love and compassion for all beings, to the rhythms of time, to the difficult harsh labor of making the unconscious conscious, and to kneading together the complex, often stubborn, rhythms of the flesh with the simpler and more elemental laws of the spirit. It cannot be done quickly and it cannot be rushed. There is no final end to its process, no place where effort can afford to relax, and no consummation that is not the beginning of a new evolution. Anyone who is unwilling to fail, and fail repeatedly, cannot begin to undertake this great alchemy. What this alchemical marriage demands, in fact, is nothing less than the humility, patience, stamina, and selfless capacity for ordeal of the Divine itself—of that Divine humble enough to risk manifestation in the first place and brave and patient enough to undertake the enormous labor of transforming that manifestation from within it and within its own terms.

The rewards of the marriage between soul and body, however, I have found, are worth all the sufferings and confusions of the work. All divisions between sacred and profane are dissolved as the whole of life reveals its divine origin and nature and becomes what Rumi called the "Marriage Feast, the Place where Soul and Body celebrate their eternal wedding in time." In every action and thought and gesture and hope and practical action, the inner passion of the soul and the outer intention of the body become one beauty, one presence, one all-transforming, focused, gentle and holy power. In this way, the banal is alchemized into the revelatory, the so-called ordinary flashes out with the holy and sublime, and what was impossible either to spirit or body on their own becomes a naturally miraculous and empowered way of being in which each serves, implements, and realizes the holiest dreams of the other.

Coming to know this undoes all the sad denigrations of Creation that the traditions addicted to transcendence have prescribed. To take on a body is not in any way a catastrophe for the soul; it is a supreme opportunity. To have a body is the soul's chance to experience the *fullness* of Divine Presence that is at once transcendent *and* immanent, unborn, uncreated, *and* created, and living and dying in time.

An amazing, mind-deranging, and heart-expanding paradox starts to become increasingly clear as the soul grows down and the sacred marriage between soul and body becomes more and more intricate, all-pervading, and conscious; that it is *because* the soul has opened itself to the vulnerability of death and to the fragile precariousness of physical life that it can be wholly divine.

What the living experience of the sacred marriage of body and soul reveals, then, is that the body is the grail cup out of which the soul drinks the wine of divine ecstasy and of a final divine love that can embrace *all* the terms of a living and dying creation and so become boundless and infinite. To know, feel, and understand the body as the grail cup is the key to the divinization of life in all of its aspects, the key to the flooding of earth life with the powers and glories of the spirit. From such an understanding flowers an immense and ultimate "yes" to life in all of its aspects that is the source of boundless transforming power.

To grow down, then, to marry body and soul, to live in simple union, is to come progressively, with humble astonishment, to know the ultimate paradox of being human—that to be fully and completely human is to be fully and completely divine, for the ultimate power of love and the ultimate fragility and vulnerability of the body are not opposites at all but two sides of one marriage, one glory, and one revelation. This is what is most deeply meant by the old Sufi saying "God speaks to the Awakened one; You are my secret and I am yours." To know and live together both the transcendent and immanent sides of this "secret" is the full divine human life. At the end of the history of my relationship to my body I found myself writing:

> Through the grace of the Mother I now know that I am divine, not despite my fragility and physicality but BECAUSE of them, and through their blessing. If I was not somewhere breakable, broken, and dying how could I begin to love all other breakable, broken, and dying creatures? How do I drink this wild and increasingly barrier-less love except from the cup of death? Isn't this what Rumi meant when he wrote, "A thousand roses are blooming in my skull"?
>
> Accepting, loving, cherishing, and honoring my dying body as the Grail I become increasingly one in non-dual suffering and bliss with all creation and realize myself as neither physical nor spiritual but both together now and always. I am starting at last to savor and live the wonder of such a paradoxical existence and to understand that if I were merely matter or merely spirit I

could never drink the wild divine wine of such a Feast; only a being that is both, like God, can drink it, for in the wine is mixed
inextricably the blaze of eternity and the blood of Creation.

LET ME NOW give some practical advice based on my own experience and study on how to knead the light into matter and "marry"
spirit and body in the heart of ordinary life. The "goal" of the sacred marriage could not be more holy or exalted; the "means,"
however, are often not at all exotic or glamorous but, as the divine
feminine tends to be, very down-home, practically demanding,
sometimes funny, and are meant to be employed constantly and
tirelessly in the heart of life with discipline, humor, and goodwill.

Diet and Fasting

ALL THE SERIOUS mystical traditions have stressed the necessity of keeping to a sensible and healthy diet; however, they have not agreed as to what such a diet is. Hindus swear by vegetarianism; certain Tibetan mystics eat meat; Jains eat hardly anything; some of the most evolved Sufis I have met eat copious amounts of richly stewed lamb and Turkish delight. Theravada Buddhists and strict Hindu Vedantists abhor alcohol, as do most Muslims; tantric Buddhists and Hindus and certain Taoist sects use alcohol freely and exuberantly. I have seen one famous Native American shaman down more whiskey sours than would have floored the toughest marine.

Quite clearly, you can become "awake" on almost any kind of diet. Given such extravagant variations between mystical traditions and given, too, the differences between physical needs and temperaments, no one diet can suit everyone. What you have to do is to experiment and discover the diet that suits you, that makes you feel the most alert, healthy, and awake.

My own opinion—and the opinion of most of the practicing mystics I have talked to—is that moderation and balance are the keys to intelligent eating. I myself prefer vegetarian food to food with meat, although I do eat chicken and fish; I find that for myself, vegetarian food keeps me light and supple-minded. At home I make sure I eat lightly three times a day, mixing grains and fibers and vegetables and taking every morning substantial vitamin supplements. From time to time I try a specific diet. What I usually discover is that I have always known better how to feed myself and keep my body and mind in harmony.

I see no harm whatever in the occasional drink, and was delighted when a group of government-sponsored doctors last year announced that a glass of red wine every day helped keep heart disease at bay. Again, moderation and balance are essential; as an old Sufi I know once said to me, "It is hard to keep up Witness Consciousness if you are drunk." She was at the time and so spoke from experience.

If I had to give any concrete advice to everyone, it would be to always eat as many fruits and vegetables as possible and cut down on desserts, which not only fatten you but string your mind out on sugar overkill. Eat simply and eat often the things you most like that are good for you, so eating is always a delight and a pleasure. Cut down on caffeine and all stimulants so as to not make your mental metabolism too nervous. Eat *less* rather than more; nearly everyone in the West overeats. This is especially important, I find, as you grow older; Bede Griffiths ate sensibly but lightly as a sparrow and lived to be eighty-seven.

I also believe it is important to break every rule imaginable occasionally, for the joy of it and to honor what Mr. Ratnasabapathy, my Hindu priest friend in Tanjore, called Krishna's Law of Excess. He—who was the most balanced and simple of men—used to say with a smile: "Everyone needs to eat and drink a little *too* much from time to time just to stay human." Once every month on a Saturday Mr. Ratnasabapathy would bathe, pray to Krishna, and consume an enormous delicious meal prepared by his wife, Kasturbai (who was the best cook in southern India). I participated in several of these wonderful, funny, and holy occasions; at the end of the last course Mr. Ratnasabapathy would clap his hands and cry out, "And now for three weeks and six days of sensible austerity!"

As for *fasting*, I have used it on and off for the last twenty years and find it very helpful—again in moderation. It is excellent for hygiene, for clearing the mind and for spiritual concentration; it should never be taken to the point where it substantially weakens the body.

When I first started to fast—in my middle twenties in India in Pondicherry—I took it, as I took everything at the time, to excess. I sometimes went without food for almost a week. I had a few marvelous prolonged meditations and minor mystical insights, but after a while fell sick. When I told a local doctor—a Brahmin lover of the Gita and Upanishads—what I had been doing, he grew very angry. "Never be so stupid again! A three-day structured fast is quite enough!" He then explained to me what he meant by a "three-day structured fast" and I have stuck to his instructions ever since.

"On the first day," he said, "eat lightly in the morning. Cereal and fruit juice is excellent. Then have only fruit juice for lunch, a cup of hot tea at about five, and nothing at all at night. On the second day, do not eat anything, but have a large cup of fruit juice for each meal. On the third day, have juice in the morning, eat lightly at lunch—perhaps a small potato and tomato salad—and nothing at night."

No one should do even such a relatively light fast without consulting their physician, and no one should fast often. Once every two weeks is enough. And you should always consume as much water as possible, at least eight glasses a day, to avoid dehydration.

Whenever I fast I increase my daily meditation and prayer time so as to take a maximum benefit from the new physical lightness I feel. One rule I always follow is not to go out anywhere on the second and third evenings; these are most richly spent, I find, in holy reading or in listening to music. A physical fast to be most effective should also involve a mental fast—from worry, the images of TV, excessive mental work or thinking. Combining these two rests body and mind; when I wake up on the morning after the fast ends, I invariably feel far healthier, more rested, and more generally hopeful and creative.

Another simple method of fasting that I use, especially during times of spiritual retreat, is known in Burmese Theravada Buddhism as *eka-tani patabai*, which means sitting in one place with one vessel and eating only once during the whole day, at noon. Traditionally this practice is undertaken for a week at a time. In the afternoon, drink as much juice as you want but no other fluids. At the end of the week, I advise returning to your normal diet slowly, eating only moderate amounts.

Reducing Daily Stress:
Eight Exercises

EVERYONE KNOWS THAT STRESS KILLS and destroys the body and profoundly imbalances the mind and emotions. But the demands of modern life are for most of us so constantly intense that we have to accept a certain high level of stress as inseparable from life. One of the first things I ask anyone I know well who is on the Path is how they *practically* deal with their stress; over the years I have collected and practiced many of their recommendations. Here are eight that I find helpful.

1. Stopping Dead and Taking Five Long, Deep Breaths

This method was given to me by my friend Anne Pennington, a Russian Orthodox professor of Slavic languages at Oxford who was at once the busiest and gentlest of people. "When life gets too much," she said, "I start to say the Jesus prayer, and if even *that* doesn't work, I stand completely still, close my eyes, and take five deep, calm breaths, trying to empty my mind completely. I find that always works."

In the twenty years since I first heard her advice, I have tried it on every continent (except Africa and Antarctica) and in most conceivable (and some barely conceivable) situations, and I have found it quite amazingly powerful and yet one more proof of how, in spiritual practice, it is often the simplest things that are the most effective.

2. Lying on the Floor or Outside on the Earth and Giving Your Stress Away

This method was first demonstrated to me by an old Tibetan beer-seller in Ladakh, who swore by it. He cleared the dirty floor of his small shop near the river in Leh, and then lay down on it with his arms and legs outspread. Then he started to intone, "I give the stress of my mind to the Buddha. I give the stress of my upper body to the Buddha," and so on, solemnly, through his whole body. He made it seem so effective that for a moment when he'd finished I thought he'd fallen asleep.

I find this method both amusing to do and effective. Obviously, it can't be done everywhere—in offices or concert halls, for example. But in the Sturm und Drang of family life it can work wonders.

I have also experimented with it out in nature, particularly in these last years in the desert where I live. I am always amazed by how powerful lying out on the earth and giving it all your stress and distress can be. It has deepened profoundly my sense of the protectiveness of the Mother and of the natural world.

3. The Hot Bath "Spa" Treatment

My grandmother, who was a world-class hysteric, used to say of herself that "the only thing that calms me down is a long hot bath." In my late twenties, when suffering from the end of a particularly miserable love affair, I decided to systematically take her advice. I found myself much more philosophical after a prolonged hot bath than before, even though at the time I was in a tub at Oxford that seemed nearly as old as the college itself.

A Kabalist real estate agent I love who works fifteen hours a day added some touches to what she calls "spa prayer." Once a week, usually on Saturday afternoons, she turns off her phone, sends her husband out to play cards with one of his friends, and draws herself a perfumed bath, surrounding her tub with candles. She then reads one of the Psalms she loves out loud in Hebrew and immerses herself in the hot water for anything up to an hour. She imagines that all her stress leaks out of every part of her into the water; when at last she drains away the water and puts out the candles, she prays that her whole being and body should now be completely clear of any blocks, difficulties, or pain of any kind.

About two years ago I was in a very tense and anguished mood and couldn't concentrate on anything or find any way to relieve my mind. I remembered my friend Bathsheba's spa prayer and decided to try it. I made the water as hot as I could stand, surrounded the tub with lit candles, and put on Gregorian chants so loudly, it echoed through the house. I decided to invent my own variation of spa prayer and imagined that the hot waters were the healing waters of the Divine Mother. As I lay in them, I felt my entire spiritual and physical being gasp in gratitude and relief; just thinking of the water in that way, I found, gave it blessing power. As I washed myself, I said the mantra *ma* in my heart-center; after about twenty minutes my mind and body were peaceful.

I recommend this form of practical spiritual creativity to everyone who asks me for advice. Sometimes, of course, people expect something a little more "exalted"—a Tibetan visualization or a Sanskrit mantra from Bhutan. Recently I was phoned by a friend who has written many elaborate and highly intelligent books on spirituality but who was feeling gloomy and listless; I told him in detail about spa prayer and what I had discovered in it. The shocked silence that greeted my explanation dissolved, after I pushed a bit, into a grudging and embarrassed commitment to "try" it. Three days later, I received a gushing phone call, rich with gratitude. Clearly, he was still reeling from the shock that something so "frivolous" could work so well. At the end of our conversation he asked me: "Do you think Aurobindo ever took long yogic baths?" I assured him that of course he had.

4. One-Minute Tonglens on Stress in the Body

On page 149 I gave instructions for the Tonglen exercise of giving and receiving.

There is a one-minute method of doing Tonglen that is very helpful with stress. Simply imagine that all the stress in your body concentrates into one big, ugly, condensed ball of sticky black smoke; take that smoke deep into the formless "space" of your heart-center and imagine it dissolving there completely. This is best done with and on the breath. As you breathe in, breathe in the black ball into your heart-center; as you breathe out, imagine it dissolving into the skylike spaciousness of your divine nature.

Do this nine times in quite rapid succession and at the end imagine yourself as a brilliant large diamond radiating calm Buddha peace in all directions.

5. Writing in Sharp, Wild, Telegraphic, Unedited Bursts Your Reasons for Being Stressed on a White Piece of Paper and Then Burning It and Burying It in the Yard

This is an adaptation of an ancient Wiccan technique for dissolving inner and outer obstacles. It was taught to me in Hawaii by two funny and learned white witches on holiday from Wyoming, and I have used it often since to real effect.

Begin the ritual by lighting a candle to an image of the Mother you worship. Pray for what you are about to do to be effective by her grace.

Now take a large white piece of paper, scatter fresh ash on it to purify it—or you can use a few drops of consecrated water. Then write on it in as fast and unedited way as possible everything in your current life that is causing you stress. Don't worry about grammar or even whether you make sense; just put down exactly what comes to you and in the way it comes. Above all, don't worry if what you are writing seems "violent" or "aggressive"; it is essential that you get out everything that is in you.

When you have finished, fold the paper in two neatly and then light it from the candle you have already placed before the image of the Mother. It is best to burn the paper in a large dish so none of the ash can escape or be scattered. When the burning is complete, take the ash out into the yard, dig a hole in the ground, and bury the ash in it. As you cover it over, pray again and again to the Mother to hear your prayer and release you from everything that is disturbing you.

This exercise, I have found, is particularly effective in situations in which stress is being caused by a blockage of energy or another's malice.

One warning: Never use this exercise for anything but good ends. It is extremely powerful and if you use it *against* anyone, it will rebound on you.

6. Opening Like a Bud in the Light of Peace

Another immediately effective exercise that dissolves stress is one that I was taught by a Dzogchen Tibetan Buddhist in Nepal. Imagine that you are a beautiful flower in bud. If your favorite flower is a red rose, for example, think that you are the most beautiful rose about to open. Revel in the richness and perfume of the imagined flower you are.

Then, in the next part of the exercise, believe with all your heart-mind that the bud you are is receiving everything it needs to open—all the sun and rain and careful watering and attention. Feel the joy of receiving so many precise blessings and allow yourself to trust that you are getting all you require.

It sometimes helps at this moment to imagine the gardener who is looking after you as the Buddha or Christ or the Mother.

Now see in your spirit's eye the bud you are opening in full warm sunlight. As it opens, think that all your sources of stress and frustration just melt away; rest in the peace and calm that comes.

I have found that the best way to do this exercise is in the open air. If you have a yard, do it in your yard. If not, find a park or a peaceful stretch of open ground and do it there.

At the end of the exercise, pray that all other human beings can also now be relieved of all forms of stress and send out the fragrance of the open flower you are as waves of light in all directions.

7. Using Rainbow Light

Another ancient Tibetan way of quickly using your own innate healing power to dissolve stress concentrated in any part of your body is the following:

First locate where the stress is crystallized—in your back, or neck, or heart-center. Then imagine that from your fingers stream rays of light of all the colors of the rainbow. Run your light-streaming fingers gently again and again over the place of stress, or, if you prefer, just lay your hand against it, imagining it being irradiated by rainbow light.

You should feel relief quickly. At the end of the exercise, pray for all other beings to be relieved of stress.

Sometimes it helps, I find, to imagine at the beginning of the exercise a source of white light in front of you that streams to you all the different colored lights of the rainbow and empowers you with them.

8. Imagine the Stress in Your Body as a Block of Ice and Let the Divine Melt It

Begin by listening to your body and finding out where your stress is concentrated at the moment. Then imagine that stress as a large lump of black ice.

Now start to pray to whomever you most believe in. Summon up the Buddha or Christ or the Mother as a being of radiant light. Open your entire self in love to the One you have called to you.

Now see that a stream of *red* warm, focused light is streaming out of the heart of the figure before you and is trained on the big lump of ice within you. Imagine the warm red light penetrating and slowly and deliciously dissolving the lump of black ice.

Continue the exercise for as long as you need until you feel relief. At the end, bow inwardly to the being you have asked to heal you and imagine the entire planet bathed in the warmth and power of the red light, healing the sufferings and stresses of sentient beings everywhere.

One Piece of General Advice

Experiment with all eight methods in different kinds and periods of stress. Take notes on which exercise works for you on what kind of stress. Soon you will have become your own "stress alchemist," able to intuit almost immediately what exercise will help you most richly attune body and spirit.

Physical Exercise

IT HAS ALWAYS BEEN KNOWN in the mystical traditions that it is helpful on the Path to have a spry, well-exercised body. I remember my Tibetan mentor Thuksey Rinpoche saying to me after teaching me the visualization practice for the Buddha of compassion: "It is not enough to practice compassion in the abstract; you must also learn to be compassionate to your own body. And the way to be compassionate to your own body is to cherish it and keep it strong and balanced and healthy."

There are three interlinked reasons for being alert to physical well-being on the Path. First, it is hard to meditate or pray with the self-forgetful attention and concentration if you are feeling sick. Second, as I have stressed throughout, there are stages on the Path when the body will be put under great strain from the intensity of the purification your consciousness is undergoing; if you haven't from the very beginning of your spiritual journey looked after your body, you could find yourself getting into serious trouble. Third, there can be no hope of effecting the kind of alchemical fusion of spirit and body, soul and matter, that the later stages of the Direct Path makes possible if reverent attention is not paid to the body and if the body is not kept as far as possible in a state of sensitive well-being.

A Sufi friend of mine once said to me in Paris, "I think of my body like a musical instrument my soul is always trying to play. If the instrument isn't constantly tuned, how can the divine music that my soul wants to play in and through my life be created?"

This need to "tune" the body so that it can be the refined, responsive, and grateful instrument of the soul underlies the Taoist and Confucian adepts' pursuit of different physical regimes, the Hindu and Buddhist mystics' cultivation of hatha yoga, the medieval Christian monks' subtle evolution of a balance between contemplation and manual labor. Many of the most evolved modern practitioners I know are convinced and capable athletes and sportsmen. One famous transpersonal philosopher I admire does an hour at least of weight lifting every day; a Zen abbot I know jogs every morning in San Francisco for at least half an hour; I know several Hindu businessmen who swear by the meditative properties of golf; my greatest spiritual friend at Oxford was a superb skier, skater, and tennis player who maintained that her deepest experiences of what she always called "the Presence" were on the sports field. Before my back trouble dramatically slowed me down, I used to find playing tennis not only invigorating but also, sometimes, exalting because of its elegance, rhythm, and need for constant concentration.

My advice to anyone who is genuinely athletic and who has always enjoyed regular physical exercise is: Keep at it and explore the *spiritual* dimension of what you are doing.

There are five interlinked ways of doing this. First, always meditate for a few minutes before you begin exercising or playing. Ask for the Divine to infuse your body with health and strength and peace and for you to remain aware of the gifts of the energies you will be using. Dedicate the joy you will feel to the happiness of all sentient beings.

Second, while you are exercising or playing, try to remain as far as you can in the witness position—that is, be aware that your body is the instrument of your divine self and "watch" and "witness" what your body and mind are doing with calm, gratitude, and detachment.

Third, be aware of the exercise or sport you are participating in as a form of divine play. Consciously revel in and celebrate the elements of what the Hindu mystics call "lila" in what you are doing.

Michael Murphy in *God and the Kingdom* has written brilliantly of
this aspect of "play" in sport; I have known passionate cricket and
tennis players also who "use" what they are doing to reinvoke the
childlike within them. For most of us, exercising or playing a sport
is a much needed break from the push and shove of "adult responsibility"; make the most of this freedom by trying to release your
playful divine child within it. You can even do this while jogging,
for example. One older lady I know jogs in a purple and green
jumpsuit, listens to Frank Sinatra on her headphones, and every
so often stops—even in the middle of a city street, to break into a
few dance steps. "Hell," she told me, "if I'm going to sweat to keep
healthy, I'm going to have a ball doing it."

Fourth, as you are playing the sport you have chosen, or exercising, remember to offer at intervals all your activity to the Divine. My friend in Oxford who was a wonderful skier used to tell
me that before she turned down the ski slope she would say to
God, "Help me make this a perfect run in your honor." When the
run went well, she said, "I would feel God smiling within my
body." If you are weight lifting, for example, you can dedicate each
lift to the Divine, ask the Divine for the strength you need, consciously thank the Divine when you find you can lift weights heav-
ier than you were able to previously. This simple act of remem-
brance can guide you deeper and deeper into the meaning of what
you are doing. Once I asked a famous old English cricketer why he
loved the game so much. He thought for a long time and replied,
"Because in its elegance, dear boy, it is a gentleman's form of
prayer."

Fifth, when you have finished what you are doing, remember
with gratitude all the joy it has given you and dedicate that joy to
all other sentient beings. One of my friends in Paris was an international rugby player who was also, rather incongruously, a passionate Catholic and devotee of the Virgin. After every game he
told me he would offer all the joy he had had in playing to her "so
that she can take it and give it away to anyone who might need it."
Once a year he would work with disabled children in the South of
France. "God has given me the ecstasy of health, a firm body, and a
game I will adore playing as long as I can still stagger around on

two legs. I want to help all those—especially kids—who don't have these blessings."

You don't have to be athletic at all to keep up a physically and spiritually satisfying regimen, however. All you need to do is exercise gently but regularly and with spiritual intelligence.

HERE ARE THREE FORMS of physical exercise that almost anyone can do: walking, swimming, and dancing.

Walking

My father told me when I was about six years old that "there is no problem that walking cannot help you solve." Thirty years later, when researching aborigine culture, I discovered that for the aborigines, walking is the most sacred of all activities, the one they consider most naturally attuned to the rhythms of the cosmos and so rich with healing and calming properties. I remember seeing Bede Griffiths—then in his mid-eighties—returning from a long morning walk down the riverbank near his ashram in South India; his joy and balance seemed to radiate from the earth itself. I asked him that morning what he thought about on his walks. He looked shocked. "I don't *think*, dear boy; I try to become one with the air and water and earth and with my breathing and I try and revel in the seamless dance my body and mind are doing with the world around me." He added, "Sometimes when I am really awake I really see that the trees are angels."

I have always loved walking and try to walk for an hour and a half every day, wherever I am. Like many passionate walkers, I find I love to repeat the same itinerary. Such repetition for me becomes an exercise in both stability and the subtle ways of change; it is like hearing the same sonata played by different master pianists.

Since walking has always been for me my primary form of exercise, I have constantly experimented with ways of integrating it with spiritual practice. Here are seven simple ways I have found to

use walking as a way of experiencing and deepening the union between spirit and body. What I suggest is that you try them all for
three or four days at a stretch and note what you experience; then
choose, if you want, the two or three methods you find work most
naturally for you.

METHOD 1: KEEPING CHRIST OR THE
BUDDHA ON YOUR RIGHT SHOULDER

This wonderful method was taught to me by the abbess of a
contemplative order in Oxford. She was a vibrant, big-boned, red-
faced woman straight out of Chaucer, and we were great friends;
because she couldn't leave her cloister and needed to exercise every
day, she had had to invent things "to spicen life up a bit."

"And this is what I came up with twenty years ago now," she
told me on a dreary winter afternoon. "I've been using it ever since.
When you start to walk, imagine Jesus or Mary [and I'll add here
anyone you deeply love or believe in] standing on your right shoulder, radiating divine light and love to you, and wanting to come on
a walk with you. As you walk, just imagine that you are walking
with them, and concentrate in your heart on their living presence.

"Another variation on this," she added, "is to imagine that as
you are walking, you are walking around a shrine to Jesus or the
Buddha or around Jesus or the Buddha themselves. This makes
every step you take an act of reverence and prayer."

This is a method I have used often and always found calming
and purifying. Another beautiful variation I have used is to imagine Jesus or the Mother actually walking silently by your side, filling you with their joy and peace and subtly waking you up to the
divine in you and around you.

METHOD 2: WALKING WITH LIGHT

This method of infusing walking with an awareness of light
and divine energy was taught to me by an English Tibetan Buddhist friend who had learned it from the Dzogchen tradition.

Before you begin your walk, imagine your entire body as being
full of light. Think of it as being a bonfire of unified light. As you

start to walk, walk as the divine human being you are, joyfully, serenely, spaciously, conscious that you are streaming invisible healing light to all the beings around you.

It is especially important that you relish the joy of being in a light-filled body. Breathe freely and let your innate divine energy shine out. Feel that walking in this way liberates you from all stress and worry.

"As you walk," my friend said, "have complete faith that everything and everyone you pass will be made subtly happier by the light radiating from you. Rejoice in the secret power God is giving you and keep saying in your heart-center, 'May all beings everywhere be happy!' Feeling and acting like this will help you make your walk an act of offering, and help you to transform your other daily activities."

METHOD 3: ENTERING INTO DARKNESS, AND LEADING OUT OF DARKNESS (ADAPTED FROM A HINDU EXERCISE)

I learned this method from a holy man in Benares and practiced it with him walking between shrines on the banks of the Ganges.

Imagine that as you are on your way to wherever you are walking—to the end of the beach or to the top of a particular hill or into town—you are consciously entering into the dark world of suffering and needy beings. Pray, "With every step I take my joy and peace be given to all those suffering everywhere!" If you want to, imagine a particular group of suffering beings—say, those with AIDS or those afflicted with extreme poverty—and imagine each step you take sends them healing light energy. As you return, imagine that you are leading out all sentient beings from the various dark realms in which they suffer. Imagine all of them follow in a dancing, joyful light-army behind you and feel their relief and ecstasy filling your heart with power and strength. Pray, "May all those my good intentions are leading out of suffering always stay happy and free!"

This is a very powerful exercise to use as you work on your resolve to be of service to all beings. It can over time give you a precise sense of how every activity can be charged with sacred power by the quality of the intention behind it.

METHOD 4: WALKING WITH A MANTRA

This is the method I use almost every day, and I find it has a tremendous power to transform even the most mundane stroll into a form of prayer.

Select a mantra you want to work with and knead into your deepest awareness and inwardly dedicate your whole walk to reciting it in your heart-center. As you keep on saying the mantra, imagine that it opens like a burning golden rose within your heart and starts to radiate healing light throughout your body, cleansing it of all sadness, blocks, and stress, and penetrating and opening and illumining every cell.

Imagine, too, that as you keep on saying the mantra, the golden light starts to spill out of your body and radiate in all directions from you in God's name. If you are passing houses, for example, consciously direct the power of the mantra and the light to the happiness and well-being of everyone who lives in them; if you are passing flower beds or fields, direct the light to keep the earth fertile and help everything blossom. Extend the mantra's light protection secretly to everyone you pass or who passes you.

When you return from your walk, pause before your door and with great love and joy send the golden light streaming from the open flower in your heart to the four directions.

I have found that the most effective way of kneading the mantra into the substance of my awareness and body is to try to combine a rhythmical recitation of it with as nearly synchronized a rhythm of walking as possible.

METHOD 5: USING WALKING AS A WAY
OF UNCOVERING SACRED MEANING

This method has a complicated-sounding title, but it is simple and used by practitioners in many mystical systems. It is especially effective during times of powerful spiritual initiation.

Begin your walk by selecting a dream, vision, or inward illumination you have received either recently or in the past and that you
want to explore and deepen. Before you begin, try to recall the
dream, vision, or insight as clearly as you can in all its detail. Then
meditate briefly and ask for divine grace and for the Divine to use
the calm and harmony of your walk to take you deeper into the
truth of what you experienced.

Now begin your walk, intuiting your mind to return constantly
and calmly to what you have chosen to explore. You will find that
the rhythm of walking will help "open up" your dream or vision or
inward experience in the most natural and marvelous way; paral-
lels and insights will suddenly flash into your imagination, and
any guidance you were meant to receive through what you are exploring will flower.

You will find too—as I have many times—that the power of
what you are uncovering will spill over into your body, which will
itself feel more and more light and relaxed. You may even find that
you, your body, and the insight you discover become momentarily
and deliciously one. If that happens, be grateful and send the joy
of unity to all sentient beings.

When you walk using this method, be sure to carry a pen and a
piece of paper. Important teachings can be given directly to you,
and essential messages can arrive from your own deepest awareness.
Try to note them as they occur, in their first and freshest form.

METHOD 6: PRACTICING MINDFULNESS
AS YOU WALK

Being mindful is being transparently and undistractedly present in whatever you are doing. You can practice mindfulness,
then, in any and every situation.

I find that practicing mindfulness while walking makes me
over time far more attuned to the ways I use my body even when
sitting still or just standing casually.

The ancient Theravada Buddhist instruction for "mindfulness
by walking" is simple to give but hard to do; an old Buddhist text
says: "When you walk, from the time you pick up your foot and

place it down again, be mindful of the lifting, pushing forward, and dropping down of the foot."

When I practice this, I devote the first half of my walk "just" to being mindful, to being aware of "lifting," "pushing forward," and "dropping down" my feet, while also trying to be conscious of my breathing. On the second half of the walk, I do what is called "noting." I count every time I lift my left foot up to ten, and then begin again, over and over again. This combination of "being mindful" and "noting" leads, I find, to increasing precision of awareness of everything, and to profound calm of mind.

If I am walking in nature or on a level piece of ground where there aren't too many people, say, on a beach, I practice "noting" by walking up and down for twenty minutes or so. This greatly helps focus and concentration and can lead to deep and joyful experiences of unity between body and spirit.

METHOD 7: UNITY WALK

I call this method "Unity Walk" because through it you attempt to experience the innate "unity" of all experience, what Bede Griffiths called "the seamless dance my body and mind are doing with the world around me."

The essential principle of the unity walk is: Consider and "know" everything you see, smell, touch, feel on your walk as different aspects of the One you are one with in the core of your consciousness. The flower you love in the flower bed is the smile of the One; the wind brushing against your arm is the One moving against you; the faces of the people you pass in the street are all different masks of the one face that is also yours; feel every tiny sensation in your body as belonging to the One living in and as you.

It helps greatly when you are doing this exercise to say the Sanskrit word for divine peace, *Shantih,* again and again in your heart-center. As your experience of inner profound peace deepens, your unity with everything inside you and outside you can naturally shine out.

At the end of your walk, extend peace and unity to all beings in the four directions, and dedicate any insights or joys you may have experienced to the happiness of all beings everywhere.

Swimming

Many people find, as I do, that swimming is as powerful and spiritually integrating a form of physical exercise as walking. I love it because it is graceful, harmonious, an exercise in elegant focus. For me, too, swimming is associated with the happiest and freest memories of childhood, with days on the beach and the fragrant warmth of the Indian Ocean. Whenever I enter the water—even of a communal or civic pool—I feel immediately both comforted and elated, as if I am entering the body of the Mother.

Last year I was bathing with my mother on a beach in South India. It was near the end of a month that we had spent together healing many things, and laughing and talking. We were swimming alongside each other, and my mother turned to me and smiled. "So here we are," she said, "being cradled together in the arms of the deep." As she spoke, I realized that that was how I always felt when I was swimming—as if the "arms of the deep" were "cradling" me.

The seven exercises for walking can be ingeniously adapted for swimming also. You can "swim with light," with a Divine Presence by your side irradiating you with joy and energy, swim while being mindful, and while working with a mantra; you can work with a dream or vision or inner insight while swimming; you can meditate on the unity between you and your divine self and body, the water, and the pool. I have worked with variations with all of these over the years and found them all valuable.

EXERCISE I: SCOOPING UP THE WATER'S POWER

A Taoist teacher taught me an exercise especially for use while swimming which I find exhilarating.

As you swim, imagine that your entire body is as flowing, supple, sensitive as the water you are going through. Ninety percent of your body is water. Imagine that the other ten percent is now infused by all the grace and flexibility of water and that your blood and life energy are circulating all around your body unhinderedly.

Continue with this meditation for ten minutes, using every

gesture with your feet and hands and every sensation of the water against your body as a way of deepening your imagination of a completely supple frame and a completely unhindered flow of blood and energy.

My Taoist friend recommended saying over and over "May every muscle in me flow like water, may my whole body have the grace of water, may my blood and life energy circulate with the freedom of water."

In the second part of the exercise she invited me to make an effect as I swam to *scoop* the "power," or chi (the Taoist Chinese word for "life energy"), of the water into my body. So as I reached forward with my arms, I was to imagine the power of the water I scooped back rushing into and through my body, clarifying and purifying it. "Imagine the water," she said, "rushing in a great wave of light from your crown to the bottom of your feet. If you do this, you will be filling your body as you swim with the chi of the water, and for a Taoist nothing is stronger than water. Even the hardest rocks yield to the power of water in the end."

When you finish your swim, take time to imagine your whole body filled now with the chi of the water and so relaxed, supple, and peaceful. Send the new strength of your body as rays of healing soft white light to all four directions.

EXERCISE 2: ENJOYING THE CREST AND THE HOLLOW

There is another Taoist exercise that is exciting to practice when you are swimming in the sea. My friend called it "Enjoying the Crest and the Hollow."

When you are riding the crest of a wave, imagine your life in flower and rejoice with your whole body; when the crest topples and you follow the downflow of the wave, imagine a cycle of life where difficulty follows success, illness health, sorrow joy, and realize that such a cycle is just as natural as the movement you are making now, and just as easy to be integrated within a "whole" vision of things. "Just as there is a time for the crest," she said, "so there is a time to follow the wave as it breaks. Reflect on the grace, surrender, harmony that allow you to do both naturally and without fear."

It is wonderful to accompany this exercise by light chanting or making sounds. When you are riding the crest of the wave, for example, you can shout with joy, and when you are following the wave's breaking, you could howl. This is a simple and elemental way of getting in touch with the cyclical nature of life; your cries of joy and howls will very soon come to seem like different aspects of the same music in the same way as "riding the crest" and "following the fall" will reveal themselves as two halves of one continuous movement.

EXERCISE 3: THE HEAT EXERCISE

One final, simple exercise that my Taoist friend taught me to use while swimming was what she called "The Heat Exercise."

"If you are under a lot of stress," she said, "imagine it as concentrated in little balls of fire throughout your body. Try to locate the position of those balls of fire exactly. Then, when you swim, imagine the water rushing through your body and putting out those balls of fire. Consciously visualize the water entering your body and rushing to the place where the stress is concentrated and utterly extinguishing it. When you shower after swimming, stand under the shower as if you were standing under a waterfall in the open air and envisage all the chi of the waterfall purifying and cleansing you completely. Imagine now that all the balls of fire are replaced one by one by balls of softly shining gold. This gold is the energy of stress transformed into divine power, the power of effortless strength. As you dress, relish your new strength and inner healed grace."

This exercise is most powerful I find when you meditate for ten minutes beforehand, offering your stress or anxiety to the Mother for healing; working with a mantra throughout is also very effective.

Dancing

I have always known that dancing was holy, a form of prayer and a marvelous way of doing what the Sufis call "drinking the wine";

savoring the ecstatic presence of the Divine in reality. From my earliest childhood I loved to dance; I can remember dancing in the monsoon rain on the roof of my house in Delhi, with the lightning crackling around me and the rain soaking my clothes, drunk on freedom. Sometimes my ayah, Mary, would join me, kicking up her legs and singing hymns in a gravelly, smoke-stained voice.

One of the reasons I love Rumi so deeply is that he knew the healing and liberating power of dance. When Shams, his beloved teacher, disappeared for the last and final time in 1247, Rumi went mad with grief and survived only by singing and dancing himself back to health. He had been a scholar and teacher; songs of mystic ecstasy now poured from him. He had been a dignified theologian; he now became an ecstatic dancer, evolving from his longing and visionary experience a form of dancing that was later formalized in the Mevlevi order as "whirling." I recommend to everyone that they learn a simple form of this "whirling" dance of the Mevlevis from a qualified instructor who can also lead them gently through all its manifold mystical meanings; it is one of the most complete ways of connecting "heaven" and "earth," "body" and "soul," that has ever been devised.

SIMPLIFIED VERSION OF RUMI'S DANCE

I have evolved for myself a simplified form of Rumi's great dance, which I would like to share with you:

Begin by ten minutes of seated meditation on the following two quotations from Rumi himself:

> One day in your wineshop, I drank a little wine
> And threw off this robe of my body
> And knew, drunk on you, this world is harmony
> Creation, destruction I am dancing for them both.

And

> Dancing is not rising to your feet painlessly like a whirl of dust blown about by the wind. Dancing is when you rise above both worlds, tearing your heart to pieces and giving up your soul.

These two wonderful excerpts from Rumi belong together; when you meditate on them, imagine in your heart-core what it would be to dance for creation and destruction, for the anguish you suffer as well as for the joy, knowing the whole of life as one unity and one gift, "tearing your heart to pieces and giving up your soul." The Sufi teacher who taught me how to "whirl" in Paris told me, "When you dance, throw away all memories and ideas, do not want to be anywhere but on the burning diamond-point of the present."

The purpose of these first minutes of meditation is to focus your whole being on the deepest meaning of the dance—that it is a celebration of the cosmic dance that God is always enacting. One of the first images I ever received of the Divine as a child was of God the dancer in the form of the dancing Shivas in my aunt Bella's house. This image of God as dancer is echoed in almost every religion, in the wild orgiastic dances of Dionysus, in Jesus being hailed as "the Lord of the dance," in a shaker hymn, in the light-dazzled "dance" that the Sufis believe every atom is doing every moment out of love for the Beloved. When you dance, you are dancing in honor of the great dance that is creating all things— the great dance of masculine and feminine, yin and yang, spirit and matter. You are dancing the dance of the sacred marriage; you and the universe both are between invisible spirit and animated matter, heavenly design and earthly fulfillment. The dance is the "place" where all opposites meet and are transformed, where agony can be transmuted into beauty and grace, loss be changed into another form of possession, "creation" and "destruction" harmonized in a rapture that contains but transcends both.

The image of the Divine as dance is one of inexhaustible richness; allow your mind as you meditate to be perfumed by this richness, and imagine, as you go deeper and deeper into the meaning of the cosmic dance, your whole body being possessed by its fierce, gorgeous, graceful energy. Imagine yourself as you would move if you were completely surrendered to the dancing power of the Divine; see yourself in your heart's eye moving freely, with sweet and wild abandon, your limbs entirely supple, your every movement electric with divine inspiration.

Now, in the closing act of the meditation, ask the Beloved to possess and use your body for his praise. Pray to be an instrument of the cosmic dance; pray for your whole being to be brought into the sacred nondual knowledge of the unity of opposites, of life and death, heaven and earth, agony and ecstasy, that is the heart-wisdom of the dance. I find it helps me at this moment to imagine myself taking on the calm eternal smile of a dancing Shiva—the smile beyond opposites, of triumph over all the games and masks of time. As I pray to be possessed by the Beloved, then, I try to smile a Shiva smile and allow it to permeate and unify my whole mind and body in calm bliss.

The movements I now do are very simple and are taken from one part of the much longer Mevlevi ceremony. Originally I evolved this form of the dance when my back was out; later I found that it could be done, with great effect, by anyone of whatever age and of almost every state of health.

I stand up and start to "turn" very gently around the room. The music I use varies—from original Sufi *ney* music from Konya to Aretha Franklin, Tina Turner, and lighter forms of rock. As I circle, I imagine myself a sun burning with divine light, radiating light in all directions.

Now I choose an imaginary center in the room around which I am "turning." This center represents the Beloved, in whose honor and praise I am dancing. Sometimes I place in the middle of the room a table with an open rose on it. Sometimes I find myself singing out loud or chanting one of the names of God I especially love.

After about five minutes of "turning" and letting the passion of the dance possess me more and more, I raise my right hand toward heaven to receive the divine grace and power and extend my left hand toward the earth to direct the divine grace from heaven to earth and all its beings. As I go on, I try to meditate beyond thought on what it is to be a human divine being, a "dancer" between two worlds, the lightning rod of the connection between heaven and earth. The more devotedly and concentratedly I "turn" and continue "turning," the more light flows to me down my right hand and the more power I feel streaming to the earth and all beings from my left.

Sometimes if a friend is sick or in psychological trouble, I will dance for him or her and direct all the divine energy coming from my left hand to his or her healing; sometimes when a world problem is preoccupying me, I will dance for those trapped in its fire.

I find that dancing like this invariably fills me with joy, peace, power, and the sense of holy accomplishment. The more you believe that grace is really streaming through your dancing body, the more joy you will feel in giving it away to those who need it in and for God.

After about ten or fifteen minutes, I come to a stop and turn off the music to savor in stillness and silence the union with all things that the dance has invoked. Then I give away to all beings whatever joy or insight the dance has given me. The most heartwarming way of doing this is by circling slowly four times with your arms extended in all directions.

You may not always have time to do the whole practice—which takes, for maximum effect, about a half hour. Don't hesitate to improvise smaller practices from it for yourself, or just to put on dance music and dance for God in exactly the way you feel most free.

I can remember at least five occasions in discos in Paris and New York when I was dancing with such freedom and joy that all barriers between myself and others melted wholly away. What had moments before been a worldly night scene became for the moments of that immersion Presence, ritual, and prayer. It isn't the music or even the place that matters; what matters is that you should try to dance in such a way that you lose your self-consciousness in the joy of moving. As Rumi says in one of his odes: "Pluck out the thorn of self-awareness and dance to shatter yourself free."

One grand older lady I know dances in the privacy of her studio to the voice of the great soprano Claudia Muzio; one day I arrived early for our lunch appointment and caught her at it. She blushed like a schoolgirl and said, "Now you know the secret of my immortal youth!" A translator of Arabic and Sanskrit texts I met in Bruges confessed to me that sometimes neither meditation nor mantra could refresh his soul; only dancing to Donna Summer's version of "Day of Independence" *always* did the trick.

Over the years I have compiled for myself a whole set of music for dance that I know can dislodge or dissolve almost any sullen and ugly mood; toward the end of our long agony with Meera, Eryk and I would dance again and again to Tina Turner's "I Don't Want to Hurt No More" in our San Francisco apartment, feeling her great generosity of soul flood our bodies and hearts, lighting our beings by the tenderly blazing torch of hers.

Once you discover the tremendous power of dance to melt soul and body together and to initiate you in ways beyond thought to your own inmost power, you will seek out as many opportunities you can to dance, and will become what a dance instructor I know calls the "magician of your own joy," knowing exactly what music will help you with what mood. For myself, I find that when I am angry, dancing to medieval polyphony calms me; when I am tired, I need rock or reggae; when I feel hungry to refine or express what I am feeling, dancing to the voice of Maria Callas almost always helps me, for her naked honesty of emotion connects me immediately to whatever I am blocking in my own heart.

Sometimes, too, when I am alone in my house and feeling dazzled with gratitude for my life and work and relationship with Eryk, I dance to the charged silence and the desert sun pouring in through our high open windows; nothing fills the body more quickly or completely with divine power and joy, I find, than spontaneously expressing gratitude in dance. No wonder the Catholic Church banned dancing at mass in the third century; the male hierarchy must have seen how simply people could connect with their divine selves through it without the need for priests or mediators. Who needs an archbishop or a guru when you can give your body to God in the dance and know God dancing in you as simply as you know your own breath?

THE LAUGHING DANCE

There is a Taoist dance exercise I was taught once by a Chinese friend from Taiwan. We were staying with friends in the country in

Italy; the instruction took place by a pool, and in swimming trunks—his had swirling dragons all over them. "Now I am going to teach you the Laughing Dance," he said. "My grandmother used to say that if you did this twice a day, you would live to be a hundred and healthy and wise." I have since discovered that the Laughing Dance is, indeed, an ancient and venerable mystic dance used for several thousand years by the Chinese Taoists and almost certainly by the shamans before them.

Begin to dance happily, in your own way and to your own rhythm, with your arms swung wide open, your face tilted upward in joy toward the sky. Kick your legs gently outward, imagining as you do so that you are kicking away from yourself all forms of stress and distress that could possibly stain your happiness. ("If you have some nasty enemies doing bad things to you," my friend said, "it is permitted by the Taoist deities to send a mild kick in their direction. Not to do them harm, mind you, but to give them a warning.")

"Now," my friend said, "as you dance with your head tilted back, laugh and keep on laughing, on and on, like the bamboo leaves in the wind."

For those of you who have never heard bamboo leaves in the wind, they make a rapid, high rustling noise that stops only when the wind has. You will almost certainly find, as I did, that my first attempts at "laughing like bamboo leaves" were rather ghoulish; but you'll soon get the hang of it.

Nothing is more important on the Path than a sense of humor. Humor is an essential facet of humility and one of the great secret occult powers; its ability to dissolve unnecessary grief and to put necessary ordeal in perspective is one of the Divine's deepest gifts to us. This Laughing Dance is wonderfully effective in helping you to find the wit in almost every situation; even if the ordeal you are going through cannot be laughed at, knowing you *can* still laugh—and laugh prolongedly and wildly and as a form of "dancing prayer"—will give you access to your own inner divinity. Anyone trying to effect change in the world will need to do this dance often. One religious editor I taught this dance to in Paris does it before she has to go and defend a book to her stone-faced money-minded bosses; a film director I know does it every morning before the shoot of the day begins and finds it helps him immeasurably with the hysterias of his "stars." I performed it in the wings before one of the most important talks I have ever had to give—at a Common Boundary conference just after my first interview telling some of the truth of Meera's abuse came out. I knew there would be a lot of hostile, angry people in the audience; I couldn't allow any of my past anguish to cloud the truth of what I was trying to communicate about the Mother; so, among the pipes and tubes of the back corridor of an airless Washington hotel, I shook my legs out, tilted my head back, and "laughed like the bamboo leaves in the wind." Then I went and gave one of the happiest, most relaxed speeches of my life.

Sometimes when I do this dance I combine it with an inward recitation of the words of Rumi: "Creation, destruction, I am dancing for them both." The laughter then becomes my attempt to mirror the divine laughter and so embody the divine laughter of my self. Divine laughter, which I have experienced in dreams, visions, and in moments of freedom and tender exhilaration, is an utterly childlike laughter, delicious, abandoned, untamable. As I dance, then I try to laugh with this freedom. Just try it; you'll be amazed at what resources of hilarity you discover within yourself.

WORKING WITH THE FIVE ESSENTIAL RHYTHMS

I first encountered this powerful method of using dance to integrate body and soul in Gabrielle Roth's superb book *Sweat Your Prayers*. When I met her at Esalen four years ago, Gabrielle said to me, "When you let your body dance, you strip away all the dogmas and lies until all you're left with is the soul." I wrote it in a notebook in large red letters and kept it for an inspiration whenever I dance.

In *Sweat Your Prayers* Gabrielle recommends working with *five essential rhythms—flowing, staccato, chaos, lyrical,* and *stillness.* These five rhythms encompass the different aspects and archetypes of the cosmic dance and the different energies of creation and destruction, masculine and feminine power.

Over the year I have been working with Gabrielle's method privately, I follow the order of rhythms that she has laid out in her book; I find that this discipline greatly helps the effectiveness of what I experience.

In *flowing* I select music that helps me discover my feminine generous energies, usually soul or classical music, and then I start to move as gracefully as I can, experiencing as fully as I can the sense of release and unboundedness that comes to me naturally when I allow the feminine in me.

In *staccato* I select music where dynamic male energy is on rich and explosive display—African dance music or sometimes the fast movements of Beethoven symphonies. Then I enter the yang side of my spirit, allowing its forceful, sometimes sweeping and jerky and fierce powers to possess me and dictate how I move.

In *chaos* I usually don't put on any music at all, and allow myself to dissolve in a cauldron of divine energy. I see this period as one in which the feminine and masculine sides of myself come together, mate, part, hiss at, and finally embrace each other. In the first two movements I feel I have been experiencing the two sides of the Godhead and of my own human divinity; now I feel I enter the burning chaotic core of creation, where these two aspects of my being can dance wildly into each other and in the process birth me afresh as a whole and inwardly healed sacred androgyne.

In the *lyrical* section I invariably concentrate on the *wonder* of being reborn in a dimension of sacred dance, in the divine dimension of purity and joy. For me, this section is nearly always the most revelatory; I feel myself a freshly born divine child roaming with infinite delicacy through a new world. I nearly always use religious music here—especially that of Josquin des Pres or a Byzantine chant. I try to make all my movements reflect and engender joy and awe.

In the last section, *stillness,* I allow myself gradually to dance more and more slowly to a halt, savoring each stage of returning to the stillness that is the birthplace of the energies of the dance. A great Hindu temple dancer, Ram Gopal, once told me: "At the end of dancing for God, I stand totally still and imagine that I have unrolled from my heart-center stretch after stretch of golden silk into the infinite. Now, as I stand with my heart open and empty, I receive it all back. All the silk that I have unraveled from myself ravels back into me. I receive back all the golden adoration I have poured out, not as my own reward but as a pure grace of God."

Remembering what Ram told me, I allow myself to stand and to receive back into my deepest self everything I have poured out and to experience the grace of God in this gift of returned power. Then, consciously and with reverence, I give everything I have felt and experienced away to all beings in all directions.

I refer all those who want to work in greater detail with these five energies to Gabrielle's book; I have found for myself that the simple exercise I have just adapted and evolved from Gabrielle's teaching is profoundly satisfying, all the more so for being simple and easy to do.

Each time I do this particular exercise, I try to be as aware as possible of what in myself needs most work. If I am feeling jagged and nervous, for example, I concentrate on the *flowing* and *lyrical* sections and prolong them until their wisdom has seeped deep into me. If I am feeling sluggish or bored or blocked, I pour myself into the *staccato* and *chaos* sections, using them consciously to arouse sacred energy and to dance myself forcefully out of whatever stasis I am mired in.

If I am furious or bitter about something, I try to use the energy of that fury or bitterness to fuel the staccato section. To be able to release rage, I find, it is essential to allow yourself to feel it; feeling it in the context of a dedicated sacred dance can be very healing; by getting out all the boiling, dark energy in a sacred context, you can possess it rather than be possessed *by* it, make it work for your invigoration and not against your health or nerves.

Dancing out your fury and bitterness can also help you *crystallize* the kernel of wise perception hidden in both and separate it from negative emotion; dancing out anger, for instance, in the staccato section can help you understand the larger terms and clarities of the situation in which your anger has been aroused. Bitterness, I find, is harder to transmute; dancing it out, however, you can often find yourself able to express the wounded vulnerability that bitterness often defends. If this vulnerability or grief appear in me, I find it helpful to switch to the lyrical section and work with them so that I can at last really let myself feel them and let my feeling them shape form and beauty. In working with anger and bitterness in this way in the rhythms of the dance, you can teach yourself extraordinary life lessons about how to alchemize negative emotions and how to use their energy for healing and greater wisdom and expressiveness.

Unifying Body,
Mind, and Spirit

I HAVE TRIED TO SHOW how walking, swimming, and dancing can all be made vehicles for experiencing the union of body and spirit. Now I want to concentrate on two particular spiritually evolved physical disciplines—yoga and tai chi—both of which are gaining hundreds of thousands of practitioners throughout the West.

Before I describe in some detail both yoga and tai chi, however, I would like to focus briefly on some exercises that can help us awaken our own healing energy.

Modern research and the work of Larry Dossey among others has shown conclusively that the power of prayer and spiritual practice over the body are extraordinary. Study after study have revealed, for example, that people who are sick and are being prayed for (sometimes without their knowing) get healthier more quickly than those who are just being physically treated. This "new" information—which is not really new at all and wouldn't surprise anyone with a mystical insight into the fundamental unity of body and spirit—is destined eventually to transform medicine.

Healing Exercises

All of the mystical disciplines have developed certain practices to help the adept awaken his or her own healing energy, to utilize and focus the healing power of the spirit on the body. I have made an extensive study of the many different kinds of techniques in-volved—from visualization to breathing to autohypnosis—and ex-perimented with all of them during my years of suffering from a bad back. I would like to give here the two exercises that I have found the most powerful of all—the first in *awakening* sacred heal-ing energy and the second in *directing* it. The first exercise is adapted from a Tibetan Buddhist practice; the second is my own mixture of several exercises from different sources—Hindu, Taoist, and modern. Practiced together, I have found they are powerful and profoundly energizing.

I think it is essential when you are doing exercises for awaken-ing your own sacred healing energy to always begin by meditating on the Divine—the Source of all healing power. The more deeply and devotedly you pray for divine power to be awakened in you, the more immediately you will feel that power and the more power will be given to you.

EXERCISE FOR AWAKENING
HEALING SACRED ENERGY

Sit comfortably and breathe naturally. Begin to meditate on the miracle that your body is—with all its interrelated organs and muscles and intricate networks of veins and nerves. I find it help-ful to have a detailed and beautiful anatomical representation of the body to look at during this part of the meditation—the one I use is highly colored and very precise, and just glancing at it awak-ens in me an awe at the divine workmanship that created us all.

I find, too, that it helps to be as precise as possible in invoking the different aspects of the miracle of the body (this is where an anatomical drawing can be helpful). Move slowly in your mind from aspect to aspect of the physical marvel you are; each time you move to a new aspect, offer it to the Divine and thank the Divine for it. Slowly you should feel that your entire body is glorious, beautiful, and holy.

Now start to make an internal image of one cell of your body. See and feel and know its extraordinary dancing vitality. Then try to imagine it growing as vast as the universe. Celebrate the beauty and shining power of the one cell you have imagined by chanting in its praise or putting on sacred music in its honor.

Still chanting or listening to the sacred music you have chosen, extend your sense of awe from the one cell you have chosen to all cells in your body. Feel how blessed your whole body is and how it is brimming with healing power.

Now return to the one cell you imagined and see it glowing with brilliant light. Feel the warmth of this light. Chant or play sacred music again in honor of the light now streaming from this illumined cell. As you chant or listen, imagine your entire body filling slowly with brilliant light.

If a part of your body is in pain, direct the light intensely to that part and visualize it entirely healed. Do this again and again, with extreme focus, reveling in the power to heal your own being that the Divine is giving you, allowing your chanting or the power of the sacred music you are playing to inspire you deeply. Imagine that as you work with the light in your body, believing in its power, it does not deplete at all; on the contrary, it grows more and more brilliant. The Tibetan monk who taught me this exercise said, "You should imagine that your body becomes brilliant as a billion suns."

Rest as this cosmic bonfire of healing energy-as-light you now are, feeling all your cells dancing in bliss and emitting healing in all directions to all beings.

The best times for doing this healing practice, I have found, are first thing in the early morning, when our powers of visualization tend to be freshest, or at twilight, when the body is often at its most peaceful.

EXERCISE FOR DIRECTING SACRED ENERGY

First relax totally by lying down on a mattress or the floor and breathing in and out deeply and calmly nine times.

Then start to be aware of the calmness that begins to pervade your whole body as you relax; be especially aware of your back resting against the mattress or floor and of how gravity is tenderly but firmly "grounding you." At the same time, be aware, too, of how boundless your calmed body now feels; relish your breathing. Feel the energy starting to move in every part of your body—with special concentration on that part of the body you want to be healed.

For the next fifteen minutes, use this awakened calm energy and direct it to the place that needs healing in the following way: Move the part you want healed very slowly and naturally backward and forward, up and down, or to the side. As you move it, concentrate completely on every sensation this moving creates; what you will become aware of is that your body is like a vast, floating sea of interconnected energy. Even the slightest "wave" of movement creates "waves" throughout the rest of you.

Now imagine that the divine being you especially love appears in divine splendor in the air above your body. His or her body should be imagined as exactly symmetrical with yours and exactly aligned with yours from above. From the being you have invoked streams of brilliant red-gold light, the light of divine healing. Feel at first that the light penetrates and cleanses your whole body in great pulsing waves that wash you from the crown of your head to the soles of your feet. Then concentrate the red-gold light on whatever part of your body you feel needs most help, and relish the blissful heat that will arise.

Now imagine that the divine being you have invoked descends from the air above you and merges completely into your body, sending throughout it waves of blissful, warm red-gold light. Offer up the part of yourself that most needs healing one last time, imagining it lit up now like a crystal with brilliant red-gold light.

Then, praying for continued divine help and thanking God for the healing that has already been done, rest in peace for as long as you can, visualizing yourself as completely whole and healed and well in mind, heart, soul, and body.

One very powerful way of ending this exercise is to say a series of affirmations. Traditionally, the mystical healing systems tell us that all affirmations should be kept in the present tense, as if what is asked for has already been granted. So say, for example, "I am completely healed of my exhaustion," or "my back pain," again and again, calmly and with faith.

This method is especially powerful, I have found, with the management of physical pain. When my back was out, I would use it sometimes four or five times a day, and especially strongly before speaking engagements. One of the most distressing effects of prolonged pain is a sense of helplessness. If you use this healing method, you will discover you are not helpless at all. Your pain will not disappear, but it will diminish and you will feel happier, calmer, and stronger.

Yoga

One of the most exquisite and beneficial ways of tuning the body to become a healthy, supple, transparent instrument of the soul is to practice the physical aspect of the Indian spiritual system known as yoga or hatha yoga. *Yoga* is a term for spiritual discipline and derives from the Sanskrit *yuj*, which means, among other things, to join, direct, concentrate upon, and union and communion. *Hatha* means "force" and represents the union of two words—*ha*, sun, and *tha*, moon. The best definition I ever heard of what hatha yoga is was given to me by my first yoga teacher, Marie-Thérèse, a Frenchwoman whom I studied with in Pondicherry over twenty years ago, and who first introduced me to the wonders of this great tradition. She said, "Hatha yoga is the ancient Indian system of physical postures and breathing exercises that balances the opposing masculine and feminine forces in the body, the 'sun' and 'moon' in you. When these are balanced, you will be healthy and supple and graceful and your mind will be peaceful."

I will always be grateful for what she went on to say next: "Never think that what you are learning with me is a series of physical exercises that are meant only to make you more beautiful and strong. They will, of course, make you stronger; they will help you digest your food better, help you conserve and enrich your energy when you want to, and so help keep you younger, and they will enable you to keep more physically and sexually active for longer than normal forms of exercise will. The real goal of hatha yoga, however, is not to reinforce or bolster your physical narcissism but to provide your divine self with a perfect violin on which it can play its marvelous music. When Patanjali first formulated the principles of yoga in the third century B.C., he stressed that hatha yoga was a part of other systems of yoga that included the yogas of action, devotion, and meditation. Hatha yoga, then, was evolved to provide the serious seeker with the best and healthiest possible vehicle for his or her search and to open up the seeker's body to the peace of mind and radiant bliss of their spirit."

Marie-Thérèse advised us from the beginning to concentrate on both the physical *and* spiritual aspects of the hatha yoga exercises. Again and again she would say, "The more you allow these wonderful physical exercises to introduce you to the peace and harmony of your spirit, the more friendly you will feel toward your body and the more you will marry your physical life with the life of divine love."

I never became a very proficient student of hatha yoga, but I did learn several simple exercises that over the years have helped me immeasurably to slow myself down, attain some measure of peace of mind in the whirlwind of work and stress, and keep my body as healthy and supple as possible. In my late forties I appreciate their efficacy more and more; you do not have to be any kind of expert or superman (or superwoman) to derive a great deal of spiritual joy and physical benefit from them.

One of the most devout hopes for the spread of the vision of the Direct Path is that hatha yoga would be taught to everyone from an early age in schools, starting with the simpler exercises, of course, and building up to more complex ones as physical and mental efficiency increases. Imagine what such a program, united with simple, nondogmatic forms of meditation and contemplation could create! Imagine what a gift it would be to our schoolchildren who are under such stress and face from every angle the pressures of a sex- and violence-obsessed world! Imagine knowing from an early age how to control stress and a wandering mind through certain breathing techniques and physical postures! Imagine what a different vision of the body and of physical exercise would result if the peaceful, contemplative version of physical activity that is hatha yoga were emphasized rather than those sports that wear out the body and treat it as a machine to be subdued!

The subject of hatha yoga is a vast and complex one, and I cannot begin to cover it comprehensively here. What I can do is to offer some simple breathing exercises (called pranayama) and physical postures (asanas) that I myself use and have found invaluable and that can be used by anyone of any age. If, through enacting them, you come to develop a taste for a richer experience of hatha yoga, seek out a competent, nondogmatic, and humble teacher who can be your guide.

Let me start with an exercise of simple stretching that I try to use every morning when I get up. I find it enormously increases my flexibility and suppleness of movement.

EXERCISE OF SIMPLE STRETCHING

Stand up straight but relaxedly. Then slowly start to bend over so your fingers touch your toes. Begin by relaxing your neck so your chin touches your chest. Then let the chest cave slowly while your shoulders move forward and your arms hang loose and limp. Do not rush any of this; let your every movement be calm and natural.

Now arch your spine and try to bend slowly, vertebra by vertebra, until your entire torso feels limp, like the body of a rag doll. If you cannot touch your toes the first time, don't worry; try to bend lower by pushing the body gently from the waist in a few easy motions. Now straighten by reversing the process—tense each vertebra in turn, this time working from the waist up.

Now do a complete stretch, breathing deeply and richly. If you do this regularly every morning for as little as a week, you will be amazed how elastic your spine will feel.

THREE BREATHING (PRANAYAMA) EXERCISES

The ancient Indian yogis who evolved the discipline of hatha yoga developed a series of breathing exercises known as pranayama. *Prana* means "life force" and *yama* comes from *ayama* or "expansion." These exercises were designed to instill meditative peace and to foster calm, alertness, and concentration—all invaluable not only for all worldly activities but also for meditation and all forms of sacred creativity.

I must add a warning here: Do not under any circumstances

overdo it when you use pranayama exercises; you will put your physical health and mental health in danger. These exercises are extremely powerful, and if you are serious about extending your knowledge of them, you should do so only with an experienced teacher who is aware of your physical makeup, its needs and weaknesses.

The three pranayama exercises I am going to give here, however, will not put you at any risk if you do them with calm and moderation. Remember the following when you practice: Breathe through your nose and not your mouth except where otherwise indicated; always breathe deeply and from the diaphragm; breathe as rhythmically as possible without forcing yourself.

Simple Exercise of Breathing Through Alternate Nostrils

This exercise is highly effective for dealing with stressful emotions of all kinds and can be done anywhere. It also greatly helps concentration; I often do it before giving a speech or starting to write, since it helps me focus.

Sit calmly with your spine straight and your hands palm-up on your knees. Enjoy the equilibrium of this posture and take a few deep breaths, remembering to breathe through the nostrils and from the diaphragm.

Now close your left nostril with the second finger of your left hand. Breathe in calmly and deeply through the right nostril. Imagine as you do so that you are breathing in a stream of light that starts to permeate your entire body, cleansing and lightening it.

Hold your breath for a few brief moments, savoring the stillness of your mind, and then, closing the right nostril with the second finger of the right hand, breathe out through the left nostril. As you breathe out imagine that you are breathing out all your spiritual, emotional, and physical stress.

Do this with calm concentration nine times, and then at the end of the practice sit as relaxedly as you can for two or three minutes before continuing with your day.

An Exercise in Dynamic Breathing

This exercise has the opposite effect of the one given above; it energizes rather than calms. It is especially valuable, I find, when I am feeling lethargic or sad; it immediately restores me to a sense of dynamic balance.

Stand straight but relaxedly. Breathe in as smoothly and rhythmically as possible, through your nostrils. When you breathe in, breathe in slowly and deeply while expanding the diaphragm; when you breathe out, push the diaphragm in and up. Take as long to breathe in as breathe out.

When you feel that your mind's normal pace has begun to slow down, visualize your limbs as hollow tubes through which the life force, the prana, is being pulled deep into your body. Imagine this energy flowing into your organs, bathing your entire body and purifying it. As you breathe out, imagine that all lethargy or grief or exhaustion are leaving you.

End the exercise by taking a purifying breath. Breathe in deeply. Then, when your lungs are completely extended, expel the breath suddenly through your nostrils, using a quick inward jerk of the abdomen to drain the lungs of all air. Do this at least three or four times; you'll be delighted by its bracing effect.

The Sitkari Technique for Improving the Vigor of the Body

This exercise is recommended by the ancient sages for bolstering the body's strength, overcoming sleepiness and laziness, and even for conquering hunger and thirst; I often use it when I am especially tired and need to fulfill some duties or tasks immediately.

Stand or sit relaxedly. Now fold your tongue so that its tip touches the upper palate and draw air *through the mouth* with a hissing sound. Retain the breath briefly. Then breathe out through both nostrils. Repeat this three times, then rest. The effect will be immediate.

FOUR SIMPLE ASANAS (PHYSICAL POSTURES)

The foundation of hatha yoga and the major source of its rejuvenating and healing power is the system of asanas, or physical postures that evolved over thousands of years. The legend goes that the god Shiva himself at the beginning of time revealed to humanity 84,000 different asanas that would promote health and spiritual peace; Patanjali reduced these to eighty-four. Many of the most well-known and useful asanas are named after animals—the cobra, lion, and ostrich, for example; clearly the Indian sages honored the genius of animals for relaxation and studied them with meticulous reverence in order to distill the wisdom of their movements for their own use. Animals have a natural unity of mind and body: The aim of the asanas of hatha yoga is to make human beings conscious again of this unity.

Here are four asanas that can be practiced easily and by anyone in normal health.

TWO DOG ASANAS: URDHVA MUKHA SVANASANA AND ADHO MUKHA SVANASANA

These are called the dog asanas because they mirror the actions of a stretching dog. You may have noticed that dogs, like cats, have an extraordinary ability to flow effortlessly from passivity into action and back again; this is because they perform spontaneously the movements that keep their bodies supple and ready for use at all moments.

Perhaps their greatest art is that of stretching; these two linked asanas, which should be practiced together, distill that art for human use.

Begin by lying on you stomach on the floor, feet slightly apart and toes pointing backward. Place your hands, palm down, on the floor by your chest. Then slowly raise yourself up on your arms, stretching your spine, tightening you buttocks, and lifting your head upward. Breathe out as you stretch upward until the entire front of your body and upper thighs are off the floor as far as they can go. Breathe naturally in this position for half a minute; then readjust yourself so that your weight rests on the balls of your feet.

Now begin to raise your hips toward the ceiling while exhaling slowly. Continue to shift your weight so that your torso, arms, and head come into alignment, and your body, bent at the waist, now form a triangle with the floor. Press your heels to the floor as far as they will go and hold this position for half a minute. Then bend your knees until you are sitting on your legs. Bend your torso forward so that your head rests on the floor and relax completely. If you do these two linked dog asanas regularly, you will find that they give you great flexibility and balance.

THE SAVASANA, OR DEATH POSE

This is probably the most ancient of all the basic yoga postures. *Savasana* means in Sanskrit "death pose"; in fact, its details were clearly distilled from an observation of the process of hibernation in the animal world that conserves, not kills, energy.

This asana is almost miraculously effective for the easing of all forms of tension and stress. It is also good to do before you go to bed at night, so the whole body can be at peace and your sleep can be deep and untroubled.

Lie flat on your back, on a rug or blanket if you wish. Keep your feet apart, turn your palms upward with your fingers curled naturally and hold your arms slightly away from your body. Lie as still as possible and make yourself comfortable in whatever way works best for you.

Once you have settled, breathe deeply from the diaphragm several times to calm yourself. What you are now going to do is to try to get as intimately acquainted as possible with the feel of your muscles so that you can control them better. My French yoga teacher in Pondicherry used to say at this point: "Imagine that you have swallowed some luminous tracer substance, and that your muscles are channels through which you are watching it flow."

Now send an order along one of these muscle channels. Move an arm or stretch a leg. Stretch hard, allowing all the muscles along the way to contract—and be aware of what is happening. You will discover that muscles other than the ones you have chosen to flex are also flexing in sympathy (and becoming "luminous" with "tracer substance.") If you clench your fist, for example, you will feel subtle contractions all the way up your arm and into your shoulder.

Now continue with the stretch while you study your sensations in detail, memorize them; next time you give your arm an order, you will be able to check whether or not it is being followed. Repeat the whole process limb by limb, until you have some precise awareness of how each one reacts.

Now start the stretching all over again, this time in slow motion. Think of a cat arching its back; build your stretch slowly. Let your imaginary luminous tracer substance show you what muscles you have put into play. Hold the pose until you are thoroughly aware of what is happening, and then let go.

As you let go, let go utterly and completely. Imagine yourself as a stringless puppet; you simply cannot hold anything up any longer. This state of utter relaxation is the key to the success of the exercise and of its power to recharge you and bring you peace.

After a few sessions of experimenting with your muscle groups and perhaps selecting one group of muscles—the arms or legs, for example—to relax, you will be ready to try the entire asana following the ancient method and sequence. The Indian yogis discovered that the most powerful way of helping yourself to relax is to begin at the top of the body and work down. So, first relax your head—let go of the face muscles, jaw muscles, the eyeballs, the lips, the tongue. Now imagine that a slow current of water is running through you, washing your body free of tension. Imagine it flowing down the length of your body and trickling out finally through your toes. Imagine it flowing down your neck, down the shoulders into the arms, down the chest into the abdomen, down your spine and through your buttocks, your thighs, and into your legs, and then on through your ankles and out through your toes. Imagine that when it has passed completely through you, your body is a totally limp rag doll.

How long you should do this exercise depends on your need and your degree of relaxation. At first, plan on fifteen minutes or even half an hour. Later on, you will find even a five-minute period helpful.

The proper way to end this asana is to work your way down the muscles of the body one last time, now reversing the process; instead of relaxing, restore tone control to each group of muscles. End the entire exercise with one large, rich, catlike stretch and rest in the dynamic peace you will feel.

THE TREE EXERCISE (VRKASANA)

This is one of my favorite asanas and I find it helps me restore both physical and spiritual balance. It is especially useful when you feel threatened by circumstances; it enables you to feel your inner strength.

Begin by standing upright with your big toes touching and your heels slightly apart. Your weight should be evenly distributed on your feet and your spine kept straight. Slowly raise one foot. Grab hold of it and place it as high as possible on the inside of the opposite thigh. Try to keep your balance while doing this; if you can't, stand near a wall so you can support yourself.

Go on, keeping the toes of your raised foot pointing downward. Spreading the toes of the foot on the floor will aid in your sense of balance. Stretch your spine, relax your shoulders, swing the knee of your raised leg as far as you can, and bring the palms of your hands together at chest level. Hold this position for half a minute, then repeat with the other leg raised.

Do this exercise regularly for a week and you should feel your sense of the balance and inherent strength of your body greatly enhanced; this, in turn, will breed a psychological force and equilibrium.

THE BEST TIMES to perform all yogic exercises are early in the morning, when your mind is at its freshest, and late in the evening, when your body is at its most relaxed. As with all spiritual exercises, regular practice is essential; even if you start exercising for only fifteen or twenty minutes a day, make sure you continue on a daily basis.

Tai Chi Chi Kung

Near where I used to live in San Francisco there was a small gem of a park, Sutro Park, that overlooked rocky cliffs and the Pacific Ocean. Every morning when I walked there I would see an improbable group of people practicing slow, trancelike movements under the trees. I say improbable because they included three affluent black women, an old Hungarian-looking gentleman with ancient horn-rimmed glasses, and several intense, ponytailed young men in expensive sneakers. What they were doing, of course, was tai chi with a razor-thin sweet-faced Korean master, Master Ko, whose face was perpetually set in a mysterious and serenely tolerant smile. After several weeks of observing them, I decided to join in. There began my adventure into the magical, spiritual, and physical discipline of tai chi chi kung, developed in China over millennia to bring balance to the body and flowing peace to the mind, and now practiced all over the West in increasing numbers.

Master Ko spoke in short, only barely intelligible sentences. One of his that I will always remember was "Tai chi chi kung good for keeping head full of air, body full of water, and feet on earth." Chinese spiritual philosophy both in its Taoist and Confucian manifestations celebrates a gentle-natured, adaptable equilibrium as the highest inner virtue and the surest and most natural way of ensuring longevity and physical health: Tai chi has for thousands of years been the discipline that promoted this equilibrium.

Chi is the Chinese word for the flows of subtle energy in the body. It corresponds to the Sanskrit word *prana* that is used for the same energy in the Indian yoga system. Tai chi is the art of using movement to direct, clarify, and balance these flows of vital energy. *Chi kung,* which literally means "breath work," is the accompanying system of meditation and breathing that can unblock, align, and purify the body's energy so that the entire being—body, mind, and spirit—can function more harmoniously.

Taoist adepts assert that there are both yin and yang flows of energy in the body. The feminine *yin* energy is cool, lunar, and essentially passive, while the masculine *yang* is warm, solar, and assertive. From early times, Taoist adepts knew that these energies—what might be called bioelectric currents in your body—are carried by the nervous system and control the immune system. If the flow of chi is blocked or out of balance in parts of the body, that part becomes ripe for disease or ailment.

Like yoga, tai chi is a gentle, contemplative form of exercise and uses slow, deliberate movement to train the body so that the chi energy flows in balance. As in yoga, great importance is placed on

awareness of the breath and on its control. In tai chi the center of
the body energy is located in the solar plexus, or *tantien* center. Chi
kung meditation is the accompanying mental component to tai
chi, in which visualization and breath control play an indispens-
able part.

What I offer here is a simple set of tai chi and chi kung exercises
that have been designed (from my own experience and on the advice of tai chi experts) to be performed in sequence and to introduce the practitioner to the basic forces of the two disciplines. I
hope that practicing these exercises—they can be done by anyone
at any age in normal health—will awaken a desire to work at higher
levels with a tai chi expert. Many people who find yoga too structured and physically demanding come to the flowing and graceful
exercises of tai chi with gratitude and find in them the ideal way to
stay healthy and self-attuned.

Let us begin by heightening the awareness of chi in the body.

EXERCISE FOR BECOMING AWARE
OF THE CHI IN THE BODY

Sit quietly and comfortably in a chair or cross-legged on the
floor. Begin by opening and closing your left hand rapidly and repeatedly. Continue this until your hand and wrist get very tired.
Both will begin to feel inflamed, sore, and numb. Then rest both
hands in your lap and notice the difference in the way your hands
feel.

Now close your eyes and transfer the sensation in your left
hand to the right. You will be amazed at how quickly, when you focus your energy, you will be capable of directing its flow through
will and concentration. You have now discovered a basic principle
on which the principle of tai chi and chi kung is founded.

Tai chi teaches that when mind, or awareness, is focused, the
chi can be brought to that focus. When energy flow is blocked by
imbalances in body and mind, there will be too much chi in some
parts of the body and too little in others; this will cause congested
areas (yang) and areas that are depleted (yin). As we do exercises,
then, to send the mind to particular parts of the body, what we are
doing is concentrating the breath energy in these parts to cleanse

the congested yang areas and to open and fill out depleted yin ones. The goal of all the practices is to become the "tai chi," the dancing, harmonious unity of yin and yang, the balance of the opposites, the living site of the sacred marriage of heavenly and earthly energy.

Here are some exercises that can be used to heal the body by balancing its energies.

THE WHITE MIST MEDITATION TO
CLEANSE MIND AND BODY

Begin by sitting erect on the edge of a chair so that your spine is erect or on a cushion on the floor. Close your eyes and place your hands loosely in your lap. Sit calmly and observe the natural flow of your breath. Notice how the breath flows into and through your body; whether it flows more heavily on the right, the left, or equally through both lungs. Notice how deeply the breath reaches in the body. Do not do anything to change the flow of your breath. Let thoughts and sensations meander through your awareness without judgment or interference.

You are ready now to begin the first stage of the meditation that is designed to cleanse the mind and body. Breathe in deeply, imagining that your breath is a softly swirling white mist that descends slowly through your body, collecting at the base of your spine. Inhale deeply and then hold your breath.

As you hold your breath, visualize that the white mist enters your spine and slowly rises upward through your lower back, torso, upper back, shoulder blades, and neck until it pours in a white flood into your skull. When the white mist reaches your skull, picture it swirling around and around your brain, then breathe out the mist through your mouth. Imagine as you do so that the mist is now colored black or gray with the toxins that are being expelled from your body and mind.

Repeat this exercise. This time around, imagine that the white mist swirls into and purifies places in your body that are not easy to reach. As you breathe out, imagine the mist darkly stained with your body's expelled toxins, hovering and swirling in front of you like small summer storm clouds.

Repeat the exercise for the third time. Master Ko used to tell us at this moment: "When you breathe out now, blow away clouds! Blow away clouds!" As you breathe out after this third repetition, then, imagine that you are blowing away forcefully all the dark clouds that obscure the clear, shining sky inside your head. Breathe normally and continue to visualize this. Picture the inside of your skull as a clear blue sky, pure, scintillating, and open. Allow this radiant blue to descend throughout the body like a slow, sparkling, all-cleansing wave. Then allow the image to fade and return to observing the flow of your breath.

THE FIVE-COLORED LIGHT MEDITATION FOR CLEANSING BODY AND MIND

This next meditation, which is wonderfully effective when performed immediately after the White Mist Meditation and reinforces its purifying action, uses five colored lights to heal the five major internal organs: the lungs, the heart, the spleen, the liver, and the kidneys. These organs are considered yin organs that store and deplete energy; it is essential, then, that they remain unblocked so they can serve as effective containers.

Sit comfortably with a straight spine. Direct your attention now to your lungs. Tune in to the normal flow of your breath for a few moments. As you continue your natural breathing through the nose, breathe in and imagine white light entering your lungs and filling them completely. As you breathe out and some of the white light is expelled from your lungs, imagine that it is taking all your lungs' toxins with it and that when it leaves you it is tinted gray. As you go on breathing in white light and breathing out gray light, notice that your lungs start to glow white as all their toxins are purged and only the pure light remains. Continue this exercise until your lungs glow completely white. Feel with all your faith that your lungs are strong, healthy, and free of toxins. Then let this image gently dissolve, and breathe naturally with no image present in your mind.

Now bring your mind's attention to the next internal organ the meditation aims to cleanse—the heart. Feel the shape and contours of your heart with your mind. While still breathing normally, visualize a red light and allow this red light to enter your heart. Let the red light fill all the chambers and valves of your heart. As you breathe out, visualize some of the red light leaving your body with a gray or black tint, carrying all the toxins of your heart with it. Let some of the red light remain in your heart, making it glow more and more brightly from within as you continue to breathe in pure, ruby-red light. When your heart is completely red and shining, hold the image for a few moments, then let it dissolve and rest your mind in imageless peace.

Now direct your energy to your spleen. Feel your spleen within your body. If this is difficult for you, focus your mind on the general area of your spleen, encompassing your whole stomach area as well. Without altering your normal breathing, begin to visualize a yellow light entering your spleen as you inhale. Every time you breathe out, picture the yellow light stained with gray from the toxins expelled from your spleen. As you go on breathing, imagine that more clear yellow color remains in your spleen until it starts to glow a brilliant crystalline yellow from the inside. Hold the image briefly, then let it dissolve.

Now direct your mind's eye to the largest organ in your body—your liver. Breathe in a vibrant green light into your liver—the spring green of freshly sprouted grass. As before, when you breathe out, imagine that the green light leaves you tinged with gray. Leave this green light to work within the liver and transform it slowly into a living, glowing emerald. Hold the image for a few moments, then let it fade away.

Now bring your awareness to the last major organ in your body, the kidneys. As you breathe in, fill your kidneys with a deep sea-blue light. As you breathe out, let the toxins in your kidneys be expelled and taint the sea-blue light gray. As you go on breathing, be aware that your kidneys are retaining more and more of the blue light and that its dark toxins are being eliminated. When this purification process has reached the point where your kidneys are glowing a pure vibrant blue, hold the image momentarily and then let it go.

You are now ready to experience the closing movement of the meditation, which brings all its fruits together. Review each of your five internal organs in your mind's eye, seeing each glow in its respective color like a brilliant network of jewels. Begin with the lungs; they are glowing a pure, satiny white, like a pearl. Then imagine the heart glowing a deep crimson from within like a ruby. Picture your spleen, a clear daffodil yellow, radiant like yellow topaz. Now shift your attention to your liver, which emanates a vibrant chartreuse green and shines like a large emerald. Finally, visualize your liver pulsing with the peaceful glow of indigo, like a living sapphire. Now let your mind's eye visualize all of them together, in a web of jeweled peace and health. Keep this image as long as you want, and then allow it to fade. Return to your basic imageless state of awareness, noticing objectively how the flow of your breath has changed.

TWO SIMPLE TAI CHI EXERCISES
TO STRETCH THE SPINE

While the intent of western exercise is often to develop muscle, eastern exercise focuses on awareness and control. It is very helpful to supplement the mental and breathing exercises I have given by slow stretches of the spine. Tai chi adepts believe that when the spine is agile, the chi energies running through the spine are unobstructed and the health of the entire being is improved.

First Exercise for the Spine

To help loosen and stretch your spinal column, begin by standing with your arms straight overhead and your feet pointing forward. Breathe in deeply, hold your breath, and grasp an imaginary parallel bar with both hands. Turn the upper torso above the waist as far to the right as possible, then slowly reverse the direction to your left. Pull yourself upward on your imaginary parallel bar while you are making these movements. Breathe out and breathe in between rotations of the torso as needed. This exercise will help you work and loosen your lower and middle spine.

Second Simple Exercise for the Spine

This exercise will help you work and loosen your upper spine and neck. Begin by standing straight and relaxedly. Draw your chin slightly inward, then give the head and neck an upward pull from this posture. After several repetitions, turn the head to look past your right shoulder, then gradually reverse the direction and turn the head to your left.

EXERCISE: BECOMING A FLAME

The final exercise of this simple tai chi and chi kung workout of body and mind energizes your entire being from its center of power known as the *hara* or *tantien*. It is a wonderful way of completing the healing work of the exercises given so far and of preparing you to reenter the world confidently and charged with subtle power.

Imagine your lower abdomen center as a dark space. Place in it a small warm flame. As you say the syllable "Ha!" imagine you are pouring oil onto the flame. Stand up now and feel the rich, sweet heat of this chi fire spread through your whole body. As you stand up, stretch in all directions, consciously directing the heat to every part of your body.

Now place both hands on your belly and let your palms bask in the heat spreading through you.

Now breathe in deeply, then breathe out, as you step forward and shout "Hwooo-awe!" flinging your arms up over your head.

Visualize your whole body now as a burning flame of pure energy, vitality, and health.

Nature as Revelation and
Source of Healing

TO AWAKEN TO THE SACREDNESS of the body and of embodiment is to know yourself increasingly, and increasingly normally, as a divine human being in a divine world. Nature is not dead or other or simply a set of gorgeously complicated interlocking systems as many scientific and some religious philosophies would have it; what mystical awakening reveals is that nature and all things and beings in it are sacred both in their origin and in all their relations and holy particulars.

As the divine light in consciousness works on and clarifies and purifies all your physical senses and divinizes them, the essential glory and beauty of nature will become clearer and clearer, more and more astounding, and more and more revelatory of the glory and beauty of the Divine that is everywhere appearing in and as all things and beings in nature. The mountain reveals itself as divine stability; the waters of the sea as the always-flowing divine power; the tiger as divine strength; the anemone as divine delicacy.

As this holy awareness deepens and as the great adventure of marrying light consciousness to the body's emotions, actions, and thoughts begins and becomes more refined, nature starts to unveil even greater secrets. What the growing marriage between body and spirit deepens is the sense of divine identity between you and every other sentient being and the knowledge of the holiness of every thing and creature in the universe. As you learn to bless your own body as the manifestation of God more and more completely, so a faculty for blessing all other creatures grows more and more rich in you until every flower, every passing animal in the street, every fall of sunlight on the snow peaks, every sudden fall of rain, becomes different notes in one long and endless symphony of divine presence and divine love. "Everywhere and in everything my Beloved appears," sings Kabir. "I see Him every time I turn my head. What wonder and what bliss!"

What this marriage between you and your body and you and your body and nature and the light Source of all things makes more and more obvious to you is two interconnected revelations. The first is that all living things are equally holy and equally sacred. I am not more holy or sacred than the worm in my garden or the little cricket suddenly lost and bewildered on my white carpet because the wind has blown him into my drawing room; I am not more important in the web of life than the slug or sea horse or ladybug. A frog appears to me as beautiful as any archangel. While it is true that I have been graced by God with the consciousness to participate in Divine Origin and see all things flame out with Origin, that does not entitle me to believe myself special; it makes me a partner in that divine humility that is manifesting itself as all beings and all creatures, in what a great Christian mystic of the thirteenth century, Angela of Foligno, called "the unspeakable humility of Divine Love that hides itself in the Creation and takes on all shapes and forms within it."

The second revelation that the marriage of body and spirit brings is that all human beings, precisely because they have been graced with origin consciousness, have the responsibility to serve and protect the creation in and under God, following with reverence the laws of the Father-Mother as revealed in and through nature in her relations and rhythms. As the child of the Father-Mother consciously aware of my origin in that light that is the origin of all things, I have a final and inescapable responsibility to treat all things and beings with divine love, divine respect, and divine tenderness. The more I do so, the more I will grow in my own human divinity and the more I will experience, with ever greater intimacy and wonder, the Divine Presence in every rose, every bird, every shifting play of wind in the grasses, every fern and poke-weed.

One of the greatest and most reassuring mystical experiences of my recent life was seeing my cat Purrball blazing softly in divine light at the top of the stairs, licking her paws. From the moment I first saw this beautiful tabby sitting resignedly at the back of a cage in the pound, my heart contracted in love for her. That love grew and grew in the weeks and months that followed; I never knew that I could feel so unconditional a tenderness for any crea-ture. I experienced each moment with her as a direct, almost de-ranging blessing that I began to know was taking me deeper and deeper into the sacred heart of the Father-Mother. It was as if she were the "worm" on the hook of divine love and that divine love, using her as bait, was drawing me into an ever deeper realization of the holiness of all things. Because I loved my cat so much so sud-denly, every animal I saw in the street or on television, even ani-mals that I had before disliked or been afraid of, such as cock-roaches, boa constrictors, and alligators, all became not only startlingly beautiful but also profoundly touching. I had known for years about the horrible ways in which we treat animals in slaughterhouses, cosmetics factories, vivisection institutes; I had also known many of the facts about the extermination of animal species that our environmental holocaust is causing. Loving my cat more and more made all these forms of knowledge suddenly inescapably real. Every time I saw an abused animal, I saw the face of my cat in pain; every time I read of the disappearance of a species of fish or insect or bird, I saw her face being wiped out by darkness. I realized that the Divine had given me my cat to open my heart finally to the living horror of what we are doing to ani-mals and the natural world.

At first the immediacy of such naked knowledge scared me. I believed that a great deal of mystical experience had already opened my heart; I was not prepared for this rending of another veil by love. But as I surrendered more and more not only to loving Purrball but to loving all animals and things in nature in her and through her, I found that I grew in heartbroken love for all things and beings menaced now by the environmental catastrophe human greed and blindness are engendering, and that from that heartbroken love came a more and more passionate desire to do everything in my power to help others awaken to what I was being shown. I remembered what an old Indian chief had told me years before at a conference in New York: "When you allow yourself really to fall in love with the world, your whole being becomes full of a mother's passion to protect her children, and a father's hunger to see them safe and strong."

And then the moment came when one evening, after I had been down to the fridge to drink some milk, I came back up the stairs to our bedroom and saw my cat at the top of the stairs surrounded by a nimbus of dazzling sweet diamond light. Every aspect of her seemed supernaturally precise in that dazzling light; each whisker, the white under her chin, the shining of her eyes, the "M" mark on her forehead, all were utterly clear; it was as if I had never seen them before, never loved or adored or revered them enough. I realized that if I completely married my body, heart, soul, and mind together, I would see all things with this sacramental passion, burning in the glory of God.

What the Direct Path has brought me to, then, is the knowledge that I am one with all things and beings in a divine awareness and energy that streams from the light. It has also brought me closer to the love of the Father-Mother for all things, and the protective passion that arises naturally from that love. I at last am really beginning to understand what the Lakota Indians mean when they say that all living things are their relations, and to feel some small part of the love that drove St. Francis to love the larks rising from the dawn fields of Tuscany and pick up the worms from the paths near his hermitage.

As the Ojibway Indians pray:

Grandfather,
Sacred one
Teach us love, compassion, and honor
That we may heal the earth
And heal each other.

To know the truth of your divine consciousness is to see it reflected back at you from all living things. To deepen that experience constantly, through adoration, wonder, insight, and direct protective service and action is why we are here.

SUSTAINING A MYSTICAL consciousness of the divine origin of nature and the resolve to protect and guard the creation that arises from it requires constant and humble work. The innate arrogance of human awareness and the tendency even of many higher levels of mystical consciousness to "sign off" from and "transcend" the real has to be, I find, constantly counteracted by spiritual practice that reminds us of our inextricable connection both to nature's transcendent Source and its immanent glory. Over the last decade I have researched and practiced the healing nature exercises of many mystical traditions and religions; what I offer now are nine of these that have helped me most.

Just as the goal of embodiment and integration on the Direct Path is the alchemical marriage of body and soul, so the goal of the following nature practices is to secure the marriage between the human spirit and the Spirit in nature. Bede Griffiths once said to me: "If only everyone could see where they are—in the house of God—they would not allow one creature or plant to suffer unnecessary pain and they would do everything to preserve the natural world so as to go on worshipping God and their own divine identity in it and through it."

Exercise One
Meditating on the Sea as a Way of Deepening Your Awareness of Eternal Consciousness

I was taught this by a yogi and pundit I met in Bombay on a boat trip to the Elephanta Caves. After viewing the great sculpture of the faces of Shiva together, Mr. P. took me down to the small beach near the jetty where we were to meet the boat back, and sat down.

"Gaze out with love in your heart at the sea," he said. "What do you see?"

"I see water appearing in a million different forms," I said.

"Exactly." He smiled. "Now meditate on what that really means."

I waited. He said nothing. The silence grew between us, and the late afternoon sun deepened to a dark red-gold on the waves. The three faces of the great Shiva sculpture in the caves kept returning to me—the vivid joyful profile of the Creator, the angry profile of the Destroyer, and the all-calm Face of the Eternal in the center out of which both grew.

Then, quite suddenly, I seemed to understand what Mr. P. was trying to get me to see. The sea was the cosmos; its waves all the different forms of the cosmos, different yet made from the same constant shifting and reappearing light energy. And I was looking at the sea with the eyes of the sea itself, the eyes of calm awareness, of that calm that always lies beneath the waves of the sea's surface.

I explained what I was experiencing to Mr. P. He was delighted.

"Yes," he said, "God's eyes look out at God through the eyes of a man or woman in love with the Divine."

Ever since then, whenever I am near the sea, I sit on the beach and do the following meditation, gazing out to sea:

First, I meditate on the waves in their infinite variety. Then I meditate on the fact that they are all water, all made from one energy substance. Then I contemplate the fact that none of the substance of the waves is ever lost, although their shape is. The waves rear and fall, but the water in the waves goes on.

When I have allowed my consciousness to become saturated by the quiet revelations of the first part of the meditation and soothed by the peace of my surroundings and the rhythmic maternal sound of the sea itself, I begin the second part.

In this part I reconstruct inwardly everything I know and have experienced of the nature of my inner divine self and its nondual connection to all things and to the Divine.

I gaze out to sea and see the sea as a living image of my own and everyone else's divine awareness—calm and serene in its depths, constantly changing on its surface, at once eternally stable and eternally self-transforming. I meditate on the fact that nothing that happens on the surface of the sea can alter the calm of its depths; all the masks and faces of nature may change, but the face of love that wears them never changes.

At the end of the meditation, I do what Mr. P. showed me how to do on that evening in Elephanta—I turn to the four directions with my palms brought together in the Indian gesture of *namaste*. And I repeat to myself quietly and reverently the words Mr. P. wrote out for me in my notebook as we traveled back to Bombay: "I am everywhere and in everything; I am the sun and the stars; when I am everywhere, where can I move? Where there is no past and no future and I am eternal existence, then where is time?"

Exercise Two
Looking into the Eyes of Creation

This is an astonishingly powerful and simple ancient Sufi practice that enables you to deepen your understanding of the Divine Presence in all things; I was taught it by an adept of the Mevlevi order that was founded by Rumi.

It is best done on a walk alone in a beautiful and inspiring place: I first practiced it on summer evenings in Paris's Luxembourg Gardens.

The principle of the meditation is simple; imagine that everything around you, above you, and beneath you is alive and has eyes that are fixed on you. The earth beneath your feet is staring at you; the rocks you pass gleam with eyes; the sky you look up into has eyes that stare unblinkingly and invisibly back at you; the trees on the horizon are small pillars of eyes that constantly search you out.

As you focus more and more intensely on the meditation and on trying to "look back in love and attention" at the things that are staring at you in divine communion, to "look into the eyes of the creation," the more you will become aware that you are moving as a part of divine life within divine life and its unity.

Exercise Three
Dawn Song of Celebration

This is adapted from a Pawnee ritual that I was introduced to by a Native American shaman.

First, get an ear of corn and bless it with some holy water or pray over it near a holy image. This ear of corn signifies the Divine Mother in the ritual that follows. If you can't obtain an ear of corn, use an image of the aspect of the Mother that you love. Many of the friends that I have shared this ritual with use the Virgin of Guadalupe.

Wake up before dawn, bathe, and put on fresh clothes. Do a simple form of meditation or visualization that calms your body and mind and opens you to the Divine.

As dawn begins, take the ear of corn or the image of the Mother you have chosen and go to someplace either within your house or outside it where you can observe the rising sun directly. Hold up the ear of corn to the sun and in your own words thank the Divine Mother for her gift of returning to the universe as the sun of joy and health and daylight.

Now, using words that you improvise on the spot from your heart, say or sing praises to the rising sun. Speak or sing of its beauty, force, healing warmth. If you find words do not come to you, then just chant the syllable *ma* to it, infusing your chanting with gratitude and worship.

Now, still carrying the ear of corn or the image of the Mother you have chosen, go for a fifteen- or twenty-minute walk in the rising dawn light. Imagine that you are at the dawn of all creation; salute each living thing you encounter with a brief song or with words of praise.

I have often practiced this in my house which is in a built-up area. Even in a built-up neighborhood, there are lovely signs of the creation—grass, flowers, small animals. Notice and praise and express your gratitude for each one as manifestations of the Mother and of her love. If you don't feel like singing or speaking out loud (even softly) then say the syllable-mantra *ma* in your heart-center and send its light energy to whatever aspect of the Mother's creation you are encountering. If I am walking on grass, for example, I imagine the syllable *ma* radiating divine golden light from my heart and flooding the grass with it; if I pass a dog or cat or child, I imagine it or him lit up with the same brilliant golden light.

Return home. By then the sun will be up. End the meditation by thanking the Mother again for her creation and vow to her to do everything in your power to honor all living creatures and to protect them and nature in general from greed and violence.

Exercise Four
Filling Yourself with the
Healing Power of Fire

This is adapted from a Tibetan Buddhist meditation. According to Buddhist understanding, the entire physical world—including our human bodies—is composed of the five elements: earth, air, water, fire, and space. Each element has positive aspects that can be connected with and used for health and spiritual vitality and insight. The one I have adapted for use here celebrates fire.

This meditation is best done outside in sunlight or around a campfire; it can also be done in an "imaginary" visualized way.

Still your mind and focus it on the brilliant, energetic, fierce, cleansing, and powerful character of fire. Imagine that every dark or negative thought in you, and every problem in your life, is now consumed by fire. Feel that your mind and body are filled with heat and fiery energy that ripen all your good qualities like green wheat in summer sunlight. Feel this fertile heat within you and become one with it.

Now imagine that the entire universe is filled with an infinite fire energy. See and feel and know it leaping invisibly in all animate and inanimate things. Hindu mystics call this infinite fire energy the *shakti*, the Force that creates all things; Hildegard of Bingen knew it as the Holy Spirit and hymned it when she wrote: "I am that fiery living essence of the divine substance that flows in the fields. I shine in the water, I burn in the sun and the moon and the stars. . . ." The more focusedly you enter into "fire vision," the more deeply you will be initiated into the unity of all things that are always "burning" in the Presence.

End the meditation by imagining your body as a living flame dancing out from a sea of flame. Now offer up the joy and power you are filled with to the happiness of all sentient beings.

Exercise Five
Using Trees as a Source of Healing

This exercise, too, is adapted from an old Tibetan Buddhist meditation.

Twenty years ago, I was taken by a young monk to a small grove of birch trees in the hills above the Hemis monastery in Ladakh. When we arrived, my friend embarrassed me by kneeling to one tall, straight old birch and then going up to it and leaning against it and embracing it with deep tenderness. I was still an Oxford don at the time; I was prepared to study the refinements of Mahayana metaphysics but not to hug trees. My young friend must have sensed my snobbery and the fear that underlay it; he called my bluff. "Come and put your arms around this tree," he said. "You will be blessed." Not wanting to lose face with him, I went up to the tree and, grateful that none of my Oxford colleagues could see me, embraced it. For a while, nothing happened. Then, quite suddenly, I felt it—a quiet, deep, warm energy streaming from the tree to me through my chest.

That night I dreamed in sequence of a series of trees I had loved in my life—of a banyan I had played under as a child, of a jacaranda in the Nilgiri hills in South India, whose wild windswept purple blossoms had intoxicated me, of a three-hundred-year-old beech in Oxford I had visited almost every day out of love for its ancient serenity and power. Trees, it seemed, had played a far richer and more mysterious part in my inner life than my outer intellect had wanted to acknowledge.

That afternoon my young friend explained to me that the powerful holiness of trees and their ability to heal and bless comes from them being "intermediaries" and "living communicators" between heaven and earth. Their roots stretch down into matter; their branches stretch high into the air and space and light; the branches that extend outward represent the generous and loving nature that being in such earthly and heavenly balance breeds in them.

My friend then proceeded to teach me the simple meditation he used when he looked for healing from a tree:

> Stand in front of the tree you have selected for its beauty, serenity, and strength and ask it to allow you, in the name of the Divine, to experience the energy of its nature. Then approach the tree with reverence, sending it silent waves of love from your heart-center. Lean forward and first gently touch the trunk and feel, as you do so, that your inmost positive energy and the positive life force of the tree are now in communication.
>
> Wait a few minutes until you start to feel a real exchange of force between you and the tree. Then, with great love, put your arms around it and lean your whole body against it, continuing to send it silent waves of love and gratitude from your heart-center.
>
> Be grateful for any healing energy you experience, and when you have "finished," bow to the tree and bless it in God's name for everything it has given to you. In this way, you establish a holy relationship with the tree you have chosen and can return to it again and again for companionship and for healing.

This meditation can also be used with other natural creations—with rocks or streams, for example. Native Americans lie facedown on certain majestic and beautiful rocks and ask them to fill their whole beings with strength; Taoist mystics build their retreat huts often near water and constantly pray for its supple and flowing nature to possess and harmonize theirs. Everything in nature has a healing force it can transmit to us if we are humble enough to open ourselves to receive it.

Exercise Six
Absorbing the Energy of the Sun

The next three exercises are ancient Taoist practices for absorbing the energy of the three self-luminous aspects of nature—the sun, the moon, and the stars. The Taoist adepts consider these effective ways of recharging life energy.

Sit outside in the sun or in a place in your home where you feel the sun on your body. Revel in the warmth you feel and open your heart and whole being to it in adoration and gratitude.

Now imagine that the warmth of the sun melts down in honey-gold light and spreads all over the outside of your body. Imagine your entire body being bathed in the golden light, as if you were taking a solar bath. Offer up any cramped or painful areas of your body to the light's warm healing.

Now open your mouth and imagine that you draw the sun into it. Close your mouth, and, as you close it, imagine that the sun's light and energy mix with your saliva. Swallow your saliva, imagining that it carries the concentrated energy of the sun down your body and stores it in the force center (called *tantien*) of your lower center, where the Taoists believe the sun energy that keeps us alive is always stored and has to be continually replenished. Do this whole part of the exercise several times, until you feel a warm, rich golden ball of energy and light in your lower abdomen.

Relish your new sun power and dedicate its use to the service of all sentient beings. Then let all images go, and rest in peaceful awareness.

Exactly this same exercise can be done with the moon, and is best performed out in nature and when the moon is full. There is a subtle difference, the Taoists tell us, between the energy of the sun and that of the moon. The sun's energy charges us with power and love; the moon's cleanses and purifies and subtilizes our entire being. If you are on a spiritual retreat in nature, you could perform both practices regularly at the appropriate times of day.

Exercise Seven
Journeying to the Moon to Become One with It and Absorb Its Chi (or Life Energy)

This marvelously poetic exercise is particularly effective, I have found, for bringing a luminous calm to the body and mind.

Imagine yourself sitting on a mountaintop, gazing across the sea. The moon is rising in the sky in front of you. Gaze at it with wonder and adoration, relishing its white purity and power.

Now imagine that from the heart of the moon starts to unfold a bridge of dazzling silver clouds that spreads across the sky toward the place where you are sitting. As the bridge of silver clouds unfurls toward you, imagine that your body becomes lighter and lighter, until it is as light as a cloud. Then, when the cloud bridge reaches you, step onto it and float up on it into the heart of the moon.

Become one with the moon, saturating every limb, muscle, and cell of your body and every part of your mind with its subtle resplendence. Rest in the lunar resplendence you now are. Then let all images go and rest in peaceful awareness.

Exercise Eight
Absorbing the Chi of the Stars

The Taoists believed that the Big Dipper was one of the most powerful of the constellations and saw it as filled with inexhaustible vital energy.

Either go outdoors to a place where the Big Dipper is clearly visible or sit in a dark room and imagine it clearly and precisely overhead.

Imagine now that the Big Dipper starts to tilt and overturn so that glowing purple amethyst light starts to pour out of its bowl and enter your body through the crown of your head. Let your whole body fill with purple light. In most mystical systems, purple light has a profound connection with the bliss and holy power of divine love; imagine then that the dipper is pouring into you the purple power of divine love, the love that creates and sustains all things.

When your whole body feels filled to the brim with this radiant amethyst light, allow the excess light to pour down the outside of your body, cleansing and purifying and vitalizing it completely. As you allow the light to cascade down you, offer up your whole being in service to all sentient beings.

Finally, let all images go and rest in peaceful awareness.

Exercise Nine
Joining Heaven and Earth to
Protect Sentient Beings

This practice is adapted from the Taoist and the Buddhist traditions and if done sincerely can both enlighten you to your true place in nature and expand your heart.

Sit in a peaceful place outdoors, and close your eyes. Bring your mind home to stillness.

Now imagine that you are drawing down the energy of the highest heavens, down through the crown of your head, throughout your body, and out through the soles of your feet, down to the center of the earth. Go slowly, consolidating each step in your imagination, and realizing fully your responsibilities as a conduit of power between the highest realms of the spirit and the deepest, most hidden, kingdoms of matter.

When you feel that the energy you are mediating has reached the core of the earth, start to draw it slowly upward, back into and up your body. Let it exit from the crown of your head, and send it back to where it came from, higher than the clouds or sky above you, into the final recesses of the light of the One.

Repeat this whole process four or five times slowly and precisely, noting carefully all the insights and inner visions that may come to you and all the subtle flows of energy in your body.

On the last time that you imagine this process, lower the energy you draw from the highest heaven into the *tantien*—the center of your lower abdomen where the energy of the cosmos is stored. Revel in your new power and thank the Divine for giving it to you.

Now, secure in your heavenly and earthly dignity and radiance, turn your mind and heart to sentient beings everywhere, especially animals. Imagine as vividly as you can their needs, their fears, the hunger and thirst and the myriad dangers they face in a hostile world. I find that it is extremely powerful here to concentrate on the lot of those species of animals that are threatened with extinction. If there is one particular species of animal that touches you most deeply, turn your heart to it as symbolic of the whole animal kingdom in danger.

Imagine now that the energy you have stored in your lower abdomen starts to shine like a great golden ball of light that radiates through your body in all directions. Send its healing, calming, strengthening power to the animal species you have chosen, wishing it protection and happiness.

To end the practice, imagine the golden light emanating from your stomach circling the entire planet and enfolding it in its healing protection. Make a vow to honor and protect the creation in all your cultural, economic, and political choices.

Tantra, Sacred Sexuality, and Relationship

BODY AND SEX HATRED have characterized and disfigured all the patriarchal religious and mystic transmission systems and created a schizophrenic split in the psyche of humanity that has led most human beings to feel subtly ashamed of having a body at all, to feel guilty and tormented about their natural desires, and to be radically alienated from, and blind to, the glory and power of nature. The wound that this terrible and false divorce between body and spirit has inflicted on the human psyche is the source of vast despair and violence, and the source, too, of that blindness to the beauty of life and the wonder of the creation that fuels humanity's current course of self-destruction and destruction of nature.

The answer to this destructive lack of balance is the restoration of the vision of tantra and of sacred sexuality and sacred relationship to humanity. Tantra is a term that derives from the Sanskrit verb *tan*—to "stretch" and "expand"—and it refers to a set of spiritual and physical exercises in Hinduism and Buddhism designed to initiate the seeker directly into the divine ground of life, to "stretch" and "expand" his or her consciousness so that it can embrace all the levels of reality in one overwhelming experience of interdependence and unity.

One aspect of tantra as practiced in ancient India was a celebration of sexuality as a way to divine initiation and divine ecstasy; tantric philosophy knew the inextricable mutual relationship of soul and body, spirit and matter, and knew that this electric dance could be experienced in all its bliss and power and healing force and ecstatic joy in the practice of a consecrated sexuality. Restoring this great secret to humanity will restore the balance to human life, give all beings a way of being initiated into their divine truth in the core of life, and empower all beings who follow it with tremendous powers of self-healing and expansion of the mind and heart.

The deep philosophy of tantra, both in its Buddhist and Hindu forms and in the reflections of this universal wisdom that can be found in aspects of shamanism, cabala, and certain Sufi mystics, has a marvelous simplicity and symmetry about it. For tantrics, the universe is a perpetually self-renewing creation of an eternal lovemaking between the "masculine" and "feminine" forces of the One; one Hindu poet, Kalidasa, describes all things as being always "wet with the golden love-sweat of the God and Goddess." This eternal lovemaking that engenders all the aspects of the cosmos takes place in an eternal rapture, a perpetual dance of bliss, and from this rapture and bliss stream incessantly tremendous energies of natural initiation and healing. Two human lovers, heterosexual or homosexual, who consecrate themselves and their lovemaking to the Divine, worship each other as living manifestations of the Divine, and surrender themselves beyond all thought or concept to the ecstasy of sexual passion infused by love, compassion, tenderness, and profound respect will know what the "god" and "goddess" know in their eternal love dance, will be swept directly, in fact, into the primal divine energies that are creating the universe and bathe directly in the glory of their all-renewing fire. And just as the universe itself is the child of the god and the goddess, so through experiencing the love dance of the god and goddess both between and within themselves, both lovers will, over time, help birth in each other the divine child.

Such tremendous possibilities and rewards demand, of course, their price. True tantra has nothing whatever to do with the semipornographic celebrations of promiscuity and indiscriminate sex often preached in its name. True tantra is, in fact, profound and difficult, as precise and exacting a discipline as true celibacy.

From my own experience and from my extensive study of all the different mystical traditions that honor the creativity of consecrated sexuality, five interlinked "laws" for the practice of tantra emerge.

The first "law" is that both lovers in a tantric couple should be spiritual practitioners dedicated to offering their love to the service of illumination and to living their love in the light of divine truth and divine compassion.

The second "law" is that the "masculine" and "feminine" sides of both lovers should be in love with the "masculine" and "feminine" aspects of the other; this means that their love must be a complete one, not merely physical but also emotional, spiritual, intellectual, and mystical. Authentic tantric couples are those in which the mind, heart, body, and soul of each partner is in love with all aspects of the other; nothing less than this can bring about the conditions for mutual interpenetration on all levels and its attendant initiation into oneness with the primal energies and truths of the universe.

The third "law" is that there must be a radical equality between the lovers; neither can have power over the other. Any inequality of power or desire for domination of any kind destroys the miraculous subtle balance that is essential for authentic abandon and mutual surrender. If both are to worship each other as equal manifestations of the Divine—the condition for the divinization of desire in tantra—then each must treat the other with divine tenderness, respect, and honor at all times and in all circumstances as far as possible.

The fourth "law" is that there must be fidelity between couples who practice it. The level of trust required for the sometimes very exposing work of real tantra demands that each knows beyond any shadow of a doubt that the other is completely dedicated to him or her. Without this "sealing of the vessel," the energies that need to be aroused and refined cannot be awakened. A Taoist tantric once said to me: "It's simple, really, this fidelity business—is like making vegetable soup. If you take the lid off, the flavors of the vegetables will not be able to run together."

The fifth "law," which includes and consummates all the others, is that the essence of tantra is not technique of any kind or even sexual pleasure (which can, after all, be enjoyed in situations that have none of the defining characteristics of tantric union) but passionate and profound love. Love is the fusing divine power in tantra, the glue without which true merging cannot take place. Without love, no amount of fancy gymnastic techniques, such as those sold in the often hilariously vulgar tantric manuals that are flooding the market, will be of any alchemical use. Such techniques when practiced without profound love may well result in heightened sexual delight—and delight is a divine gift; but the radical emotional, physical, and spiritual fusion that is the goal of true tantra goes far beyond even the most delicious and health-giving forms of pleasure. When in the service of profound love, however, these techniques, perfected over centuries of practice, can help tremendously in taking both lovers to heights of initiatory ecstasy. As an old Hindu once said to me in Benares: "Lust without love can be very wonderful but the heavens will not open for it. When lust streams from love like the rays of light do from the Sun, then heaven comes down on earth and the body is lit up with the fire of the Eternal."

It is necessary to know and honor these laws of authentic tantra not only because they are the conditions for true soul and body fusion but also because the work of tantra can sometimes be difficult and exhausting and will require tremendous stamina, faith, and commitment from both partners. This is because the kind of final exposed intimacy that tantra demands and engenders necessarily brings up all the "dark" and "shadow" aspects of both partners. The all-embracing physical, mental, emotional, and spiritual healing that tantra can give necessitates this bringing up all of the broken, tortured, and manipulative sides of the self and all the projections and games that spring from them—how else can they be seen and healed? Facing the pain and humiliation of this process—and the violent feelings of despair or resentment it can engender—demands of both partners in the couple a sustained level of spiritual practice. Without this, neither will be able to remain in the crucible of the relationship and the intricate, many-leveled alchemy that tantra is designed to produce cannot take place.

Let me share with you now one simple technique that can help consecrate lovemaking, and one powerful practice that can help couples deal with personal difficulties that arise on their Path together.

Technique to Consecrate Lovemaking

My general advice to lovers is always to make love in an atmosphere of holy joy and calm. Always prepare for your lovemaking by praying to the Father-Mother to infuse it with their presence: Always offer it in whatever way comes naturally to you to the Divine and ask for the Divine to reveal itself through it.

When you have done this, either out loud or silently, separate or together, sit facing each other, with your bodies touching and hands intertwined. Gaze deeply and lovingly into each other's eyes and savor the depths of Divine Presence in them. Silently offer your whole being, mind, heart, body, and soul to each other.

As the mood of tenderness and passion deepens, start to visualize the other as surrounded by divine light. At a certain state you will not need to visualize this anymore; the divine light will be evident to you. Until it is, however, imagine that the other is appearing to you as he or she must appear to the eyes of God—utterly bathed in divine white light, totally beautiful, precious, and holy on all levels. As you continue to gaze deeply into each other's eyes, say out loud or silently your gratitude to the Divine and to the Divine in the other.

Now, if you have some holy water or consecrated oil, anoint your human beloved in the name of divine love. As you anoint each other, kiss deeply, with your whole being, and begin.

You will find that if you perform this simple ceremony—or develop your own sacred ceremonies—every time you make love will be another divine initiation. From the beginning of your lovemaking every gesture, every emotion, will be saturated in the atmosphere of divine love, and every nuance of the abandon to follow will be illuminated by the divine light.

A Practice to Help Heal Difficulties Together

Meditate first together in silence and call for divine help for the difficulties you are experiencing with yourself or with the other. Then light a candle and place it between you to symbolize the Divine Presence at the core of your love. Now, honestly, and, if possible, calmly and tenderly, explain to the other what you are experiencing; listen deeply and without interrupting to the other as he or she explains to you his or her feelings in response.

Sometimes what you have to say or what you will hear will be painful. Note where the pain reflects itself in your body. Usually you will find it will appear as a constriction in the chest or lower stomach. Note where it is and try to relax your chest or stomach, breathing deeply into the pain-constricted area and inviting the divine light in with your breath to heal the suffering.

After you have both finished what you need to say and have both agreed that everything that needs to be said has been said, meditate in silence again, this time holding hands.

Slowly, and taking turns, attune your breathing to the breathing of the other. Listen deeply to how and in what rhythm the other person is breathing and attune your breathing accordingly. Both should do this with and for the other, back and forth, about five times each for periods of about two minutes.

Note as you do this breathing exercise what resistances, resentments, or angers arise and offer them all up to the Divine for healing. As the culminating part of this holy practice, take turns in leaning your head against the other's heart-center. As you do so, imagine that from your partner's heart-center streams brilliant golden light that cleanses your entire body, heart, mind, and soul and washes them free of all tension.

Shorter variations of this practice can be done when circumstances require them. Don't hesitate to experiment with whatever feels most naturally healing for you; the more creative and inventive you are with the powers of divine love in the heart of your relationship, the more completely they will be able to go on healing, opening, and irradiating it.

Creating Sacred Space

LIVING AND WORKING in spaces that have been "consecrated" and "made sacred" are essential to the success of the Direct Path. The Direct Path aims, after all, at the integration of the transcendent with the immanent, and at the sacred marriage of the Divine with the human in all activities and at all levels; to stay inspired and centered in the Divine, it is vital to make wherever you live or work reflect, as far as possible, divine beauty, harmony, and power and to arrange the space around you in such a way as to attract the healing and invigorating forces of the universe to you at all times. Everywhere we live or work should be a kind of temple, a living mandala of simple divine truth that constantly reflects back to us our richest and happiest possibilities.

Whenever I think of space made sacred, I think of the ancient house of an old Indian scholar friend of mine, Mr. Ratnasabapathy, in the old part of Tanjore. I first met him twenty years ago; in return for my help in preparing a catalogue on South Indian bronzes for the Tanjore museum, Mr. Ratnasabapathy would invite me to lunch at his house every day. He was not a rich man, and it was not a grand house, yet it remains in my memory as one of the most beautiful and holy places I have ever been. Outside the ancient wooden door in a small courtyard with a statue of Hanuman, the monkey god, in it, his wife would every day draw sacred diagrams in chalk to sanctify and protect the house and its occupants; inside, every room was kept shiningly clean: The kitchen pots especially, I remember, arranged in neat rows above the charcoal stove, shone with an almost surreal brightness, like that of the noon sun on the ocean. In every room, except for the bathroom, there was a small altar with a different god or goddess on it, and bowls of fresh water and small food offerings and flowers and, usually, one small stick of incense burning. In such naturally sacred surroundings, every act became subtly heightened; eating became a sacred ritual, washing your hands afterward a purification and a prayer, listening to the sounds of the city drifting in through the white curtains a form of meditation. One afternoon I told Mr. Ratnasabapathy how much the sweet holiness of his house moved me. He smiled shyly and said, "For ten generations my family have worshipped at all the altars in all the rooms and seen to it that there was always a stick of incense burning somewhere; for ten generations the women of my family every morning have made sacred diagrams outside the door. My house is my temple in which I worship the Father and the Mother in everything I do; I never feel I need to go on pilgrimage because my Benares, my Himalayas, are here all around me."

Ever since my meetings with my dear friend in Tanjore, I have tried to put into practice the lessons being with him in his house taught me. When I lived in a maid's room in Paris, I surrounded myself with icons and pictures of my favorite saints and holy beings and always tried to keep fresh flowers on the small altar I erected under the window. The first thing that Eryk and I did when we moved into the new house we bought three years ago in Nevada was to construct a shrine for the Virgin in the broom cupboard under the stairs; in so doing we consciously consecrated the whole house to the Mother as her temple, her temple of divine and human love. There isn't a room in our house except for the bathrooms where there isn't a sacred image of some kind; Kwan Yin rules our bedroom in serene splendor; Krishna stands behind me in rough mango wood, as I write, playing his flute on the top of one of my stereo speakers; wherever I look, as I work, I see faces of holy friends, cards of the Black Madonna or the Sacred Heart or Tara; I am surrounded and enveloped and protected by the sacred at all moments and in all situations. Whenever I am exhausted or uninspired, all I have to do is raise or turn my head to be able to draw strength from one representation or other of the holy. Even when I travel, the first thing I do in any anonymous hotel room is to put up a picture of the Virgin and put a small flower before it; even the bleakest of rooms is immediately transformed by her smile.

Having at last a house of my own has made me even more aware than I was before of how essential it is to infuse everything around you with sacred beauty and also of how vital it is always to see that the energy of the house remains at all times clear and open to divine power. I have come to know my house as the body of a living spirit and to love and respect that body and that spirit; I have discovered that if I do, my own inner and outer lives become richer and more serene. Slowly, where I live and what I am are becoming one ordinary divine dance.

Let me share with you now a few hints on how to construct and maintain an altar, two simple purificatory practices that can be used to "clear the energies of the house," and some essential tips from the ancient Chinese science of fêng shui that aims to balance the chi, or sacred energy, in the relationships between us and the objects around us and our surroundings.

On Making Your Own Altar

Above all, proceed slowly. Every object you put on your altar should have a deep sacred significance to you and be arranged, if possible, in such a way as to bring you to your own deepest knowledge of, and feeling for, the sacred. So place on your altar only those images or objects that truly speak to you.

Keep your altar clean and, if possible, place fresh flowers, or even one fresh flower, on it every day. In this way you will signal your own intention always to keep your state of prayer and adoration vital and alive.

Choose one central shrine in the house where you can always

go for peace or strength. If you like, make smaller altars in other rooms too. At one you might put photographs of loved ones you want to pray for; at another you might place natural objects or emblems and worship there the force and splendor of the Mother in nature. You might even consider doing what several of my friends of the Direct Path do—leave an empty space at the corner of one room as an altar for the formless; sitting in such an empty space can be marvelously refreshing.

Don't hesitate to experiment and improvise and change the objects on your altar or altars. This way you will always keep the spirit alive and come more and more to appreciate your own sacred powers of self-inspiration.

Whenever Mr. Ratnasabapathy passed one of the altars in his house, he would bow and raise his hands in prayer. "In this way," he told me, "even when I don't have time to pray long I can still pray a little." It is astonishing, I find, how powerful such a simple practice is; it helps you to remember that all the activities that take place in all the rooms of your house are inherently sacred and waiting to be divinized by your attention.

Two Simple Practices of Purification, or Clearing the Energy, of Your Subconscious

Our surroundings and the objects around us absorb our negative thoughts and griefs and store them; all ancient cultures are aware of this and have developed simple ways of clearing such effects and restoring clear balance. The two I use myself are extremely simple and powerful.

PURIFICATION BY WATER

This is adapted from an ancient Hawaiian practice taught to me by a kahuna in Maui.

Say a favorite prayer, asking for divine protection, and then pour some water into a clean bowl. Place your right open palm over the water and moving it clockwise, imagining rays of all the colors of a brilliant rainbow streaming from it and penetrating and consecrating the water. Hawaiians, like many ancient peoples, believe that rainbows are signs of divine protection and that their combination of all colors is extremely powerful.

When you feel that the water is charged with sacred force, take a sprig of sage or cedar or a freshly cut rose and dip it into the water. Then walk clockwise around all the rooms of your house, flicking the sacred water from the sprig or flower seven times in all directions. As you do so, pray that all negative spirits and energies leave immediately and all serene and strong spirits and energies immediately take their place.

The most powerful time of all to do this practice is during the full moon.

PURIFICATION BY SALT

Salt has been used as a purificatory agent by almost every religious civilization. It has long been one of the most powerful symbols of eternal life and purity, because it does not decay or change composition. Tibetan rinpoches, shamans, and Catholic exorcists all use it in some of their holiest rituals.

My advice is to keep some rock salt or sea salt in a special sealed bowl under your main altar, where it can collect the power of your devotion. Then, on the same day every month, say, the first Monday, take out that bowl, pray over it, ask for divine power to infuse the salt, and walk clockwise around your house, flicking it seven times, as before, in all directions.

As you do so, imagine that the rooms you are cleansing fill up entirely with a brilliant divine white light that emanates from the holy power of the salt and cleanses them of all negative influences.

At the end of the ritual, when you are returning the bowl of salt to its place under your main altar, visualize the whole house as having walls of a radiating brilliant white light that fills every room with healing divine power and pray again for you and your family and pets to be kept safe from all danger.

Nine Essential Tips from Fêng Shui

Fêng shui is the ancient Chinese science of arranging our objects and surroundings in the best possible way to balance sacred energy and attract toward us all the benevolent forces of the cosmos. It is currently having an astonishing revival all over the world, and anyone interested in it need only visit their local bookstore to find a plethora of excellent books about its nature and use. I myself have been studying it for over two years now and have rearranged my house along its guidelines; the results in inner serenity and outer strength and prosperity have been remarkable.

Here are nine tips I have myself put into practice and find helpful:

Hang a wind chime in your doorway; not only will its ringing enchant you but it will also disperse bad chi.

Ensure that your main staircase faces away from the entrance of your house, so that good energy and prosperity do not "run out."

Place a small fountain at the entrance of the house; it will not only purify the air of the house and delight your ears but entice into your life good chi and prosperity.

Make a prosperity corner in the southwest corner of your house, where every day you pray humbly to be given by God everything that you need. In my southwest corner, following the advice of a local fêng shui expert, I have placed a potted plant and a statue of Lakshmi, goddess of prosperity and abundance. In a small bowl in front of her I have folded some dollars as offering and as a symbol of material health. Every morning I worship the mother of abundance by passing a stick of incense clockwise around her and thank her for all she gives me and ask her to grace me what I need to live without worry.

Arrange the desk in your office so that it faces the door. This conserves mental and spiritual energy and symbolically protects you, it is said, from treachery or unforeseen difficulties.

Place your bed in a diagonal facing the door, so that the energies of love remain in the room to charge it with power.

Always replace flowers the moment they die, because keeping dead flowers in the house attracts negative energy.

Make sure that the kitchen—the center of the house—is well lit by natural sunlight and always clean and bright so as to honor the Mother, protect you from disease, and celebrate the life-giving power of the food prepared there. Always see that the refrigerator is not directly opposite the stove, since water and fire are elements that oppose each other and you want to ensure harmony in the place where life is constantly renewed. If they are opposite each other, place a mirror in such a way as to create deflection.

Keep a pet and love and honor it as the Mother. For me, Purrball is our temple cat; her being and needs are sacred; her presence is a divine blessing on our house to be kept vibrant by tenderness and attention. As the expert I learned fêng shui from told me when he saw her lying asleep on the stairs: "If your pet is happy, the house will smile. And if your house smiles, all your hopes will flourish."

Rites of Passage:
Advice and Practices for Dying

ALL THE AUTHENTIC mystical systems tell us that to "die" into living union with the Divine before dying is the aim and goal of the Path. They tell us that for those who enter the deathless in time and while still in a body, who know their light Origin and innate divine consciousness, and who have lived consciously and normally in its radiance, death can have no terrors. As a Hindu poet, Tukaram, wrote: "For those who have been kissed by the Face of Light, Death is just a moving from one room to another." The Tibetan adepts call those who die knowing their divine light nature "those who die like a newborn child." When Rumi was on his deathbed, a friend tried to cheer him up by saying he would soon recover. Rumi smiled and said, pointing to his nightshirt, "When only this piece of cloth is between me and the Beloved, why wouldn't you want the Light to unite with the Light?"

The mystical systems also inform us in different but related ways that for those who have lived in a body in nondual awareness, losing the body is not a disaster but in fact an opportunity for supreme liberation. Teresa of Avila knew her death as the moment when she would at last meet the Christ fully beyond "this interfering curtain, the flesh." In the Tibetan system—perhaps the most accurate and "scientific" of all—the moment of death sees the dawning of the light of Origin, what is called the "ground luminosity," in brief but extraordinary splendor; those who have learned to see and know this essential light of consciousness through spiritual practice recognize it immediately and merge with it, achieving Buddhahood. For the Sufi lover, too, the moment of death allows the Beloved to flame out in final glory and offers the one who has already in life started to die into love to die into it forever. As Rumi wrote:

> When lovers die in their journey
> The spirit's king comes out to meet them
> When they die at the feet of that moon
> They all light up like the sun.

The evidence of the millions of near death experiences that have been reported and investigated over the last forty years also confirms what the mystical traditions have informed us—that when we die we will have the chance to merge with the light we came from, if we can recognize it and approach it without fear.

For most of us, however, whose spiritual practice and mystical knowledge are incomplete, the final integration with the light that death offers will involve a demanding rite of passage. Even here, however, we have nothing to fear; the great mystical traditions have handed down to us wonderful sane advice and highly useful practices that can enable us to seize the opportunities for revelation and liberation that death will unfold.

The essential advice of all mystics can be summed up simply: When you come to know that you are dying, strip yourself as far as possible of all attachment or aversion and try to focus with your entire being on the Divine, using those practices that have meant most to you in life. I was lucky enough to be present during the last months of both Thuksey Rinpoche and Bede Griffiths when they knew they did not have long to live; both plunged into incessant and simple spiritual practice. Thuksey Rinpoche and Bede Griffiths were both, as far as possible, in constant prayer, always centering their being in divine awareness. My father, when he was dying, also prayed all the time, and not out of fear, but from a passion to stay inspired by the spirit and to surrender to the divine will.

Two kinds of practice are particularly helpful at this moment of passage—those that open the heart, and those that dedicate whatever suffering you are experiencing to the healing of the suffering of others. Opening the heart to God and keeping it open whatever is happening to the body enables you to keep your mindstream always saturated with the Presence and so open to the grace and guidance constantly streaming from it. Any heart-practice can be invaluable here; whichever one has worked best for you in your life will help you most in your dying.

If you have never done a heart-practice before or want in this hour of crisis one that is particularly powerful, I recommend the following one, which I have taken from the ancient Tibetan practice of phowa and used with many dying people, including my own father. One of the most joyful moments of my life was when I was able to share this practice with my dying father; another was when I heard a year after his death that he had done it repeatedly and told my mother, "Andrew told me that if I did this practice I would see and feel the presence of Christ, and I did."

Adaptation, or Essentialization, of Phowa Practice (Phowa Means "Transference of Consciousness")

This practice of the transference of consciousness is particularly powerful for the dying because it can help acquaint them with the immersion into the Divine Presence that death will unfold for us; the more we are used to practicing merging with the light before death, the more completely we will be able to merge with it *in* death.

If you can, take a meditative posture. If that is not possible, don't worry. Just stretch out and relax completely.

Now imagine in the sky in front of you the embodiment of whatever truth you have believed in during your life in the form of blazing radiant light. This form can be that of Buddha or Krishna or Jesus or Mary. If you do not feel associated with any of the world's religions, imagine a form of pure golden light in the sky before you. What is important is that you know that this form represents all the love and wisdom and goodness of God.

Now focus your whole being—heart, mind, and soul—on this radiant presence and pray that it will guide you through everything you are about to experience in dying; that it will heal you of all your negative karma and purify you completely of all the dark things you have said and done during your life; that it will help you die a calm, peaceful, illumined death that can benefit all other living beings and help you yourself enter into final liberation.

Imagine, now, that because of the sincerity of your prayer, the light presence is moved. Smiling a sweet smile of love, it streams toward you brilliant white light from its heart-center. See and know these rays of light as totally penetrating and saturating your body; offer your whole being, in fact, up to them again and again. Know that as they enter you, these rays of light from the heart of God cleanse and purify all your negative karma, all your dark emotions, everything in you that has caused you and others suffering. See and feel that you gradually come to be totally immersed in light.

Be confident now that you are totally healed and purified by the light. Feel that your body itself is now starting to dissolve into light and melt into its light Origin.

In this new body of light you are free and peaceful. Soar up into the sky and merge into the blissful presence of the light. Try to stay in this living sense of oneness with the Presence as long as possible.

THE SECOND TYPE of spiritual practice that can be of most help in dying is that of dedicating our suffering to the healing of the suffering of others. Using our own pain and fear as a way of opening deeply to the pain and fear of others and dedicating whatever we undergo to the healing of the anguish of others is a powerful way of initiating ourselves into the depths of our own divine nature and its boundless compassion and so helping ourselves to meet and rest in our true Christ or Buddha nature. It also helps us not to feel alone and abandoned in our last agonies, or—worst of all, perhaps—that they are without meaning.

Of all the many practices of dedicating suffering to the healing of others, I believe that of Tonglen (which I have described in detail in the sixteenth sacred practice for transformed spiritual living) to be by far the most powerful. Tibetan mystics value its truth and effectiveness so highly that they pray to be able to perform it consciously until the moment of death itself; many Tibetan adepts dedicate their very last breath to the healing of the pain of the world and so enter the dying process itself with their hearts and minds clear of clinging and naked to the light.

It is best, of course, to acquaint yourself with this wonderful practice while you are well and healthy; doing it, then, when you are dying will be all the more powerful. If you have not, however, don't worry; in their compassion for all beings, the Tibetans have developed an essentialized form of Tonglen for those who are dying that can be done by anyone, whatever their previous acquaintance with this or any other spiritual practice.

Essentialized Tonglen

Imagine all the others in the world who are suffering like you. Fill your entire being with compassion for them and pray to whom you believe in that your suffering should help soften theirs.

Say to yourself in your own words, with profound compassion: "May I take on the suffering of all those who are suffering in the same way as I am. May they all be permanently freed from their afflictions!"

Imagine that their illnesses now leave their body in the forms of grimy black smoke and dissolve into your illness. As you breathe in, breathe in all their pain; as you breathe out, breathe out to them all peace and healing and health. Each time you do this practice, believe with deep faith that everyone you are doing it for is healed.

I have witnessed the astonishing power of this practice to transform the dying many times. I think especially of several young gay friends of mine who learned this practice and performed it as they died of AIDS in their late twenties or early thirties; without exception, it helped them transform fear and rage into acceptance. Through its healing power they came to feel themselves no longer victims of a meaningless and horrible fate but agents of transformation and healing even in the midst of their own "destruction." I think of one in particular, whom I shall call François, a French singer and writer, who whispered to me a few hours before he died (he had been practicing Tonglen for two months): "I never used to believe that the Buddha nature lived in me; I was both too vain and too self-doubting. Now I know it does and I know that death can do nothing to destroy it." François died sitting up and smiling and saying the mantra of the Buddha of compassion, *om mani padme hum;* there was an unmistakable atmosphere of deep joy and peace around his bed.

Let me end with a few words of simple advice for those who look after the dying.

Again, the heart-wisdom of all the mystic traditions about how to look after the dying can be summed up simply. Try to allow the dying to die in as deep a peace as possible; do everything you can inwardly and outwardly to ensure that nothing you do or say disturbs them as they travel toward their meeting with the light. Try at all moments to be as positive, encouraging, and unconditionally loving as possible; listen to whatever the dying need to communicate to you with as open and receptive a heart as you can. Above all, pray, and pray deeply and passionately for them; you will find if you do that the power of your prayer to effect the atmosphere of their death will be extraordinary.

One of the most powerful ways of praying for the dying, I have found from my own experience, is to do the essentialized phowa for them. Imagine whatever form of golden light you want to irradiating the person who is dying, again and again, with healing light, and purifying and cleansing them of all their negative karma and fears and destructive emotions; imagine, then, that he or she merges with the light and rests in its bliss and peace. This is an especially powerful practice to do while the person you are looking after is actually dying or in the seven weeks after death when, the

Tibetans tell us, the consciousness of the dead person is traveling through different realms, or bardos, and can very easily be contacted by us. The more you can imagine the dead person "merging" with the light presence, the more the dead person's consciousness can be inspired to try to do so and the more the benevolent powers of the Divine will be constellated on his or her behalf.

If possible, too, see that the dead body is left alone as long as you can. The Tibetans claim that the body should not be touched for three days, so that the consciousness can have the best possible chance of uniting with its light ground. This is not always feasible in the modern world. What should be avoided at all costs, however, is any invasive procedure during or just after death; nothing could be more damaging to the peace of mind of the being who is undergoing his or her transition to other worlds.

One final piece of advice: Never feel that just because the person you love is dead you can do nothing more for them. As Thuksey Rinpoche once said to me: "If you feel like praying for someone who died a thousand years ago, don't hesitate to do so. What is a thousand years? Who knows where they are now? Even if he or she is a Buddha, they will still need your prayers to go on helping all beings."

Four

The Passion
to Serve

By thinking intensely
of the good of others, by
devoting yourself to their service,
you will purify your heart
by that work and through it
you will arrive at the vision of
Self which penetrates
all living things.

VIVEKANANDA

IN ALL THE SERIOUS mystical traditions, the final aim of the Path is not ecstasy, or revelation, or the possession of amazing powers, or any kind of purely personal fulfillment, however inspired or exalted, but to become the humble, supple, selfless, and tireless instrument of God and servant of divine love. The consummation of the mystical path lies not in a selfish "freedom" from reality or in any kind of magical domination of it but in a transparence to the divine will, a dedicated hunger to put its orders into effect in any circumstances and against any odds, and a calm passion to put divine love and its laws of radical equality, all-embracing compassion and justice into practice on every level of reality.

This truth that the proof of authentic awakening lies in works of profound loving service illumines the greatest and highest visions of all the major mystical transmission systems. Shabistari, the sixteenth-century Sufi mystic, sums up the heart-wisdom of the Sufi Path of Love when he writes "the perfect being is one, who in all perfection, acts like a slave despite his Lordship." The core of Taoism is expressed in the phrase from the commentary of the *I Ching* on hexagram seventeen; "He who wants to rule must first learn how to serve." In the Hindu scripture the Bhagavad Gita, Krishna the Divine Lord tells his devotee Arjuna that those who love him most perfectly live "simple, self-reliant lives, based on meditation" and "use speech, body, and mind to serve the Lord of Love." At the heart of cabalistic Jewish mysticism is a fierce and glorious vision of the necessity of putting mystical awareness into practical action so as to help "mend" the broken Creation. As Ben Gamliel, a rabbi of the third century, writes: "Study is not the goal, doing is. Never mistake talk for action. Pity fills no stomach, compassion builds no house. Understanding is not yet justice." In everything he did and said, Jesus gave us all the message that divine illumination was not real unless it was put into direct and passionate action; the kingdom he saw with the eyes of ecstatic vision and worked and hungered to create was not in any way some otherworld state but a real kingdom of God-inspired love and justice in the world.

It has never been more important than now to listen to these divinely inspired voices and to put divine love into action at all levels and in all arenas of reality with all the gifts, passions, and intellectual, spiritual, emotional, and organizational powers at our disposal. The goal of the Direct Path is, as I have said, the divinization of the whole of life and the bringing of the whole of our human existence—social, sexual, economic, and political—into living dynamic harmony with the will and love of the Divine. This demands of all who take it that they place their whole being into service of the Divine's plan for a unified, integrated, self-empowered humanity and that they work selflessly, inspired by divine wisdom and divine love, to release in the heart of a burning and endangered world the truths of divine equality, justice, and compassion for all beings.

What does this mean in practical terms? It means, I think, the linking together of five different but interdependent forms of service, all of which need to be pursued and fulfilled together to be fully empowering and effective. These are: the service to the Divine, the service to the self, the service to family and friends, the service to the community, and the service to the world, all sentient beings and the cosmos in which we live.

In service to the Divine, through adoration and meditation, study of sacred texts, and different kinds of spiritual practice and ritual, we empower ourselves with divine grace, wisdom, and love.

This service of the Divine leads naturally to the service of the self, the divine part of us—to seeing that we remain in as constant as possible inner contact with our own Christ or Buddha nature and reflect its wisdom and compassion in our relationship to our own bodies and in an integration and embodiment of its truth in all our thoughts, emotions, and actions.

If we are truly serving the Divine and truly serving the divine self within us, we will be led to want, with all our heart, mind, body, and soul, to serve those who we spend our lives with—our friends and family. Service to friends and family means, in its highest and most beautiful sense, that we see our mate, our friends, our pets, and our relations all as divine beings, potential Buddhas and Christs, who deserve the utmost tenderness, respect, compassion, and honor.

Serving our mates, pets, friends, and family in this way leads, naturally, if we allow our hearts to be constantly expanded by the direct experience and practice of divine love, to embracing the whole of our community. To be on the Direct Path is to know yourself responsible not merely for yourself or your immediate friends and relations but also for the well-being of the community you find yourself in. This means being aware at every level of how your village or town or city actually works, making responsible civic decisions within it, and trying if possible to make real contributions to the happiness of those who live in the same place as you do—whether through hospice visiting or helping out in old people's homes or with soup kitchens or working to improve housing or medical or road conditions. One seeker I know gives two hours a week to working in an animal shelter; another who is a doctor donates five hours a week to helping patients who cannot afford to pay for medical treatment; a real estate agent friend of mine donates one afternoon a week to helping people who have suffered sudden financial loss or bankruptcy obtain feasible house loans. We all, whoever we are, have gifts or skills that can be of use to others; donating them in service to others can be the source of great joy as well as deepening spiritual insight and power.

Serving our immediate community can never be wholly effective if we do not try to keep as well informed as possible about the state of things in the world in general. I am always shocked when spiritual "seekers" tell me they do not read the newspapers or listen to the news on the radio or watch it on television; what world do they imagine they are living in? It has never been more important to be as informed as possible on what is happening; the media and the Internet open up to us unparalleled possibilities of mutual communication and awareness that would be madness to waste. It is essential for every human being to become aware of global warming, poverty, environmental degradation, the role of the corporations in creating and engineering poverty, the struggle of women and of minorities everywhere to obtain equality and be treated with dignity. One very important form of service to the world is to stay as informed as possible about it; how else can you buy or vote responsibly? How else can you be aware of what factors affect what you eat or consume? How else can you practice living compassion to those you share the world with, which includes, of course, all the laboratory animals being tortured in cosmetic factories and all the endangered species being killed by corporate greed?

Having the most up-to-date information about what is happening is only the beginning, however; then we have to find ways to act upon it. If we don't we run the risk of becoming impotent and hopeless. Such ways include voting for parties that take the threat to the environment seriously, scaling down our personal needs so as to consume less, sending money to groups who combat political, economic, and social oppression. If you take the Direct Path, you consider every sentient being on the planet your brother or sister; what affects him or her directly affects you because they are part of your heart-family; if you really allow yourself to be affected like this, you will be passionately restless in your hunger to find ways to be productive in whatever way you can. The two greatest enemies of the changes that we as a human race have to put into practice if we are going to preserve ourselves are apathy and a sense of helplessness; both in the end serve ignorance and evil and allow them to continue their work of destruction. The radical self-empowerment that the Direct Path brings opens up new areas of creativity and invention for us all if we are really prepared to open up to them.

I know that it is possible to serve in this all-embracing, all-comprehensive way because I have met people who have. I think of the friend whose love transformed my sometimes miserable youth, Anne Pennington, the humblest and gentlest of beings, who was a true mystic, a brilliant professor and translator, a tireless fighter against communism, and a great, faithful friend; her whole life in all its facets was one long prayer. I think of my beloved Tibetan mentor Thuksey Rinpoche in our last summer together; he was so sick with diabetes he could hardly walk, yet he never stopped radiating to all who came to him the most exuberant affection, or teaching long into the night on the nature of mind and compassion even when he was so weak he could hardly speak. I think of the human being I have spiritually loved and admired the most, Bede Griffiths; his whole long, glorious life was lived out of a vision of service that embraced the Divine, his own divine human self, his intimates, his community, the world he loved so profoundly and for whose fate he was so deeply worried.

I had the honor and grace of being with Bede Griffiths for two weeks during his protracted and painful dying. One night, when I was watching over him, he woke up with a start from fitful sleep, sat up, lit from within by an unmistakable mystic ecstasy, and cried out twice, "Serve the growing Christ! Serve the growing Christ!" By the Christ I knew he meant nothing that could be expressed within the confines of any one religious system; I knew he meant the divine human being within each one of us and the supreme love consciousness that creates and sustains the creation at all times.

Those four words have come to be for me the key to service on the Direct Path, the key to understanding its aim and goal. The divine power of love consciousness is within each one of us; we all have the potential to grow into its possession and to act with its wisdom, courage, and intense hunger for justice in reality. To serve God, our divine human self, our friends, our community, and the world with all our gifts and energies and powers is to serve the growing Christ and to help birth a new creation, a new world.

A Vision:
The Flowering Earth

AS I WAS NEARING the end of writing this book, I went on a pilgrimage with my mother to the shrine of the Virgin of Guadalupe in Mexico City. For me, this is the holiest and most powerful place in the Americas, the Americas' Mt. Sinai, the source of a continuing, immense revelation of the universal presence, love, and power of the Divine Mother. The woman clothed with the sun and pregnant with the new who appeared to the native Indian Juan Diego, and who manifested the image of her on his cloak that still survives in all its tender and dreamlike radiance, cannot be confined to any one religious interpretation, whatever Catholics might claim; she is the mother of all things and all beings and all revelations, the full divine mother, companion, and friend to us all, standing humbly to meet us and raising her hands to us in prayer for the fulfillment of all our richest hopes. To be in the presence of the image of the Virgin of Guadalupe is to be in the living eternal presence of the Mother herself; no other image or statue or shrine I know anywhere in the world radiates with so much divine power. Gazing up at her, all things suddenly seem possible, and the wonderful description by St. Paul of divine love that it "bears all things, believes all things, endures all things" becomes a living reality in the heart.

After meditating in her presence, I walked up the hill of Tepeyac, where she had first appeared to Juan Diego, to the small church at its top, where Juan Diego is now buried. As I entered the church, I nearly keeled over with the overwhelming scent of roses that came from the hundreds of bouquets of flowers flooding the nave of the church. For a moment, it was as if I were participating in the miracle of four hundred years ago, when the mother told her Indian son to go to the top of the rocky, thistle-infested mountain and pick flowers there in the middle of winter. In my heart echoed words I had always loved from the Aztec text the *Nican Mopohua* that describe Juan Diego's first reaction to seeing the mountaintop covered with blossom: "As I arrived at the top of the hill, my eyes became fixed; it was the Flowering Earth." In Nahuatl, the expression "the flowering earth" means "the place where ultimate truth resides."

In the splendor of that long, divine moment I saw, felt, and heard in a way no words can describe the new world that is now possible for the entire human race, the "flowering" earth that we could, even at this late, dangerous moment, still co-create with the Divine in the world. I realized with a tremendous joy that only our lack of faith, our laziness, and our addiction to the forms and rituals of the past now separate us from extraordinary new powers and possibilities.

And as this blessing poured over me in wave after wave of joy and gratitude, I understood clearly how the human race now has everything it needs, not only to preserve itself and preserve nature but also to enter into a fruitful and creative and unified future. It has the scientific knowledge, the technological skill; and now, in the great worldwide return to mystical awareness and in the restoration to the forefront of human consciousness of the world's wisdom traditions, it also has all the necessary spiritual knowledge at its disposal, all the mystical "sciences" waiting to be synthesized, lived, and applied. What is possible—and for the first time in human history—is an integration and fusion of the highest and most practical wisdom of all fields and disciplines to engender a new world and to work consciously and humbly with the Divine to uplift the whole of humanity and the whole of nature into divine harmony, beauty, unity, and power. Now at last our sad, tormented world can become the flowering earth of Juan Diego's vision and the promise of the mother's flower miracle; now at last heaven and earth, divine grace and human intelligence, soul and matter, science and meditation, can marry, make love, and birth endless new possibilities of healing and justice for all living beings.

Ranged against this astounding but real and practical possibility that every day becomes clearer to those who dare to open to it, stand nothing less than all the forms of thought, philosophies, elites and hierarchies of the past, all religious, mystical, social, sexual structures that claim "exclusive" truth, eternal justification, or "natural" validity. Ranged against this possibility, too, stand all the arrogant nihilisms spawned by a narrow vision of science and the materialist cults of a world addicted to power.

Clearly, we have now reached the decisive moment in the evolution of humanity. Are we as a species going to choose the sublime adventure of the Direct Path that empowers each individual whatever their color, status, or sexuality with their divine nature and God-given passion and creativity? Are we going to embrace the challenge of the Direct Path to integrate all useful forms of knowledge, marry vision and economics, a mystical passion for justice with political practice, a love of the creation with precise and structured efforts to save and preserve the environment? Or are we going to go on embracing the limited divisive religious, mystical, social, and political philosophies of the past that have so blatantly and so horribly failed us, and that are plunging the world more obviously each day into a deepening maelstrom of suicidal greed and violence? Are we going to go on clinging to the dogmas that in both spirit and material matters have so clearly created the misery and helplessness and despair that we see all around us?

All liberations are costly and no one can doubt that going beyond all the limiting forms and definitions of the past will call upon our deepest resources of humility, vision, and courage. But the Divine is always inside us and around us, longing to pour its powers and graces into us, and the possibility of an integrated humanity and healed nature that the Direct Path opens up to everyone is too real and too marvelous to ignore.

May you who embrace the Direct Path know the urgency and

responsibility of what you are undertaking! May the mercy of divine love fill your hearts with sacred passion and your minds with sacred wisdom! May the entire planet be transformed into the mirror of love and justice—the flowering earth—it has always been in the heart-mind of the Father-Mother!

Resources

Aurobindo, Sri. *Letters on Yoga, Volumes One to Three*. Pondicherry, India: Sri Aurobindo Ashram, 1971.

——. *The Life Divine*. Pondicherry, India: Sri Aurobindo Ashram, 1977.

Baring, Anne, and Jules Cashford. *The Myth of the Goddess: Evolution of an Image*. New York: Viking Press, 1991.

Berry, Thomas, and Brian Swimme. *The Universe Story*. San Francisco: Harper-San Francisco, 1992.

Cleary, Thomas, trans. *The Essential Tao*. New York: HarperCollins, 1991.

Cooper, David. *God Is a Verb: Kabbalah and the Practice of Mystical Judaism*. New York: Riverhead Books, 1997.

Dossey, Larry. *Healing Words: The Power of Prayer and the Practice of Medicine*. New York: HarperCollins, 1993.

Easwaran, Eknath, trans. *The Upanishads*. Petaluma, CA: Nilgiri Press, 1987.

Fox, Matthew. *Sins of the Spirit, Blessings of the Flesh*. New York: Harmony Books, 1999.

Govinda, Lama Anagarika. *Foundations of Tibetan Mysticism*. London: Rider Press, 1972.

Hillman, James. *The Soul's Code*. New York: Random House, 1996.

Moore, Thomas. *Care of the Soul: A Guide for Cultivating Depth and Sacredness in Everyday Life*. New York: HarperCollins, 1992.

Myss, Caroline. *Anatomy of the Spirit: The Seven Stages Power and Healing*. New York: Crown Publishers, 1996.

Nikihilananda, Swami, trans. *The Gospel of Sri Ramakrishna*. New York: Ramakrishna Vivekananda Center, 1942.

Nisargadatta Maharaj, Sri. *I Am That*. Durham, NC: The Acorn Press, 1982.

Osbourne, Arthur. *The Teachings of Ramana Maharshi*. York Beach, ME: Weiser, 1995.

Radha, Swami. *Mantras: Words of Power*. Timeless Books, 1976.

Rinpoche, Sogyal. *The Tibetan Book of Living and Dying.* New York: Harper-Collins, 1993.

Roth, Gabrielle. *Sweat Your Prayers.* New York: Tarcher, 1998.

Shapiro, Rabbi Rami M., trans. *Wisdom of the Jewish Sages: A Modern Reading of Pirke Avot.* New York: Harmony Books, 1993.

Shaw, Miranda. *Passionate Enlightenment: Women in Tantric Buddhism.* Princeton, NJ: Princeton University Press, 1994.

Tagore, Rabindranath. *The Religion of Man.* London: George Allen and Unwin, 1953.

Tarnas, Richard. *The Passion of the Western Mind: Understanding the Ideas That Have Shaped Our World View.* New York: Harmony Books, 1991.

Wilber, Ken. *The Atman Project: A Transpersonal View of Human Development.* Wheaton, IL: Theosophical Publishing House, 1980.

——. *Sex, Ecology, Spirituality: The Spirit of Evolution.* Boston: Shambhala Publications, 1995.

Yogananda, Paramahansa. *Autobiography of a Yogi.* Los Angeles: Self-Realization Fellowship, 1987.

Index